FOGGY

FOGGY

The Explosive Autobiography of the Four-time
Superbike World Champion

CARL FOGARTY
with Neil Bramwell

CollinsWillow
An Imprint of HarperCollins*Publishers*

First published in 2000
by Collins Willow
an imprint of HarperCollins*Publishers*

1 3 5 7 9 8 6 4 2

A CIP catalogue record for this book is available from the British Library

ISBN 0 00 218960 7

Set in PostScript Minion by
Rowland Phototypesetting Ltd, Bury St Edmunds, Suffolk

Printed and bound in Great Britain by Clays Ltd, St Ives plc

Photographic acknowledgements

All photographs supplied by the author with the exception of the
following: **Chris de Beer** p 10 (centre); **Double Red** p 3 (centre right),
7 (top and centre), 16 (bottom); **Kel Edge** p 4 (top – main pic),
5 (top and bottom), 7 (bottom), 11 (centre and bottom), 14 (top
and bottom), 15 (top); **Gold & Goose** p 4 (inset), 9 (centre right
and bottom), 11 (top); **Terry Howe** p 2 (bottom); **Lancashire Evening
Telegraph** p 12 (centre), 13 (top); **Keith Martin Photography** p 9 (top);
Annabel Williams p 6 (bottom).

*Dedicated to the memory of
Vera Fogarty and Hannah Walsh*

Contents

Acknowledgements

I would like to thank Michaela for her love, patience and support; my dad for all his backing early in my career; Alan and Pat Bond, whose help in looking after the kids and the house while we have been away has been invaluable; Davide Tardozzi, who re-motivated me at a time when I could have walked away from the sport; Slick, who put my needs before his own for seven years; Raymond Roche, for showing faith in me at the right time; and Neil Bramwell, for his assistance in writing this book.

Introduction

THE ALFRED HOSPITAL, MELBOURNE – 8pm, Tuesday, 25 April, 2000: I'm so pissed off. I should be on a plane to Japan, ready to step up the fight for my fifth World Superbike title. Instead, I'm sat in bed in a private room in an Australian hospital, knowing that my chances of the title are buried in the gravel of the Phillip Island circuit. Still, I suppose I have to be thankful that I'm not about to be buried back home in Blackburn.

I don't remember a thing about the second race. I only just remember starting. It had been a shit day and tyre choice had been crucial for a wet first race, where I was a comfortable second behind Anthony Gobert – who gambled on wet weather tyres. For the second race, a couple of hours later, the track was drying and I made a bad start. But, as my tyres warmed up, I was charging through the field with the on-board camera on my bike for the first time ever!

I've not even seen the incident on video. But I've been told that I was about to pass an Austrian rider called Robert Ulm on the outside. The theory is that his engine was cutting out. I think he must have been concentrating on that and not on what was happening around him. So he was already pulling out into my line before it cut out again. There was nothing I could do to avoid him and I ran in his back. The TV picture was all grass and sky until they cut to my slumped body. I was apparently unconscious for 10 minutes before coming round in the track medical centre. X-rays showed that the humerus, the bone that connects the shoulder to the elbow, was fractured in three places near the joint with the clavicle and had jarred up into the muscle. The first thing I remember is being put into a helicopter and I couldn't work out why. And I don't even remember

1

the flight because I was pumped up with morphine while I was flown to Melbourne with Michaela.

The surgeons took about an hour to fix seven screws and a titanium plate to the bone the next morning. A lot of the muscles were torn and there were fears that a nerve might have been stretched. I was told that I wouldn't race for a minimum of six weeks. That was hard to take. So I asked Michaela if there was any chance at all that I would make Donington in three weeks' time. She just looked at me as if I was mad.

I had given her, the team and everyone back home a real fright. It was a 150mph fall and you don't always survive those. But that thought has never crossed my mind at any time of my career. Before the start of this season I said I would quit if I suffered one more big crash. But there's no way I'm going to quit like this. Despite all the problems I was suffering at the start of this season, I have shown in the first two rounds in South Africa and Australia that I'm still the fastest out there. The bike was good and I was riding well. So I'm even more determined to go out and win more races.

That's my problem sometimes. I want to win too much. Other riders would have accepted that they had had a bad start and aimed for a few points. But there was only one thing on my mind: to finish first. So maybe I was riding on the edge. The same thing happened in South Africa, when I crashed out in the second race but wasn't injured. Maybe I was pushing too hard again, because I had been battling against another shoulder injury all week, and I lost the front end and slid off. But I still managed to finish third in a tight first race of the season. All things considered, I would probably have settled for that at the start. But I'm a superstitious guy and, whenever I've gone on to win the title, I've always won the opening race. So I was even more determined to win in Australia before going to Honda's home the following week.

It had been bad enough recovering from that first injury, a damaged right shoulder from a testing fall in Valencia. It was one of the reasons why I had struggled to motivate myself all winter. My body is starting to show the wear and tear of 20 or so years of competing in a gruelling and dangerous sport. There are only so many times that you can dig down and ask it to keep going through the recovery process. It gets harder every year and you have got to listen to your body. I've got aches and pains everywhere, on top of the agony that I'm in now.

And there comes a time when you have to say, 'Forget it, sonny. You ain't getting any younger.' I might have to say that at the end of this year. We'll have to see. It's different for the younger riders, because they still have everything to aim for – to prove themselves by winning trophies.

The only thing that keeps me going is winning races. And if this injury prevents me from doing that, then there'll only be one thing for it. Because the life of a bike rider, apart from the obvious danger, is not as easy as it may seem to some.

The travelling used to be exciting 10 years ago but now it has started to become a real ball-ache. It all seems very glamorous from the outside, because the sport is very colourful and there are lots of girls in bikinis in beautiful climates. But tell me what's glamorous about flying to the other side of the world, hanging round a track and living out of a hotel for a week. As far as I'm concerned, it's now a case of get in, do the job, and get out. I would have been away from home for 16 days when we were due to return from Japan and both myself, and my wife Michaela, are aware that we are missing the kids growing up.

Don't get me wrong, I have been lucky to make a very good living out of fulfilling my dream. Not many people can say that. All I ever wanted to do was ride a bike and become world champion but, when that happens, you find out that it's not as easy as you thought it would be. There's a massive responsibility because people make demands on you everywhere and everyday.

Then, on top of all my problems I have had with motivation, there has been a complicated legal battle with my uncle over merchandising rights, which has got everybody down. There was no way that I wanted to be risking my life like I did on Sunday when there was a chance that he could make money out of it.

There are a lot of people who think that I'm deliberately negative because it makes me look even better when I go out and win against all the odds. But I've nothing left to prove – I'm the best superbike rider there has ever been. If the World Superbike championship had not grown into arguably the biggest championship today, and I hadn't grown with it, I might have regretted not moving to Grand Prix.

It always used to be said that the 500cc Grand Prix bikes were harder to ride, but there's only a handful of people saying that now. In my opinion, there will be no such thing as the Grand Prix championship as we know it in three years' time. It's going through such a bad patch and is no longer convincing. All it will take is for superbikes to pinch a couple of the top riders. Then the 500ccs will become four-strokes, like the superbikes. When that happens, I'll be able to say I was world champion, anyway.

I don't really care how I compare to stars of other sports. But, if I'm ever asked who has been the best British sportsman of the last 10 years, I'll say me. I've won five world titles, and there aren't many who can match that. Stephen Hendry, maybe, but snooker is a leisure pastime, not a sport. I couldn't argue with the rower Steve Redgrave because he has had to train incredibly hard to achieve success in a sport which, like mine, has struggled to attract mainstream publicity.

I admire guys who do well at motorcross because it's so physically demanding, although nobody has dominated it in Britain like Jeremy McGrath has done in the States. In the high profile sports, there aren't many sportsmen who, when you look into their eyes, want to win like I do. They might want to do well, but they don't want to win.

The ones who really wanted to win are people like John McEnroe. He had the same spoilt brat type of bad-tempered attitude when he wasn't winning. I would have thrown my racket down if I had been a top tennis player. If Ayrton Senna didn't win he had a face like thunder and punched people. Tiger Woods is like a big kid whenever he loses. In football, there's Roy Keane. He has the kind of determination to win that I can relate to – to try and score a goal and then to make sure he's back defending.

And I have seen it in very few other riders. Mick Doohan would sulk and blame something if he didn't win. I've seen it in John Kocinski and Scott Russell. And I'm starting to see it a little bit in Colin Edwards, who was second in the championship last year and is second after Sunday's races. It's that special something that separates you from the other guys who just enjoy being out there, getting paid good money. If they win, then it's a bit of a bonus. I don't care about the money. I would do it for food if I had to.

Sure, there are times when I sit back and think, 'You've done bloody well for yourself.' This is a cut-throat world that is very difficult to break into and I had a lot of other bad injuries and set-backs early on. So I'm not ashamed to celebrate the fact that I'm the best. I wear a gold number one earring and a necklace with a gold number one pendant. I drive a Porsche Carrera with a personalised number plate, FOG IE, and I have my own official Website.

Some people might think all that's flash and big-headed. But I don't care what people think. If you take 100,000 people, 95,000 might think I'm ace and 5,000 might hate my guts because I'm outspoken. There might be people who are upset by some of the things I say in this book. All I can say to them is that they are the honest opinions I held at those specific points of my life.

Actually, I have no idea what the other riders think of me. There's a lot of jealousy and back-stabbing in racing because it is an individual sport. There are not a lot of people who I can trust. They might say nice things in public and then, behind my back, make up some excuse about why I have always won, such as the fact that the Ducati is a better bike. That really used to annoy me. And it used to upset me when I got criticised.

But now I quite like it when I wind people up and it doesn't bother me when riders moan because the same thing was always said about other champions. They said that Valentino Rossi's Aprilia was miles better than everyone else's. They said that Doohan's Honda was miles better. They said the same thing about Barry Sheene, Kenny Roberts, Giacomo Agostini – all the top riders. But the people in second, third, fourth and fifth have to say that. If they said, 'He's better than me', their team would just get rid of him. The only person who ever said that about me was Troy Corser, who, in 1999, admitted that nobody could beat me at Assen. He was axed by Ducati a month later!

I genuinely feel that I have very rarely been beaten on equal terms on a dry track. I admit that I'm not as good as some other riders in the wet. But the day will come when a rider does beat me in the dry without having a better set-up on his bike. Then I'll just have to say, 'Shit, Foggy, you rode really well but you were well beaten.' I'm honest enough to do that. And when that day happens, I will stop racing. Until then, it might appear that nothing has ever been my fault. But it never is! If I lost a race because a fly splattered into my visor, as it did at Assen in 1997, what am I supposed to say? That it didn't happen?

Even as a kid I hated the fear of losing. When I raced other kids at the back of our house I always had to be first. They treated it as a bit of fun but I always had to have the last word. And if anyone asked me when I was 12 or 13 what I was going to do when I grew up, the answer was, 'I'm going to race motorcycles.' Even when I was

5

motocrossing, as a teenager, I knew I would never be good enough to win, so it was a question of filling time before I was old enough to satisfy my addiction for road racing, at which I always knew I could be the world champion.

It's strange, because my dad was never a bad loser when he was racing. If you beat him at snooker or darts or dominoes, he hated it. But racing was just a hobby for him. He was nothing like me. So I suppose it's just how you're created. I was born with this desire to win. If you put six or seven guys in a 100m race, one will go faster than the others and go on to be a good runner. I grew up around bikes and I happened to be faster than the other guys. I was crap at everything else in life. When I won, I wanted to win more and more until I became such a bad loser that I would say things about another rider or criticise his bike.

There's been many a time that I've cried after winning an important race or championship. But I'm not ashamed about that, either. Why shouldn't everyone see just how much it means to me? Yet crying is not something I can do at other emotional times like after a tragedy. It shows just how dedicated I am to winning.

I just don't see the point in doing anything unless you are going to be the best at it. Whoever came up with the saying, 'It's not the winning, it's the taking part that counts' was obviously someone who couldn't win. That's an attitude that can make me a bit of a monster. And there are definitely two sides to my personality. People who meet me think I'm some scary highly tuned idiot who just goes out to win races and doesn't care what it takes.

But there is also the other Carl Fogarty, the one who wants a quiet life at home and who is still probably a little bit shy and embarrassed at being called a superstar. It's nice to be recognised, but a lot of the time it can be awkward. Someone asked me for an autograph on the plane on the way out here and, from then on, everyone was looking at me. The way I see it is that I'm no different to anyone else just because I can ride a bike fast. It's one of the reasons I don't enjoy racing any more. I just don't have my own space.

The organisers, Flammini, need to take some lessons from Formula One. I have no area where I can go in the paddock to get away from it all. And when I've got to think about winning, I need to have some room. I can't stand it when people lean into the Ducati hospitality area and ask for my autograph. So, at a race meeting, I'm the worst person in the world to be around. I don't like talking to anybody and I'm snappy with people, even with those closest to me like Michaela and the mechanics. I want to win so much that I just don't have time for other people. So, when people try to get at me all the time, I'm very ignorant and bad-tempered.

You look at all of sport's winners, they are always difficult characters. But the fans do get to see the other side of me as well. After I've won two races, then I'll sit down at the back of the hospitality tent and sign autographs and drink beer with them. I just love sending so many people home happy – my family, my team, my sponsors and thousands of fans. But, until that point, I am just a focused machine, who will say anything or do anything to get his own way.

In any case, I've never wanted to be the good guy. When I won the first world title there was a lot of aggression building up and it stayed there when I had to prove that I could retain it. Sure, I've changed as I've got older. When you win, and win again, you can relax a bit. There's no need to call people names. I'm now a lot quieter and more thoughtful about life. I can now devote more time to other hobbies and business interests. Before, I was so wrapped up in my racing that I couldn't break off to go and do something in the garden, for instance.

In some ways I can't wait to give up racing so that I can do these other things and spend more time with Michaela and the kids. But I'll always be busy doing something. I'll probably be a fitter person, too, as I'll have time to go into the gym or to go mountain-biking. There's even talk of a movie deal, a bit like Vinnie Jones in *Lock, Stock and Two Smoking Barrels*, although it's still very hush-hush. At the minute, I've no time to do any of this stuff because I'm pulled from pillar to post doing promotions, interviews, prize givings and official functions.

I've worked really hard since I started racing, so I deserve some time to myself. I don't even really know England that well, so there's so much to see and do. I will always live in England, that's for sure. Whether we will stay in the north is a different matter, because it's always wet and rainy. But I need to be speaking English and eating English food, near to my friends and family.

People ask me if I would miss putting my knee down on a corner or going at 190 miles an hour. But all that adrenaline buzz stuff means nothing to me. Sure, I've always liked anything with an engine, where I can push a button and have power. I drive fast, so I suppose I quite enjoy being on the edge. But I don't enjoy racing. I enjoy winning. Ask me what it's like to win a race and I'll tell you that there's nothing like seeing that chequered flag. That feeling was exactly the same when I was first to cross the line at Assen in 1999 to all but clinch my fourth World Superbike title, as when I won that first race on the fields behind my house.

And I want that feeling again. Because winning has been the story of my life . . .

CHAPTER ONE

Cock of the North

Let's start with a confession. I was born at Queen's Park Hospital on 1 July, 1965. Yes, *1965*. Not 1966, and not even 1967. The confusion is my fault but I've no idea why, or when, I decided to subtract a year or two whenever I have been quizzed about my age. I'm sure I'm not the only sportsman who has ever lied about their age and racers are particularly notorious for doing this. But it reached the point when it became too awkward to backtrack. So you can guarantee that now, whenever my age is quoted in newspaper or magazine articles, it's almost always a year or so out.

Dad, George, made his money by basically working his balls off from the day he left school. When I arrived, he was a panel beater for East Lancashire Coachbuilders, but at night he would earn a few extra quid by clearing rubbish from people's backyards. Together with his brother Phillip, they scraped enough together to buy a truck and slowly moved into the demolition business. Before too long, P&G Fogarty owned another truck and then needed a warehouse for storing equipment. So dad packed in his day job to concentrate on the business full-time, which was soon successful enough for us to move from a terraced house on Linley Street, in a working class area of Blackburn called Mill Hill, to a semi-detached – 595, Livesey Branch Road – in the Feniscowles district. That was the scene of my first ever bike accident at the age of three, and I still have a small scar on my forehead to remind me of the time I rode my three-wheeler off the edge of the patio and split my head open. I've been reminded of the incident so many times by my mum, Jean, that I've almost formed a mental picture of the scene, although I'm sure that I've no actual memory of it.

My days at Feniscowles Junior School are also something of a blur, so much so that I don't even remember being in too much trouble! I might have had to stand outside the headmaster's office a couple of times, but Mr Painter was a really nice man, who died shortly after I left, and not the type to go over the top with punishments. I had a big crush on a girl called Donna Pickup, but was scared to death of saying anything to her. My only contact with the girls at junior school was hitting them with rubber dinosaur toys tied on elastic under the desk. The monsters were confiscated, but that was as far as the teachers went.

I vaguely remember thinking I was fourth 'cock of the school', the honorary title given to the best schoolyard fighters. The undisputed cock was Paul Dinham, who I got on okay with most of the time. For some reason, I once roughed up one of his mates, who went running to Paul for protection. Paul stuck up for him and tried to sort me out but, instead of giving me a pasting, struggled to land his punches as I was too quick for him. And, while he was off balance, I sneaked in a few kicks, which wound him up even more. I was saved by the playtime bell and ran back into the safety of lessons while the going was good and, luckily, he didn't come looking for revenge.

The school was so easy going that the football team's fixtures were limited to two friendly matches a year against the two neighbouring schools, St Paul's and St Francis's. We beat St Paul's about 7–1 – I scored four or five – but Mr Painter did not think that was fair and, when we played them again, he took out all the best players, me included. We only won that game 2–1, which was how he liked it. I was gutted in my second game against St Francis's when, after leading 1–0 at half-time, we lost 2–1. Even at the age of eight, I did not like to lose one little bit.

Those reasonably happy memories were in total contrast to the start of secondary school at Darwen Vale High School. The place was huge, the older pupils were huge and I was absolutely crapping myself on the first day, despite the fact that a few of my classmates from junior school were starting at the same time. I was devastated when we did not receive a carton of milk at 10.30 on that first morning and I hated the place from that first day until the day I left. The teachers were stricter and I found it very difficult to keep up with the work. To be honest, I did not fit in at all. I had always been shy with new people, even though I was quite loud around any bunch of lads that I knew well. Maybe a few of the other kids in that class mistook the shyness for being spoilt. Mind you, I didn't help my own cause when we moved to a bigger house called Verecroft, on Parsonage Road, in the fairly affluent area of Wilpshire, when dad's business started to really take off. Thinking it would be cool and clever, I bragged that our new house had a swimming pool. But instead of impressing the other kids, it backfired and they thought I was a cocky git. When anyone came to visit, I bullshitted that we had to have the pool filled in, so that we could extend the lawn.

That typified the way that I tried too hard to be in with the in crowd. There were times when the other lads would tolerate me, but I was only ever on the fringes of the main group and, all of a sudden, they would give me a slapping to put me back in my place. If I'd had a fraction of the confidence that I have now, I would have turned round and hit one of them so hard. That would have earned their respect. And I'm sure I could have beaten any of them. Instead, I sort of curled up into a ball and took whatever abuse was coming my way. I wasn't picked on, but the boys that I wanted to mate around with would pick and choose when to include me, and when to drop me like a stone. It didn't help that the rest of the lads lived in the Darwen area, whereas I was now at the other side of town and pretty isolated. I could have moved to a school nearer to home but I was far too shy and insecure to try and meet a totally new set of friends. I would have cried my eyes out if it had been suggested.

In a nutshell, I just hated school and counted down the minutes of every day to when I could get home and ride my bike around the fields. Ever since the age of 11, I had been inseparable from the couple of Honda XR75 field bikes that I rode on a stretch of Tarmac near the poultry cabins at the back of our house. When I was around 13, dad bought me my first proper motocross bike, a two-year-old second-hand RM100 Suzuki, and we started to visit some local motocross tracks on the outskirts of Blackburn.

Until then, my only taste of racing had been to follow dad around the country watching him race. He was a good rider even though he didn't really have a decent bike until towards the end of his career. Still, he beat some big names and the thrill of the racing circuit made a big impression on me. Even at that early age, I somehow knew that was what I wanted to do.

I also found that I could hold my own against the older lads down at those tracks near Blackburn, which whetted my appetite for racing. Later that year, I dropped down to a smaller bike, a very fast Honda CR80, which I could ride really hard. Dad rented one of the fields behind the house and invited four or five other lads down one night, to ride their 125cc bikes against me. I absolutely blitzed them. It was my first taste of racing against other riders, and I loved it.

There was nothing at school that I loved. In fact, there was only one subject which interested me – and no prizes for guessing that it was PE. But I even lost interest in that. For the first couple of years I played football for the school on Saturday mornings as a tricky left winger, but only for the 'B' team which pissed me off. When I was eventually picked for the first team, the game was on a weekday after school. But I could not stand the thought of hanging round school one minute longer than necessary, so I told the teacher that I had an appointment to get my hair cut. When I turned up the next morning with my hair still all over the place, it didn't take him too long to realise that my commitment was less than 100 per cent. I was never picked for any side again after that.

I absolutely loathed maths and couldn't understand why I had to sit through English lessons when I could already speak the language. The attitude of my parents wasn't helpful, either. Neither of them ever checked whether I had done my homework; they just didn't seem to care. So I got away with murder. I tried to keep up for the first couple of years but, after that, I can't remember doing one bit of homework. The more I fell behind, the more pointless it was actually turning up and I started nicking off school altogether. I spent many a day just wandering aimlessly around the nearby canal and Witton Park, or mucking around with my mates who had also played truant. Nobody seemed to bother and the teachers never rang my parents to tell them that I hadn't been at school. I just caught the bus home at the usual time and was never found out. And the more I got away with it, the more I would do it.

So, when it came to exams in the fourth and fifth year, I was moved down a class into one of two groups of lost causes, along with one of my best friends, Andrew Shepherd. It didn't bother me because I was also back with some of my mates from junior school. And I was out of the way of the bigger lads from my previous class, who I had grown to hate. So, while they were doing their O-levels, me and Andy were sent out to a local mental institution, Calderstones Hospital, to gain work experience for some kind of City and Guilds qualification. It was the best week of my school life.

We were given all the shitty jobs, literally. As well as taking a few patients out for walks and exercise, we also had to take them to the toilet and bath them. We realised that one particular guy needed a lot of help which obviously led to an argument.

'I'm not taking his pants down,' Andy said.

'Well, I'm not bloody well going anywhere near him,' I argued.

But I drew the short straw and undressed him before he sat on the toilet. What we didn't realise was that he didn't know that he had to lift the toilet seat. So he sat on the lid and, before we knew it, there was shit everywhere. We were splitting our sides laughing, but we had to get him back to the ward.

'I'm not wiping the mess,' said Andy.

'Well there's no way I'm going to do it,' I argued.

In the end, we both pulled his pants back up, without cleaning him, and it went all over his back and his clothes. When we had calmed down enough, we returned him to the nurse, still stinking the place out.

Another of the patients never spoke, but you could tell when he was pissed off because he grumbled and muttered loudly. When it was our turn to bath him, we soon cottoned on that his level of grumbling rose when he was splashed with water. So, neither of us wanted to scrub him and he didn't get much of a wash. Then came the problem of drying him, as he wasn't capable of doing it himself. His shoulders and legs were no problem, but we weren't keen on towelling his bollocks. So we devised a method with Andy holding one end of the towel and me holding the other, rubbing it between his legs as if we were sawing down a tree. We must have been a bit rough, though, because his grumbling was deafening. The noise attracted the attention of a nurse who suddenly burst in. She was furious when she discovered friction burns in a particularly sensitive part of his body.

It was hilarious at the time, and still quite funny looking back, but typical of the cruel streak that I've still got. And, as the week went on, we became quite skilled with these patients. Not at looking after them, but at winding them up! As well as the grumbler, there was a woman who used to scratch her wrists so hard that she needed bandages for the wounds. Then there was a man who would swear violently at the slightest thing. And, finally, one of the inmates would just slap the nearest person when provoked. So, if you lined them up in the right order, it produced a spectacular chain reaction – like a line of dominoes toppling over.

Andy lit the fuse by slapping the slapper round the back of his neck. He turned round and slapped the swearer. 'You fucking bastard, you fucking bastard,' he shouted, which upset the grumbler no end. And that made the woman scratch her wrists furiously. All the time we were almost pissing ourselves laughing.

Part of their exercise routine was in a kind of bouncy castle. But, when we put them in the middle of the room, they just sat down and refused to bounce around. So we jumped around the edges, which made them clatter into each other – with predictable results. Slap. 'You fucking bastard.' Grumble, grumble. Scratch, scratch, scratch.

The frightening thing is that, three years later, someone told me that I had passed the course!

One year on and Andy was dead – the first person that I knew really well to be killed in a bike accident. I had been the one who actually got him involved in motorbikes, as he used to ride on the fields behind my house. He was very frightened the first time he sat on a bike, but soon became quite quick. Then, when we left school, we drifted apart. He lived on one side of Blackburn and I lived on the other. In June 1982, the year after we left school, he was riding with a pillion passenger during a lunch break as a trainee mechanic. The bike ran in the back of a van carrying eggs. Andy's passenger was also badly injured. I didn't even find out until a week after it happened. At the age of 17, death didn't mean much to me and I didn't even attend the funeral. It didn't really sink in for a year or two, when it suddenly hit me that my best mate throughout my time at school was dead.

On my last day at Darwen Vale, I turned up in my school uniform, but all my mates were in their normal clothes. I had a Harrington jacket, with a tartan lining, so I turned it inside out to show that I was a rebel as well. Nobody was going to learn anything on their last day so we just roamed around, disturbing other classes and trying to cause trouble. The headmaster, Mr Strafford, tried to chase us off the premises and my last contact with a teacher was telling him to fuck off. So much for an education.

I left school, in 1981, having never sat a single exam. I had sneaked through a back door of the system and the whole education thing just passed me by. It was amazing how it had been allowed to happen. And it was wrong. At the time, it seemed brilliant that I got away with doing so little but, looking back, I wish my mum and dad had made more of an effort. Dad was always late home from work and would then start messing with his bikes in the garage. Mum was never strict enough with me, even with little things like checking if I had brushed my teeth. She had lost a baby girl, who was stillborn a couple of years before I arrived. I didn't find out until I was 10 years old and it wasn't something that was often talked about. Maybe it caused her to spoil me, and my sister Georgina, a bit.

Whatever the reasons, they didn't push me to get involved with anything, inside or outside school. I would have kicked, screamed and cried if they had made me go to the cubs, or for extra football training or for swimming lessons, but I would probably have enjoyed it in the long run. Maybe it's because I was left to my own devices as a kid that I pushed myself so hard later on in life. When you are older, you realise when you've got the opportunity to do something with your life. Sometimes it's too late and the chance has passed. Luckily, when I realised that I had a talent for riding bikes, I still had time to be successful at it. But all the way through school I was quite happy lying in front of the fire watching *Scooby Doo* or *Grange Hill* on the telly, or getting into mischief with my mates.

At first that mischief was all fairly harmless teenage stuff, like pinching apples and pears from the garden of a grumpy old git who lived quite close by. On one occasion, he caught me and two other lads red-handed, marched us back into his house and rang the police. It was a complete over-reaction but they turned up and took our details. It was no big deal for me, but one of the others was about three years younger and, when the copper asked for his date of birth, he broke down in tears because it was his birthday. 'Don't lock me up, I'm supposed to be going out with my mum and dad tonight,' he blubbed. We were also crying – with laughter, until the policeman said he would be visiting our parents the next day. Stupidly, I believed him and spilled the beans to mum and dad that night. It earned me a few days in my room although, of course, the copper never turned up.

That punishment must not have made much of an impression on me though, because a few weeks later we were in deeper trouble. The day started off in all innocence – four 14-year-olds cycling into town with nothing much more in mind than to kill time in the summer holidays. I'm not even sure whether anyone actually made a conscious decision to go stealing. But, in any case, we tied our bikes up and headed for the big newsagents, Lavell's.

There was no big plan of action, no look-outs or decoys. We just wandered around the store filling our pockets with pens, lollies, sweets, a torch and some batteries. Then we scarpered back to the bikes and started pedalling furiously back in the direction of home. We had got away with it. 'Let's stop and have a look at what we've nicked,' I shouted to the others.

Me and my big mouth! On the outskirts of the shopping centre we were sifting through our haul when a woman strolled casually up. 'That's a lot of stuff you've bought there, lads,' she said. 'Have you got receipts for it all?'

Just our luck. We had been rumbled by an off-duty store detective, who worked for Boots. 'I think you had all better come with me,' she said.

Not bloody likely.

We made a dash for it and I managed to wriggle out of her grasp, but one of the lads was collared. As the store detective marched him off to the police station, it was obvious that he would grass us up. So me and a lad called Les McDermott rode as fast as our legs would pedal. The direction was not important, as long as it was out of Blackburn and away from home.

We did not pause for breath until we were in the Mellor area, near to where I live now, about three miles away. 'I'm not going home, no way. I will be in for a huge bollocking. I'm going to run away,' I told Les.

It seemed as though there was no other option. It was at this point that we started thinking like desperados. It had been a warm summer's day but the evening was closing in and it was starting to get chilly – and we were starving.

We spotted a small general store near to the Fieldings Arms pub and entered, pretending to be buying some sweets. But, by now, we were a couple of artful dodgers and, while I bought the sweets, Les sneaked away with the cheese and bread, and a newspaper to discover whether our crime had made headline news.

The next move was to find somewhere to sleep for the night. So we cycled a bit further into the countryside and through a tiny village called Balderstone, in a pretty well-to-do farming area. Just before the lane ended, in a farmyard near to the river, we spotted a tree house at the bottom of a huge field. I remember the exact tree to this day. The tree house was impressive with a proper roof but, after hiding the bikes and climbing up, we discovered the floor sloped badly. It would have to do, though. Having tucked into the food, which was impossible to eat because it was so dry, we tried to catch some sleep. But the temperature was falling rapidly and, even though we wrapped ourselves up in the newspaper, it was too cold to sleep. And, to add to the discomfort of the sloping floor, the noises of the countryside gave me the creeps. I could not have slept for more than a couple of hours all night.

By daylight, I was really thirsty and heard a milk float stopping further down the lane. So, adding to the growing list of crimes, we nicked a couple of pints and climbed back up the tree. We were starving again and absolutely filthy. It didn't take too long to realise that the outlook was pretty bleak, so we decided to head for home with our tails between our legs. To cap it all, I had a puncture a mile or so away from my house, and had to stop off at a phone box and ring my mum. 'Carl, is that you, love?' she answered. 'Where are you? We've been out of our minds with worry.'

I was lost for words and broke down crying and, when mum turned up in the car a couple of minutes later, she was in tears and couldn't stop hugging me. The police had been in touch and told mum and dad about the theft. They had been up all night, ringing round hospitals. Mind you, my dad couldn't have been all that bothered because he had gone to work as normal that day. Mum rang him to say that I was safe and well. So, while I was having a bath and restoring some feeling to my fingers and toes, dad marched in with a face like thunder. 'You're in so much trouble, boy,' he snarled. I knew I was in no physical danger, as dad never once hit us. But, even so, he could be pretty scary when he wanted to be.

We were forced to attend the police station that night, where I got away with a stern lecture before dad grounded me for ages. My only other scrapes with the law, apart from motoring offences in later life, were all bike-related. Some of the neighbours would ring the police if a few of us were hanging around outside their houses on our mopeds. I think they found us a bit menacing.

In many ways, it's quite fortunate that I didn't go off the rails completely because, for as long as I can remember, I was pretty much left to do as I pleased. The same applied to our pets. When we lived in Feniscowles, we had a beautiful Alsatian dog called Sheba, who lived in a world of her own, and was allowed to wander off whenever and wherever she wanted. Before too long, she roamed off and was never seen again.

Her replacement was my favourite pet, another Alsatian called Rebel, who was named after the dog in the *Champion The Wonder Horse* telly series. He was a typical man's best friend who used to go everywhere with me and do anything I wanted him to. He was very obedient where people and kids were concerned – but loved to kill other animals. I've always been an animal lover, but I hated cats. And I had that warped sense of humour of a typical teenager.

Behind our garden there was a poultry farm, so cats ventured into the garden quite regularly. As soon as I saw one, I would let Rebel out. Eight times out of 10 he would catch them straight away but, if the cat escaped up a tree, I threw stones or shot at it with my 177 airgun, which I had for hunting rabbits. When the cats tried to run away, Rebel would grab them and shake them so hard that they were dead within seconds. It sounds horrible, looking back, but it seemed perfectly normal at the time.

We also had another dog, a fat little scavenging mongrel called Trixie. She thought she was the boss and started all the trouble, only for Rebel to bail her out when the going got tough. On one occasion, Trixie squeezed through a gap in the fence of a pen, which contained a few sheep and two big, mean geese.

The geese fancied their chances against Trixie, until Rebel jumped over the fence and tore one of the geese to pieces. I got him out as quickly as possible and ran back home, acting all innocent. Then the phone went and the owner of the pen wanted £20 from my dad for his dead goose. Yet another bollocking – and we didn't even get to cook the goose!

Rebel loved our midnight poaching expeditions to the reservoir and would sit loyally next to me for hours on end while I fished for trout with little fluorescent floats. One night, the peace and quiet was shattered when a warden pulled up and scanned the banks with his searchlight. I grabbed Rebel and tried to sit perfectly still, hoping he would not spot us. It took me a while to realise that the lights had cast a shadow of a young boy and his dog, 20 times their normal size, on the wall next to us. We fled down the steep banking, again thinking

I had given the warden the slip because I was out of the light's beam. Unfortunately, though, I was still carrying my rod and the fluorescent float was trailing behind, allowing him to keep track of all my movements. So I ditched the rod, sneaked back home and, for once, got away with it.

Our house opened up onto acres of spare land, so the dogs often slipped away on their own. Many a time dad would come across them on his way back from work. Trixie had usually nicked something like a loaf of bread while Rebel brought up the rear, dutifully watching her back. Nobody seemed to complain that the dogs knocked around on their own, although nowadays a dog warden would probably pick them up. But it did mean that Rebel was free to attack any of the chickens or turkeys that escaped from the poultry farm. They were easy meat for Rebel, so the farmer bought two Dobermanns to protect his livestock. That was just a new challenge and Rebel used to take them both on, usually coming out on top.

We were inseparable for around 10 years, until I noticed that he wasn't his normal self in those fights with the farmer's dogs. Within six months, his back end went and he developed heart problems. When the vet came round, I knew it was the end and he injected Rebel as I held him in my arms. It was probably the most upset I have ever been at losing something dear.

It was around this time that I was learning to survive with girls. The one good thing about having a younger sister was her friends. Even though I was at a different school to Georgina, I used to catch the same bus home with her mates. As a teenager, I was very shy around girls and would sooner torment them than talk to them. I was interested in them, but much more interested in riding my bikes, and probably a bit of a late developer when it came to chasing them. The last thing I would do, if I fancied a girl, would be to approach her.

Georgina's birthday was one day after mine, on 2 July, so we often had joint parties like the one at Holy Souls youth club near home for my 16th. All Georgina's friends were there, and it turned out to be the sort of night that every teenage boy dreams of, when birds are coming at you from all angles. I snogged several, although only one, Christine Alsop, actually meant anything at the time.

First in line was a right pest called Jane McGarry. She was a good few years younger than me and the granddaughter of a guy called Tommy Ball, who had built up a massive shoe empire by selling

seconds from a warehouse in Blackburn. She had always wanted to go out with me because I was a few years older, but I didn't really pay her much attention. I only kissed her at that party to shut her up, as she was crying her eyes out because she knew I fancied someone else. By the time she was 16, she was absolutely stunning. I suppose I went out with her on and off for a while after that party, but it was always more off than on, as we always seemed to end up fighting. It was great to be seen with her, though, because her clothes didn't leave much to the imagination.

Ironically, Jane was to make headlines in her own right later on in life. Towards the end of 1993 she fell for a dangerous conman called Paul Bint, who had been jailed several times for offences which included pretending to be a doctor and even operating on a man's stab wound. Jane, who was by then called Griffiths, went to the *News of the World* with her story of how she blew his cover to the police. The last time I heard of her, she was in the newspapers again, this time the subject of an undercover exposé!

Next up at the birthday party was a girl called Michaela Bond who would, many years later, become my wife. She had met my sister at a fashion parade and was a year older than Georgina. She lived in Mellor and had started to visit our house more and more. At that time, it kind of registered with me that she was okay, but I was still at a stage when I would rather annoy her than do anything else. I liked to pin her down on the floor and squirt Fairy Liquid in her eyes, or chuck her shoes into the stream when she was in our tree house.

If she stayed over with Georgina, I would bang on the ceiling with a snooker cue to make sure they couldn't get to sleep. Then, when they came downstairs to shut me up, I would be hiding under the stairs and scare them half to death. I thought Michaela looked like Rory the Lion in the kids' programme, *Animal Kwackers*, and always greeted her with the show's catchphrase, 'Rory, Rory, tell us a story'. Anyway, at that party, I became the first boy she had ever kissed. It lasted all of 15 seconds before she ran off because her dad was picking her up.

Last, and by no means least, was the number one target, Christine Alsop. She also lived on Parsonage Road and was the same age as me. Again, even at the age of 13 when I first clapped eyes on her, I had thought she was nice. We went out together, on and off, for a while before getting together seriously, four or five years after the party. She

was fairly clever as well as attractive and worked at the Royal Ordnance Factory in Blackburn after leaving school.

My own time at school had not prepared me for the outside world in the same way. As it turned out, no classes could have taught me the skills that I have ended up using while travelling the world, facing the world's media or handling all the money and contracts. These were all things that scared me in the early part of my racing career. Life itself was my best teacher. That said, I wish I could turn the clock back and sit in a classroom knowing what I know now. I would have loved to have been able to put my hand up and answered a teacher's question with confidence, or just to have had enough self-belief to say 'I'm sorry, but I don't know the answer.' Even when I thought I knew the answer, I was too embarrassed to volunteer.

Now I am exactly the opposite and have so much confidence that I shout my mouth off all the time and am not afraid of anything. And I can't help thinking that, if I had had an ounce of that confidence as a teenager, I might have got in more trouble, but I would have breezed through school. It's for these reasons that I push Danielle and Claudia to take their education seriously and we have paid for them to go to Westholme, the best school in the area. I'm just dreading the day when their homework gets a bit more complicated, because I'll be useless then!

My dad didn't even push me into starting to ride bikes. Racing was something I had grown up with, and gradually turned into something that I wanted to do. Other lads had started riding motocross when they were six years old, but my dad didn't urge me on in the same way that other dads did. I could, and should, have started riding competitively at a much earlier age. As it was, I finally plucked up the courage to enter races when I was 15, but I was absolutely shitting myself. My attitude was: 'I don't really want to do this. What if I come last?'

Maybe dad was consciously making me stand on my own two feet. I suppose he might not have even wanted me to be a racer. But I felt as though I needed a bit more encouragement. If I'd had a little boy, he would have been on a bike at the age of six, if only to see if he wanted to do it. Then, if it was obvious that riding wasn't for him, he could try something else – no problem. In my case, I was left to make my own decisions and, at that age, did not have the courage of my own convictions to give anything a real go.

And, when I did, it was a disaster . . .

CHAPTER TWO

Boy Racer

There is no doubt that I am not the first rider to have crashed in his first race. And I'm probably not the first to have had a blazing row with his dad after that first fall. But, it's safe to assume that this would have been the first time it was over a packet of Polo mints.

For Christmas in 1980, I got a brand new Yamaha 125G, made that year. The 1981 'H' models were already out, the first year of the water-cooled bikes. Mine was air-cooled, but it was still pretty fast and I badly wanted to test it in a proper schoolboy race.

But I could still not pluck up enough courage to enter that first event. I didn't have anywhere near enough confidence to conquer the fear of losing and showing myself up. So it was almost inevitable that, when my dad eventually entered me for a 125cc motocross event at Carnforth, it would end in disaster.

My mouth was dry as I lined up behind the elastic starting tape, waiting for the 80cc race to finish and the first of our races to start. All the other kids had brand new gear, which didn't help my confidence. And it was dented even further when I realised that I was not wearing any gloves. I waved to dad and he dashed back to the van and brought them over just in time. Right, this was it, now or never.

When the tape went up, it was obvious from the first lap that I was in for a right pasting. One guy shot off into the lead, skimming over the bumps. I was following every contour, like a rollercoaster. My former mechanic, Slick, calls it 'Charlie Browning', because the ups and downs are so exaggerated, like in a cartoon.

Coming down a steep hill, I misjudged one of the bumps, the front wheel hit the up-slope and my chin smashed into the handlebars. I bit straight through my tongue. Blood was gushing from my mouth, so I pulled up at the side of the track and laid on the floor. Dad came rushing over. For some unknown reason, he suddenly started shoving Polo mints into my mouth.

'What the hell are doing that for?' I spluttered.

'It will help you spit the blood out,' he said.

'I'm not having a problem spitting the blood out,' I coughed back at him.

I still have the scar on my tongue. I cannot even remember where I came in the other two races, but I managed to stay on and the accident had not dented my confidence enough to stop me wanting to give it another go.

At my second attempt, back at the Carnforth club, I won my first ever trophy, which I still keep in my garage, for coming tenth overall. That was against some good riders, who went on to become top British motocross racers, and I started to win trophies regularly after that.

The main focus for my racing was the Vale of Rossendale club, which was the nearest club to home. Their meetings were not quite as competitive, so I would usually finish around the top five. I was gradually improving, but could not quite manage that first win.

Then, on a sweltering day at the end of June, at a local track next to a quarry in Hapton, where I only ever raced once, it all seemed to be clicking into place. I was leading the first race and pulling away from the pack. But the excitement got the better of me, I lost control and ran through the ropes around the track. And it was bound to be at the exact spot where dad was marshalling. He rushed over and was frantically trying to unravel the rope, which had become tangled in the bike.

'Come on, come on! They're getting past me. Hurry up,' I shouted.

'I'm doing it as fast as I bloody can,' he yelled back.

It wasn't quick enough, though. I couldn't stand the thought of letting my first win disappear, so I let the clutch go and sped off, with my dad still holding the ropes. The friction burnt all the skin on the palms of his hands, so he wasn't too chuffed, especially when I fell off again a few yards further on because the ropes were still wrapped around the bike. I was so pissed off, and felt a bit guilty about dad's hands, so I tried to repair the damage in the second race of the day, but could only manage fifth.

There was one last chance to make amends, in the last race of the day. Christine Alsop was there, as I went out with her for a few weeks that summer. She gave me a hug on the line and stuck a grass reed in a crack in the seat. 'There, that's for luck. Now go out and win,' she said. Sure enough, I led from start to finish. And Christine was there at the finish line to give me a big kiss, which was highly embarrassing because all the other lads started to jeer and wolf-whistle. But I wasn't too bothered because it was the first time I had felt that unique thrill of winning. It was such a fantastic feeling.

I couldn't wait to get back to 'the caravan', the meeting place for all the teenagers on Parsonage Road and Warrenside Close, to tell everyone. It was a big six-berther, which dad had used for travelling to race meetings. When he stopped racing, he parked it at the back of the house on some spare land near the poultry cabins. There would always be somebody in there. It could have been three people, it could have been 12, because it was such a cool place to hang out – even for people I didn't know all that well.

So, when I got home from Hapton, I charged straight down to the caravan and burst in shouting, 'I've won, I've won my first race.' Quite a few mates were in that night and they joined in, 'Hey! Foggy's won his first race. Good on you. Brilliant!' I think they were probably taking the piss and laughing behind my back, because most of them were not really that interested in bikes.

The caravan played a major part in all our lives for a couple of years. While I was still at school, I would come home, wolf my tea down and head straight for the caravan to see who was there. It was a great place in which to get away from mums and dads, so people would smoke their fags in there or sneak the odd can of beer in.

I just experimented with cigarettes in those days and I only ever smoked properly when I moved into my first flat. I gave up in November 1989 and now I find it disgusting. I didn't even like the taste of beer, and I have never really been a big drinker, although I went along with it at the time, so as not to feel left out. The smell of whisky still makes me feel sick following one night as a 14-year-old, when mum and dad were out, leaving Georgina and me alone with the drinks' cabinet unlocked. I drank nearly half a bottle of the stuff and spewed all over the bathroom. My sister thought I was dying.

As for drugs, I wouldn't know one if it jumped up and bit me on the arse. I have never been offered them and I don't know anyone who does them. The Australian rider, Anthony Gobert, has been caught out, and I've had my suspicions about a few others. But I don't know the difference between grass, cannabis and weed, or whether to smoke or inject them. But I do know they are no good for you, so what's the point getting involved?

As well as being a great place to hang out, the caravan was also a great place for me to show off my riding skills. While the other lads were inside chatting up the girls, I would try and impress them by riding up and down as fast as I could, hanging my knee off the bike like I was a superstar road racer. It was the summer of 1981 – the best summer of my youth.

It all went downhill when I started work as an apprentice HGV mechanic for a company called Holden's, where I stayed for nearly three years. I hated the job from the word go. I had no interest in wagons and I also hated the fact that everyone else was probably in the caravan, while I was grafting away. I couldn't stand the fact that I didn't know what I was missing out on. And, because I was covered in oil all day, my face became really spotty. Like most teenagers, I was really conscious of the acne. If there were any girls around, I would try and hide in a corner, or sit in the dark so that the spots were not as noticeable.

It didn't stop me trying, though. When one of my mates, Ross Duncan, passed his driving test, he wanted to show off his new skills but his dad would not lend him his car. My mum and dad were away, which gave me an idea.

'Come on, we can take my mum's car. Let's call on Michaela Bond. I haven't seen her for a year, and she's really fit,' I suggested, remembering her from my 16th birthday party.

She agreed to come for a ride and Ross had hardly reached the end of the block before I was trying it on and groping away. She was not having any of it. When we dropped her back at her house, I asked her if she wanted to go out on a date that weekend. She made some feeble excuse like she was washing her hair. I didn't see her again for five years as she moved down to Oxford to live with her mum, who had left home when Michaela was 10.

Another part of my growing pains was that I was also a bit weak at that age, which is probably why my racing was so inconsistent and I didn't win another race for the rest of my first season in 1981. I finished around seventh in the Vale of Rossendale championship, because I lacked the strength to ride more aggressively. Motocross is a very demanding sport and, even now, I still use it for training. I cannot think of a better form of exercise, as your whole body gets a good workout and you can finish the day with your arm and leg muscles really pumped.

Towards the end of the year, I had become a good mate of a lad called Gary Dickinson, a fellow Rossendale rider. During that summer his dad, Tony, who was a friend of my dad, had been killed at the Southern 100, a race that is held on the Isle of Man about four weeks after the TT races. I was at the meeting, because my dad was also competing, and it was my first experience of tragedy in racing.

The accident happened in the 250cc race on 15 July, when Tony braked hard to avoid another rider and crashed. He died the following day. When I heard the news I just stared out of the window of my room at the Empress Hotel, trying to take it all in. Our room overlooked Gary's and he also appeared at his opened window. 'I suppose you've heard,' he said. I nodded.

There is nothing that a 16-year-old can say in those circumstances although Gary, who was a year younger, seemed to be handling it better than me. Rachel, his nine-year-old sister, was hysterical and it took her ages to get over it. From that day onwards, my dad took Gary to all the motocross meetings in Tony's old van. Dad kept Tony's leathers and I cut a piece off the sleeve for good luck, although I didn't tell Gary as I didn't want to upset him any more. Our friendship grew stronger over the years and he ended up being the best man at my wedding.

For the 1982 season, we both rode brand new bikes, which probably cost my dad and Gary's mum around £900 each. That was a fair amount in those days, but this was a sport where you needed cash if you were to have a chance. That year I was second in the Vale of Rossendale championship, the series of races run by the club, but I should have won it. I was inconsistent again at the start of the season, but came on strong later in the year. I was also second in the Newton-le-Willows and North West championships.

Second place was becoming a habit, which was made worse by the fact that Gary, who was probably a better rider than me, won two of the three championships in his class, a year below the schoolboy experts' class that I was racing in. But I was slowly becoming hooked on motocross and, because dad wasn't racing as much on the roads, was quickly losing interest in road racing. I preferred to watch the British Motocross Grand Prix on telly and only read the motocross press, like *Trials* and *Motocross News*.

That was the last year I was eligible for the Auto Cycle Union (ACU) schoolboys meetings and, in 1983, I decided to ride in the rival Amateur Motorcycle Association (AMCA) championship. My club, Rossendale again, was a lot stricter than their ACU equivalent. Every rider had to attend the weekly meetings and miss a race every so often to marshal. At this level there were no age group categories, just different levels of expertise – juniors, seniors and experts. Gary could have done another year at schoolboy level as he was a year younger, but he would have cleaned up because he was much better than everyone else. If I'd had that choice, I would probably have stayed at schoolboy level, so that I could win the championship. But he wanted to carry on racing with me. I passed my driving test the previous November, so we could travel to meetings on our own, as it was no longer cool to have dad in tow. I bought the latest CR125 Honda, but Gary kept his 1982 Yamaha for our first season of racing against each other.

The first meeting was at Park Hall, Charnock Richard, in Chorley. We started in the junior class against people of all ages and for bikes of any size. The guy next to me on the starting line was huge, riding a 500cc Maico. It was all very intimidating, as we didn't know what to expect. But, when the catgut went up, I found myself leading at the first corner, with Gary tucked in not far behind. We blitzed them. I think I won one race and was second and fourth in the other two, to finish second overall for the day. We could not believe how easy it was.

The next race was at a top track near Preston called Cuerden Park and we were too good for the opposition again. I won the first race and Gary won the second, so we were tied on points going into the final race. A guy on a Suzuki had cleared off way in front. I finished third but Gary was second and so he won overall. That was the story of the season, the bastard always beat me. He was more aggressive and, while I would perhaps win one race, he was more consistent and still came out top on points.

Some of the meetings were too far away from Blackburn to travel to on the morning of the race, so I would drive there the night before. The transit van, which doubled up as a caravanette, was quite well kitted out. There was a sink, a small cooker and the seats became beds, with just enough space for the bikes. It also had a CB radio.

After parking up for the night before a meeting at Leigh, Gary scanned the airwaves looking for someone to talk to. He made contact with a girl, whose 'handle' was Barbarella, and persuaded her to let us pop round. I wasn't up for it at all, but he talked me into driving to her scruffy council house. She offered us some red wine and, soon enough, Gary was drunk and coming out with all the chat. 'I think you're really nice,' he slurred. For once, I was acting grown up and trying to calm him down. 'Come on Gary, I think you've had a bit too much to drink.'

Then, out of the blue and without any warning, he dived onto the settee and tried to snog her. 'I think you'd both better go,' she screamed, as I tried to steer him out of the house.

Despite his hangover, he had a great day and won all three races in the pouring rain and horrible muddy conditions. I felt as right as rain the next morning, but didn't finish one race because I kept getting stuck in the mud.

The organisers had been noting our performances and eventually decided we were too good for the juniors. But, instead of going up one level into the seniors, we were moved straight into the expert class. Funnily enough, I could beat Gary at that level. I maybe only finished around sixth, but it was usually ahead of Gary. Our final race together was in Cumbria and, significantly, the day before I was due in the Isle of Man to watch my dad race in what was to be his last TT.

When I got to the Isle of Man, the thought hit me like a hammer. What the hell was I wasting my time in motocross for, when this was what I had always wanted to do? I couldn't believe that motocross had caused me to forget the thrill of road racing. The fact that dad was now late on in his road racing career made the fact that I wasn't riding even more frustrating. I was furious with him because he was lapping slower than 114mph, the absolute minimum speed he should have been achieving.

As a kid, I had been in awe at the big names like Joey Dunlop, Mick Grant and Roger Marshall. Now, after my motocross experience, I was thinking, 'I can beat this lot.' Maybe it was the size of the bikes, the crowds or just the sheer glamour of the event, but there was no turning back from that moment in 1983. My mind was made up and I went to find dad. 'I want to stop motocross,' I told him. 'I want to start road racing.'

It's not unusual for good motocross riders to convert to road racing.

For one thing, young riders have no other way of starting, as they are not allowed to race on the roads. Some riders leave it until their mid-twenties before making the switch, a bit like Chris Walker has done recently to become one of the most respected riders in the British Superbike championship. I think that is too late – you miss too much time to develop. But I was only 17. I still had time on my side.

On returning from the Isle of Man, I spent a couple of weeks in the South of France near St Tropez with my mate John Jefferson, as his dad, who owned a chain of bookmakers, had a place down there. That was my first holiday abroad without my parents, but all I could think about was starting to race bigger bikes on the roads. When I got home, I went to watch Gary racing motocross at Cuerden Park. He was dreadful. I felt guilty, as it seemed that he no longer had the motivation because I wasn't there for him to race against. He quit soon afterwards, which was a shame because he had a real talent.

After I had turned 18, in 1983, dad sent off for a licence for the road racing novices' orange jacket (which you must wear for the first 10 races) from the ACU and I joined the nearest club at Aintree, Liverpool. During that year, dad was riding a beautiful Formula 2 600cc Ducati, a version of the road bike bought direct from the factory, as well as a 500cc Suzuki. The plan was for me to ride the Ducati, which was fitting.

The first race of the 1983 season was only two weeks away, so dad took me to Oulton Park in Cheshire for some much-needed practice. I started off on a road bike, a 500cc Honda, while dad was on the Ducati racer. The plan was for me to follow him round the track and learn the best racing lines. After a few laps doing this in the pouring rain, he dropped behind to have a look how I was doing. His version of the story is that I was all over the place, taking the inside line when I should have been wide, and lucky not to crash at every bend.

It's a pity he didn't pay more attention to what he was doing as, unknown to me, he fell off at Lodge Corner, a tight right-hand bend. I carried on lapping, totally wrapped up in getting to grips with the bike, while dad frantically tried to catch me up. His only option was to cut across the short circuit – but he fell off again. When I reached that point, I noticed that he was in a spot of bother and pulled up.

'What's the matter?' I said. 'Are you all right?'

'Of course I'm all right. I was trying to catch you up, you bloody idiot. You were all over the show. You'll kill yourself if you ride like that in a race,' he shouted.

'What are you on about. I was enjoying myself,' I replied.

'Shut up and go and get me a 10 millimetre spanner, my gear lever has jammed,' dad growled.

I was still killing myself laughing when I got back into the pits. After we had mended the gear lever, it was my turn to try the Ducati racing bike, in preparation for the Aintree race. It was my first time on board a racing bike and I absolutely hated it. My feet were in a strange position behind me and my arms were tucked in at my side. I did a few laps and called it a day, wanting to return to the road bike.

But the following day was an open test day at Aintree, and dad forced me out on the Ducati again. 'You've got to get used to this bike, and get rid of all those bad habits,' he said. By the end of that day, I started to feel comfortable on it and was looking forward to the race – and half expecting to win. I had never been that confident in motocross. But this just felt right. 'I'm going to show everyone next week,' I thought. Ironically, my first ever road race turned out to be one of dad's last ever races.

There is no denying that dad had been a decent rider in his heyday, in the late seventies. In 1976 he rode in the Spanish 250cc and 350cc Grands Prix, his only Grand Prix races on foreign soil. It was at a road circuit near Barcelona, called Montjuich Park, and we combined it with our first holiday abroad. This was the scene of my first dice with death.

While playing in the sea, I was hit by what seemed to be a huge tidal wave and dragged out of my depth. The currents were pulling me under as, in a blind panic, I struggled to catch deep breaths. I was thrashing around furiously but didn't really realise which way I was swimming. Then a stranger grabbed me round the neck and dragged me back onto the beach. I was semi-conscious but coughing my guts up and, when I came round, could not work out why my trunks were bulging with sand. Mum and dad rushed over. 'How did this happen? We only took our eyes off you for a second,' they insisted. More likely, they were fast asleep in the sun.

Despite all the drama, dad did pretty well in the race, finishing 12th, and could have done better had he been riding a more competitive machine. By the next season, he finally had enough money to buy some decent bikes and 1977 was the only year he had a real go at making a name for himself. He rode two Suzukis – a 500cc and the 750cc bike that Barry Sheene had used the previous year. He hadn't really had enough money to compete at a higher level during his early career so, when he was eventually able to compete, he was probably a lot older than the other riders, which didn't help. Even so, he was second in the Isle of Man TT and flew past former world champion Giacomo Agostini on the first lap of the British Grand Prix at Silverstone before crashing out, when a top six place looked on the cards.

That run of good rides was dramatically stopped when he crashed and fractured his skull at an airfield circuit at Carnaby, near Bridlington. Mum and me had not travelled to the meeting and, while I was watching telly, the phone rang. It was my dad's mechanic, Ben Westall. 'Oh my God! Oh no!' mum groaned. She started crying so I sprang up and, tugging her arm, frantically asked, 'Is he dead? Is he dead?' Thankfully the injury did not prove too serious and, after two weeks in a hospital in Hull, he discharged himself.

For the next two years, he rode for Sports Motorcycles Ducati along with one of his big heroes, Mike Hailwood, who was returning to road racing after more than a decade away from bikes, during which time he took to racing cars without too much success. Hailwood made an immediate impact in the TT, winning and breaking the lap record in that first year back. It was a big thing for dad to be racing with a guy who was possibly the best rider in the history of the sport and had no fewer than 76 Grand Prix wins in all classes to his name, not to mention nine world titles. Some of that quality must have rubbed off because, in 1978, dad won an international race in Scarborough and hit the headlines in the 1979 British Grand Prix at Silverstone – for all the wrong reasons.

British hero Barry Sheene and his American arch rival Kenny Roberts were involved in a ding-dong battle for the lead on the second last lap, and were about to lap dad. He was actually still in the points, although his bike had started misfiring and he was running on three cylinders. Dad was blamed for obstructing Sheene as the leading pair tried to pass, but Roberts went through without a problem, pulled away and won the race. The newspapers made dad a scapegoat, but Sheene told him after the race that he wasn't to blame.

Later that year, he fractured his skull for a second time, coming out of the final corner at Aintree – and right in front of me. When he came round in hospital, the first thing he asked was whether the bikes were ready for the next meeting. But, even at that early age, this sort of incident didn't really affect me. It was more a case of 'Oh no! Dad's crashed. I hope he's all right' rather than crying or screaming in the ambulance on the way to the hospital with mum. After all, it was not unusual for dad to be involved in big crashes.

His worst ever was at the bottom of Bray Hill in the TT. If you fall off there, you usually do not live to tell the tale. He didn't even break a bone in that fall, or at any other time apart from those two fractured skulls, which caused no lasting damage other than to make him quite forgetful at times.

Dad could have been a very good rider, especially if he had decent bikes in his twenties. When he eventually rode better bikes, he did not ride aggressively and go all out to win races because he had a business to run. Even so, he was second in the TT and second in the North West 200 four times, and should have beaten Tony Rutter to the Formula 2 World championship in 1982.

Strangely, I do not think I have learnt anything from him. While you can study and copy techniques or styles from videos, your own ability has to come naturally. You are either good enough or you are not. I think my talent was largely natural, rather than copied from watching dad. It's hard to say how he would have done these days, as racing has changed so much since. For a start, the tyres were different back then and riders now slide the bikes around corners a lot more. These days racers put their knees down on the ground, whereas I don't think my dad's knee ever touched the ground once with his tucked-in style.

When the big day at Aintree eventually arrived, dad entered the 500cc and 1000cc open class races. I entered the 500cc four-stroke class, but also put my name down to ride against him in the 500cc open class. That meant I was on a road bike, up against other out-and-out racing bikes such as 350cc Yamaha two-strokes. So I didn't have a cat in hell's chance. That was not the point, the race would provide invaluable experience. It also counted as one of the 10 races that I needed to complete in order to lose the orange jacket and the tag of 'novice' in time for the following season.

I finished around 11th and, as expected, dad won easily to clinch the Ace of Aintree championship. He was, after all, an international class rider up against club riders. But I still felt that I had a real chance in my class, the 500cc four-stroke, even though I was as nervous as I had ever been.

Numbers were drawn out of a hat for starting positions on the grid and, just my luck, I was on the back of the grid. Electric starts weren't allowed but there was no way I was going to be able to bump start the Ducati, as I would have had to run for miles. There seemed nothing else for it. Before the flag dropped, I hit the electric start button and was off before the rest of the grid had time to blink. I weaved through the others and straight up to the front, as my dad and his mates held their heads in embarrassment.

It was so obvious that I had used the illegal starting mechanism. I was oblivious to this and felt pretty pleased with myself. I even tried to give dad the thumbs up. The rest of the riders, although their bikes were probably not as good as mine, were a lot more experienced. So they were even more annoyed when this kid started cutting people up and veering all over the track. At one point I dropped down to fourth, but managed to claw my way back to finish second. I was the only person at the track surprised when I was disqualified, not for reckless riding, but for using the electric start. I was devastated, and fuming. 'It's bloody disgusting,' I shouted. 'I made it back to second from being fourth. That proves I didn't need the electric start.'

My dad didn't know where to look – he was the main man at Aintree and his son was showing him up.

I had wanted to win so badly, though. That was something I had never felt when I was racing in motocross. Perhaps I always knew that I would never make a great motocross rider. But, ever since I had been a little kid, something inside had told me that I would be a great road racer. It seemed somehow destined that my whole life would be dedicated to being the best at the sport that I had grown up with, following my dad to events all over the country.

The next meeting was at an airfield in Northumberland called Ouston. In all honesty, my bike was way better than the others in the 500cc four-stroke class. But that didn't matter when, having come second in the first race, I notched my first road racing win in the second. Again there were protests, that I had been knocking over the cones that marked out the track.

By this time a few people were also moaning that my bike was too good for the class. They had a point, as it was, after all, a 600cc competing against 500cc bikes. There was no way, though, that they would be able to get that first trophy back off me and I made up some excuses, like the bike had been sleeved down, a modification whereby smaller piston barrels are added to reduce the capacity of the engine. And the Ducati was based on a street bike, so not much faster than a 500cc four-stroke, in any case. The rest of the season was just a mad rush to be rid of the orange jacket, racing every week at places like Mallory Park, where I won two races and was second in the other.

This road racing business seemed a bit of a doddle – until I travelled to Cadwell Park in Lincolnshire. During practice I was over-confident and, instead of parking up after practice to concentrate on the race, I kept joining the queue to go out for another session to show that I was so much faster than the other riders. There is a fast right-hand corner on the circuit called The Gooseneck. As it tightens, you have to flick the bike back into a chicane – a tricky manoeuvre.

I was flying as I approached the bend and realised I would not be able to get round. So I lifted the bike a bit to run over the grass, which suddenly dropped down a slope. The bike went lock to lock, where the rider has no control over the steering, and threw me off. There were no broken bones, but one badly broken bike. The frame was bent and there was no chance of me making the race. A few of the wise old heads in the paddock said, 'It might be your first crash, lad, but it'll not be your last.' Dad was not quite so philosophical. He went mental.

I also raced at another airfield called Flookburgh in Cumbria, where a friend's father, Derek Shutt, was killed the following year in a sidecar race. I was one of the last people to see him alive, when he had told me that he didn't really want to race there that weekend, but owed the organisers a favour. His passenger was badly injured. Usually the passenger would have been his son, Steven, but he was not there that day for some reason. His absence possibly saved his life.

Despite having seen my dad fracture his skull, and having experienced the effects of tragedy at first hand when Gary's dad was killed, I did not know the meaning of the word fear. The consequences of crashing just never entered my head. That attitude probably shone through in my best result that first season, at a wet Oulton Park in a 1000cc open class race, against some experienced international licence holders. I was only fourth but that meant a lot more than any novice or four-stroke victory. Maybe I was not as bothered by the wet as some of the other riders because of my motocross background.

I raced at Aintree one more time that year, and I was already starting to love what had become my home track. But word was getting round the circuit, not about my ability, but about the size of the engine and the fact that I cheated by using the electric starter. By then I had learnt to blend into the pack, and to try and make it look a bit more like I was letting the clutch out to bump start the bike. I ended the season on a high note with an epic win and, despite all the usual protests that I was kicking up too much dust and riding dangerously, this time I was not disqualified. If I am honest, I think the rest of the older riders at Aintree hated my guts. They didn't like being beaten by a young, raw upstart. But, having completed the 10 races, the orange jacket was now a thing of the past.

I was no longer Carl Fogarty the novice, I was Carl Fogarty the road racer.

CHAPTER THREE

Moving up a Gear

It was ironic that Barry Sheene retired in what proved to be my first full year of racing. The comparisons and debates have never stopped since. But, for me, there is no debate. I know that I am a far better rider than Barry Sheene ever was.

The year in question was 1984. The Australians and Americans came over here and showed the Europeans how to ride bikes. And it was a good job that Sheene got out when he did. The face of racing was changing and he was not up to it. All of a sudden the Yanks and Aussies, such as Wayne Gardner, Freddie Spencer and Eddie Lawson, were sliding their bikes everywhere. Sheene did not know what had hit him. I was never a big fan of Sheene – my big hero was always Kenny Roberts. There's no doubt that Roberts was also a better rider. For a start, he won three consecutive Grand Prix world titles. But that didn't matter as a kid. I liked the sound of his name and the colour of his bike, and that was good enough for me.

In my eyes, Sheene was only famous because he had set out to make himself famous. It helped that he came from London, had a model girlfriend and a pretty face that sold Brut Aftershave. And, when he crashed, he really crashed. More often than not it was in a big race, so the crashes would be on *News at Ten*. When he smashed himself to bits at Silverstone, in the British Grand Prix, the whole country was gripped by his recovery as it was the first time people had seen legs put back together by pins and screws.

He was a good rider, don't get me wrong. After all, he won the world title twice, in 1976 and 1977. But that was at a time when some of the better riders, such as Phil Read and Giacomo Agostini, were past their best. And the up and coming riders like Virginio Ferrari, were still a bit too young to mount a proper challenge. As soon as Roberts came over to Europe in 1978, where the world championship was largely based, he won the title in his first year. Until then, he had only raced on circuits and dirt tracks in America and had hardly any experience of riding over here, except for annual challenge matches between Britain and the USA.

There were also a couple of other riders who looked like they would become better than Barry. But Pat Hennen didn't race again after he suffered head injuries in a crash at the Bishopscourt section of the TT circuit in 1978, and Tom Herron was killed at the North West 200 in 1979. Before 1975, there was really only one rider who was any good – Mike Hailwood – and he was brilliant. The way he came back to win the Isle of Man TT was incredible. I have no argument with people who say that he is the best British rider of all time, even the best rider the world has ever seen. And I can see why some people might argue that Geoff Duke and Phil Read were better than me.

But I don't rate any of the others before that time. People like John Surtees weren't the legends they were cracked up to be. In those days racing just consisted of a bunch of gentlemen travelling around Europe, racing on a few road circuits and claiming the world title. Then they thought to themselves, 'Oh, we'll have a go at driving cars now and win the world title at that as well.' It was so easy to do, then, but there is no way that it could be repeated now. These guys weren't athletes, their bikes were not fast and they could even use the same tyres all year. They weren't great riders. There is no such thing as a great rider before 1975. If people like Surtees were around today at the age of 28, they would be just another rider on the grid.

Getting back to Sheene, I think one of the main reasons he had the success he did was because his bikes were better than the rest. If you didn't have a factory Suzuki, you could forget it until Yamaha produced a quicker bike for Roberts, although that bike seemed harder to ride. Having said all that, I do like the guy. Barry lives out in Australia now and we regularly bump into each other as part of his work for television. He is a lot like me in many ways; he doesn't really care what he says and is not afraid of upsetting people. We always have a laugh and a joke and some good-natured rivalry. He is quite protective of his status in the sport and believes that, if the two of us were to walk down Oxford Street tomorrow, he would be the one who would be pestered for autographs. I think he would be very surprised!

Our records just do not bear comparison. I've won more world titles than Sheene, and on more bikes. I have won on road circuits, which Barry didn't do, and I have won the *Motor Cycle News* 'Man of the Year' award six times, compared to his five. He might have been famous in his time but, unless you are over 30, you are not going to remember Barry Sheene too well. I think our achievements will stand the test of time, but I would put myself in the top two or three British riders of all time, whereas Barry would be in the top five or six.

And 1984 proved to me that I could make it to the top.

Preparation for my first full season was poor as I spent the winter going out with my mates. There was no fitness regime and we couldn't even work on the bike, as it didn't even arrive in time for the first race at Oulton Park, one of a series of club meetings up and down the country. We were concentrating on the 250cc class and bought a one-year-old Yamaha, which had been used for Grand Prix races, off Tony Rutter, a former team-mate of dad's. It probably cost around £3,500, which was a decent price, and was as good as the new 1984 models.

There was a baptism of fire in store for me when the bike turned up for my first actual race, down at Snetterton in Norfolk, in the middle of a rainstorm. Dad, who was officially acting as my mechanic, my mate John Jefferson and me were all trying to sleep in the back of the van, while the bike was outside, covered by a tent that spent more time being blown around the fields than keeping the rain off. We were up all night trying to keep the bloody bike dry. But all that hard work was for nothing because on race day, at the first corner of the third lap, the throttle stuck wide open and I ploughed straight on and through a potato field. I expected another bollocking, but dad was quite impressed. 'You were going really well. It was my fault, really. Someone has just told me that we should have put oil on the slides,' he panted, after dashing over to the bike, which was stuck in three feet of mud.

In truth, neither of us really knew what we were doing. I was new to riding and dad was new to being a mechanic. So there were some tense times. At another meeting at Carnaby, we couldn't even get the bike to start so I hurled my helmet into the van, nearly smashing the front windscreen.

That was typical of the flashpoints, which were triggered when I wanted something for the bike and dad either didn't agree or couldn't deliver. If I wanted fresh tyres, dad would argue that there was enough tread left. The other riders were all using 'trick' parts, the expensive after-sales bits that made so much difference to the bike's performance. So other bikes had magnesium wheels while I was still on spokes. Racing technology was starting to change, but I felt as if I was being left behind. It wasn't until later on in the year that we decided to buy some Hans Hummel-tuned barrels for the engine, which were a lot better than our Yamaha powervalve system's barrels and had improved performance for other riders. If you didn't have HH barrels, you weren't cool.

But I wasn't really in a very good position to complain about dad not buying me stuff because I hadn't been earning myself. In February of that year I had started working at my dad's warehouse after realising my apprenticeship at Holden's had been a waste of three years. It just dawned on me one day that I was going nowhere so, out of the blue, I decided to clear off. When it came to the lunch break, I stopped steam-cleaning a truck, packed my toolbox into the back of my van, drove down to the local park and sat on my own all afternoon. Most of the time I was wondering, and rehearsing, what I was going to say to dad. When I finally confronted him his reaction was much as I had expected. 'That's bloody clever,' he said but, when he realised how much I hated it there, he offered me a job at his warehouse on about £50 a week.

Dad didn't really have anybody to look after his trailers and, while I didn't really know what I was doing, I could at least get them ready for their MOTs in the workshop. My cousin Chris came to work as a mechanic with me later that year, as well as a lad called Graham Wilson, known as Taste for some reason, who was as daft as arseholes. I had worked with him at Holden's and persuaded my dad to hire him. He didn't last long because he was used to an ordered way of doing things at Holden's where, if there was a fault on a wagon, the storeman would provide a new part. At my dad's works, you had to try and repair it first, with welding or tie-wraps. In some ways it was similar to the racing, but dad's company was putting nearly all the money in, so mostly I just had to put up with it.

P&G Fogarty was a true family concern and, at some point or another, all three of dad's brothers were involved in the business. Uncle Jimmy worked there for 20 years and Brian, who I was to grow to despise for his attempt to cash in on my success years later, was also there, on and off. Three cousins, Mark, Chris and Andy, were also employed during my time and my sister worked in the office. She was probably thicker than me and tried to do a bit of typing in the office, but she was pretty useless and only lasted a few years. Even my gran, Vera, did her bit. My grandad, Richard, was the warden of Witton Park and died when I was about eight, so I don't remember too much about him. But I was very close to my gran. She lived a short drive from the warehouse, on Cartmel Road, and cooked dinner every day for me, my dad, Chris, Mark and, more often than not, a couple of dad's brothers. This wasn't soup and a couple of butties. It was a proper lamb or steak slap-up, served in old-fashioned dishes with a flat rim, with chips, peas and beans.

Working for dad meant that I could sneak in a few hours' work on the bike during the day, and disappear on a Friday afternoon when I had a meeting to travel to. I guess that caused a bit of jealousy among the workforce, and there were a lot of two-faced blokes who wished me all the best only to slag me off behind my back. That wasn't the type of rivalry that was worrying me, though, as the 250s proved to be a very tough class.

There were a lot of new lads starting out, not to mention the older experienced riders who were still knocking around. I can't really remember many of my opponents, although one lad called Steve Patrickson did go on to be British champion at 250s and 125s. Another rider, Darren Dixon, went on to be TT Formula One British champion in 1988. A few of the others made their mark on the national scene, but nobody else made it on the world stage.

At that point, I had no career path mapped out to the top, although the 250ccs seemed like a good class for serving my apprenticeship in. If I wanted to be good, I knew that I would have to make a consistent impression at this level. It was a steep learning curve as I tried to get to grips with some fairly major changes to my technique, such as moving the handlebars further and further in from a sort of motocross position, to the more orthodox cramped racing style. It was also a huge jump from riding the bikes of the previous year, which were effectively road bikes in a racing bike's frame, to these out and out two-stroke racers. Suddenly, racing was all about carrying a lot of corner speed, and the experience I gained at that time has stood me in good stead right up to the present day. Something must have clicked, because I got better and better as the year went on and, by the end of the year, I was winning consistently at a lot of different tracks and breaking club lap records.

I was just getting into my stride when I suffered my first major injury, on my 19th birthday of all days. It started a weird sequence of events featuring the number 19, but more of that later. I had won the first race at Cadwell Park but, in the second, came out of the hairpin first corner and high sided the bike. High sides seem to happen to a rider more nowadays, and I don't really know why. Maybe it's because, in those days, the tyres were a different shape. The modern tyres are thicker and, when the wheel slides underneath, it suddenly seems to find grip and flips the bike the other way, sending the rider flying. It usually results in the worst injuries.

This time, I landed on my collar-bone, but it wasn't a bad break and I raced two weeks later at Aintree, when I was strapped up in a figure of eight bandage and wore my dad's baggier leathers for extra comfort. I finished second, which was not a bad result with a broken bone. The next meeting at the track was my best of the year – I won both races and smashed a race record that had stood for three years. Then I capped off the year with another win in the final meeting of the year at Aintree, but I didn't win their championship because I hadn't been consistent enough early on.

The biggest series for the best young riders at that time was the ACU Marlboro Clubman championship, staged all over the country. A lot of the tracks were new to me, such as Donington, where I crashed out at Redgate, a second gear right-hander where a variety of possible lines can confuse riders on their first visit. The final race of the series was at Silverstone and was live on television, another new experience. I was in the lead for about two seconds, eventually finishing fourth as four bikes crossed the finishing line virtually side by side.

By 1985 the goalposts had changed. I'd had enough of a taster to know that I could win the Marlboro series. And there was another target, the Manx Grand Prix, which was a major step towards entering the TT. To do all this I would need the right equipment, and that meant a Yamaha or Rotax engine, in either a Harris or Spondon frame. It was also the first year that Honda were back competing in the 250cc class, and they went on to win the 250cc world championship with Freddie Spencer. But those bikes were not for sale on the open market and were therefore not an option for me. So, at the start of the year, we sold the 1984 bike and bought a new Yamaha. We also got hold of a 350cc Yamaha, which was starting to become obsolete, so that I could ride in a wider variety of classes. There was no point having such good bikes, though, without a top mechanic and someone pointed us in the direction of John Gibbons. He had previously worked for Yamaha and had also been involved with Charlie Williams, who won the TT several times. I had also attracted a bit of backing from sponsors including Shell, who provided a few products, and had started to receive discounts on tyres from Michelin.

Everything gelled from the word go as I won at Oulton Park and Snetterton, when another sponsor, Dave Orton from Appleby Glade, a fruit machine company, first noticed me in their club races. He had seen me win the 250cc race and ride rings around the 500cc riders on my 350cc, only to be passed every time in the straight because of their bigger engines. Appleby Glade had been involved in the sport for a long time and it was a good sign that people like Dave Orton wanted to help out. It was only a few hundred quid, but his name carried a lot of clout. I don't know what Dave made of my first race in the Marlboro Clubman series at that same Snetterton meeting, as I was leading the race when I crashed at the end of the back straight after dropping down too many gears and locking the back wheel. My mechanic, John, was not one to moan, but I could tell how disappointed he was. 'The guy behind you had already settled for second,' he grumbled.

It was the first in a series of crashes because, by now, I was pushing that bit harder to win races in order to live up to the growing expectations. In my first national race, at Oulton Park, I was pressing the leaders on the 350cc when I crashed out. This time John found it harder to disguise his disgust. I overheard him saying, 'I get the bike set up perfectly for him and then he goes and throws it away like that.' It upset me to hear this, but he had a point and I was still too shy and insecure to fight my corner. I just wanted to ride the races, pack up and then go home.

There wasn't much of a social life through biking, although, by then, I had started going out with Christine on a serious basis and she came to a few meetings. I was no longer quite as shy as I had been with girls. Racing had started to bring the best out of me and I had more freedom. The start of my racing career had coincided with the time when I was becoming more and more interested in what they had to offer. So I probably missed out on the peak chasing years around 17 and 18 years old, as I was away racing a lot at the weekends – often with my dad for company! And, if I did go to a nightclub with my mates, I hated asking girls to dance. I was always too scared that they would tell me to get lost. My sister was probably responsible for pushing me and Christine together, and the rest of my family approved as she only lived a couple of houses away and was almost part of the family anyway.

After most of the meetings we faced a long trip back to Blackburn, where we would meet up in a small nightclub that had started to sponsor me, called Harvey's Disco Bar, where I was quite well-known. It was my idea of showing Christine a good time, though I'm not sure she appreciated it. If we had raced at Aintree, though, we got back earlier and headed for a Chinese restaurant in Blackburn town centre with a few of the other lads that had come to watch. They were a lot older than I was – and a bit rough. But I thought they were cool, especially when they started a fight and got us chucked out of the restaurant, which happened quite often. There was one giant guy called Dave Tate, a real hard bastard with a heart of gold, who loved coming to the races when he wasn't in some kind of bother. He was so big he could carry the bike back to the van on his own. Funnily enough, he was the one who usually stopped any fights, because people took one look at him and decided it wasn't worth it.

At the Aintree club dinner that year, some guy was trying to move in on Christine on the dance floor while I was nodding off at the table. Chris, my cousin, didn't like this and walked over to the lad and said, 'That's my cousin's bird, leave her alone.' Before the lad had a chance to walk off, Chris butted him. All hell broke loose and everyone piled in. Then Dave coolly wandered over and, with one in each hand, picked up two of the main troublemakers and marched them out.

In general, I didn't mix with the other riders or seek attention. If anyone ever tried to interview me over the tannoy at the track, I would run off and hide. My first real press coverage followed the first race at Aintree that year. *Motor Cycle News* was covering the meeting, at which I had won the 250cc and qualified for the 500cc final on my 350cc. But during the 350cc final, it seized up and I was left without a bike for the 500 final. The rules stated that the engine capacity had to be between 251 and 500cc, so 250cc bikes were ruled out. In my eyes, riding a 250cc in a 500 race was not cheating, so I went out for the final regardless.

It was one hell of a race and everyone went mad when I won. But, incredibly, one of the blokes that I had beaten made an official protest. I was livid and couldn't believe that anyone would embarrass himself so much as to complain after being beaten by someone on a smaller bike. 'Where is he? I'm going to rip his bloody head off,' I shouted. The headline in MCN read something like 'Mighty Mouse Fogarty disqualified'.

The second Marlboro race was at Thruxton and I thought it was about time that I started to pay back the faith that had been shown in me. I won that race, but was then only seventh in my first race at Brands Hatch the following week. I was still too inconsistent and proved that point spectacularly in the next meeting at Mallory on 19 May (that dreaded number again!). I was riding that 350cc bike during practice and lost control of the rear coming out of a corner. As I was coming off the side, I made the mistake of trying to hang onto the bike and found myself being dragged towards the tyre wall, with my hand still full on the throttle. I just shut my eyes . . .

. . . The next thing I knew I had won the Spanish Grand Prix. The crowd was going mental as I stood on the podium, spraying champagne everywhere. I was actually lying in the middle of a patch of nettles and the hallucination had been caused by concussion. I was numb everywhere but knew that my arm was broken. I had also cut the inside of my thigh as, when I hit the tyres, I had been thrown over a fence and into a bush. My leg must have caught the top of the fence on the way over.

I was very dazed and confused and, when I started to come round in the hospital, the doctors were asking me the standard questions like, 'What's your name?' and 'What town do you live in?' Even with those questions I was doing a Homer Simpson, pleading with my brain not to let me down. Then they asked, 'Who is the Prime Minister?' I couldn't think of the answer for the life of me, because I wasn't the slightest bit interested in politics. It wasn't due to the blow to my head, I simply didn't know. It took a couple of attempts before I remembered Mrs Thatcher and the doctors let me out the following day. That was my first serious injury and the last time I rode the 350cc bike, as it was smashed to pieces in the crash.

Recovering from that broken arm, a clean fracture that healed quickly, was nothing compared to coping with the death of my gran, from a tumour. It was a big shock because, even in her seventies, she was as fit as a fiddle despite the fact that the first of her four sons was only born after she had turned 40. I still miss her, even now, as she would do anything for anybody. I appreciate that fact more now than perhaps I did at the time. At the funeral, everyone was crying and I couldn't understand why I was the only one who wasn't. Again, I put it down to the fact that I was at an age when death didn't really affect me.

If it had happened later in life, I would have been much more upset. But I really wish she had been able to share in some of my glory. It would have been nice to buy her things, to show how much I appreciated everything she did for me as a boy. At the time, though, the only tribute I could pay her was to win at the next meeting. Fittingly that was Aintree, where she'd just started to enjoy watching me, standing with everyone else at the start-finish line. I managed to win both races, but it felt strange without her there to congratulate me.

Despite the injury and gran's death, I was still in with a shout of winning the Marlboro series at the final round at Silverstone. I had only won two other rounds, at Lydden and Thruxton. So I had to win, and Darren Dixon had to break down, for the title to be mine. It was an incredible race, again live on BBC *Grandstand*, and I passed him on the last corner to win. He won the championship, but I felt that winning that race was more important. I watched the race on video every night for the next three months.

Another highlight was the Manx Grand Prix newcomers' race in September. I had travelled over to the Isle of Man with Chris a couple of days before the race. We did 12 laps a day in the car, that's 37 miles each time, so that I could learn the circuit – and it paid off. I was leading by about 30 seconds at the start of the last lap of the race in which, like all TT races, riders set off at timed intervals. So I slowed up to make sure that the bike would finish. Another rider, who wasn't in contention, came past me over the mountain. I thought, 'You cheeky bastard' and decided to tag onto him a little bit. If I had not speeded up by doing that, the guy in second place would have won because I had slowed down so much that he closed to around seven seconds. In the main open race I was third, setting the fastest lap of the race, which was a real feat.

During celebrations later, we ran straight from the hotel sauna into the freezing Irish Sea with some champagne and, at the presentation ceremony, the lads carried me up to the stage on their shoulders, where I said a few embarrassed and drunken words of thanks.

But I saved the real fireworks for the final race of the year, at Darley Moor. I was riding in the support race for the main event, the Stars of Darley. Someone from Preston had leant me his 350cc Yamaha, which was a beautiful bike to look at. I never really discovered what it was like to ride because, as I came out of the first corner, something shorted and smoke billowed out from the bottom of the bike. I threw it on the floor before sprinting away. The marshals, who looked like something off the *Camberwick Green* kiddies' programme, were not quite so quick to react and the bike was burnt out by the time they got there. The guy from whom I borrowed the bike wasn't all that happy when I returned a heap of scorched metal.

It was an ironic end to the season, because I didn't think I had set the world on fire in 1985. I was quick, and I was winning a few races on a good bike, but I had let myself down on too many occasions. I was vulnerable away from my favourite circuits, Oulton Park and Aintree. This was all going to have to change in 1986 because, almost overnight, I had decided there was no point just going through the motions – I had to start winning all the time.

To achieve this, there would have to be a new approach. So this time around, I did not waste the winter. I studied a lot of magazines, videos and photos of myself and realised that I was not hanging far enough off the bike around corners. Dave Orton had provided a caravan and helped out with some more cash, along with a few new sponsors. We bought a new Yamaha 250cc – one of the best bikes I had ever owned. John Gibbons had agreed to carry on as mechanic, even though he'd been involved in an accident during the winter, when a bit of metal flew into his eye. He was sure that it wouldn't get in the way of the racing. Also, during the previous year, I had built up enough national results to apply for an international licence. So this was it, I was all set.

It was obvious that I had moved up a notch in my first outing at Oulton Park. When I turned up, everyone else's attitude was, 'What the hell is Fogarty doing here, he's got an international licence?' Sure enough, I won all four races in what was a warm-up event for me. But John was struggling with his eye, which he was eventually to lose. We all decided that it would be better if I looked for a new mechanic.

Somebody put me in touch with Tony Holmes, a Blackburn lad who raced a bit. I had no idea whether he was any good with bikes but he seemed confident enough, so we decided to give him a go. He certainly knew his bikes, but the two of us never really got on. I thought he was a pain in the arse. It was a real effort for him to get out of bed before 10 o'clock. And, while the bike ran well, he never wanted to clean it or put new stickers on. He knew that we couldn't afford to pay him anything, yet he was always moaning about money. By the same token, I don't think he was too keen on me. Perhaps I wasn't the easiest person to meet for the first time and he thought I was a bit spoilt. So he was always putting me down, which I didn't like.

After a few national races I was beginning to find my feet and entered a three-race international series called the 250 MotoPrix championship, in which foreign riders were paid to take part. I was third in the first round, which was an unbelievable result. The second round was in the pouring rain at Thruxton, which had a really abrasive and stony surface. For some reason, I used intermediate cut slicks (racing tyres with hand-made grooves) instead of the expected grooved wet weather tyres, which have a far better grip in these conditions. I always fancied my chances in the wet, probably because I was a bit daft and didn't realise how fast it was safe for me to ride. I led the race from start to finish, beating Grand Prix riders like Alan Carter, Donnie McLeod and Andy Watts.

For the first time, the press wanted my opinion. 'You're leading the series with one round to go, Carl. Can you go out and win it?' I gave a pathetic answer, something along the lines of, 'Well, I have done it twice, so I don't see why I can't do it again.' Nobody would be stupid enough to ask me the question today! I thought I would be on the front page of *The Sun* the next day. No such luck, but I did earn around £500 for winning a round and there was £2,000 up for grabs for the overall winner.

The final round was at Mallory on a hot day. I needed to finish in the top three to win the series and was sitting comfortably in third place when my gear lever broke. But, as I pulled in, another rider crashed and the race was stopped. While the other riders were making their way back to the grid, I frantically managed to fix the bike and rushed back to the line.

Just as the race was about to restart again, Chas Mortimer, the team manager of the factory Armstrong team, which included McLeod and the injured Niall Mackenzie, made an official complaint. He was well within his rights, as I had broken down before the crash and so wasn't allowed to carry on. I was pulled off the line and was out of the championship. My moment of glory had slipped through my fingers and my reaction was predictable. And it wasn't 'Ah well! That's life.' I wanted to send Dave Tate round to their garage to sort them out, but dad calmed me down.

When the dust had settled, it was obvious that people were starting to see me as a real talent. Suddenly, I was being tipped to do well at the Isle of Man TT, which was an event that I had wanted to compete in ever since I was a young kid. There was no point entering just one class, as that would have meant spending two weeks on the island for one race. So all the riders tried to take as many bikes as they could, and enter as many classes as possible. I had the 250cc, a Formula 2 bike based on the 350 Yamaha RD LC that I had already ridden in the F2 national championship, and a horrible 400cc which sounded like a sheep baaing. I had another new sponsor, a bike cleaning product company called Magnaseal. They gave me new leathers and resprayed the bike and, for the first time, I felt part of a proper team. Another of their riders was a really good lad, Gary Padgett, who won the 400cc production class that year, but was killed on the road a few months later.

On the ferry over to the island, I was casually flicking through a motorbike magazine, which included predictions from various journalists for that year's races. Then I saw it. The words leapt from the page. Someone had tipped me to win my main race, the 250cc, ahead of top riders like Joey Dunlop and Brian Reid. Within about five minutes of us docking, I bought as many magazines as I could get my hands on. 'That's me, Carl Fogarty, predicted to win the 250cc,' I told anyone and everyone who cared to listen.

One of those included a waitress who I pulled after a night out in Ramsey during the practice week – and before my girlfriend Christine had travelled over. My mechanic, Tony, shagged the waitress's mate in the other bed of the hotel room, but we couldn't wait to get rid of them in the morning. Take it from me, Ramsey is one of the easiest places in the world to pull. In fact, that kind of thing is fairly common during TT week, as the island just buzzes. The pubs are full, there are wet T-shirt competitions everywhere, and just about anything goes.

It must be something about the TT meeting, but riders didn't seem to care about being up bright and early for morning practice. So, when another conquest called Angela, if I remember rightly, asked me to walk her home, I was more than prepared to sacrifice a bit of sleep. She was pretty nice and I didn't moan, even though she was staying right at the other end of the capital, Douglas, near a place called Onchan. It was starting to get light and the seagulls had begun to fly around.

When we finally reached her hotel door she said, 'Thanks for walking me home. I think you're really nice, Carl. Can I see you again tomorrow night?'

'What are you on about?' I replied in shock. 'I thought I would be invited in for a shag.'

She was horrified. 'Oh no! Never on the first night. I didn't think you were like that.'

Bloody right I was like that. I couldn't believe it. 'Well, can I still see you tomorrow night?' she asked again.

I tried my best to be polite. But it was a good job there were no dogs and cats up and about to kick during the long and lonely walk home.

It was after four in the morning and I was due to go practising within an hour. When I got back to my hotel, the mechanics were just getting up and, after a quick cup of coffee, I went up to the circuit, put my leathers on, hopped onto my 250cc Yamaha and I was away. I didn't properly wake up until I hit the bottom of Bray Hill. Looking back, it's amazing how I got away with it but, when you are younger, you don't think about the dangers.

Clearly my cousin Chris and Dave Tate didn't think of the dangers when they thought they would do a lap of the circuit on the 600 Yamaha that someone had leant us for running errands. I was a bit annoyed, because they were both big lads and it was obvious it would all end in tears. Sure enough, Chris lost control and ran wide into a bank. Dave smashed his ankle and spent the next week or so in hospital in Ramsey, while Chris escaped with cuts and bruises. Later the same week, my uncle Brian took the 400cc Honda road bike out and fell off at Quarter Bridge, the first corner, and broke his collarbone.

In many ways, I was also unlucky throughout the whole TT. But, in another, I was one of the luckiest riders on the island. I was lying around sixth or seventh, which was not bad going in my first appearance, when my bike seized up on the far side of the island. As I was waiting for help, I heard some piercing screams from about a mile further down the road. A horse had strayed onto one of the fastest parts of the track and was hit by one of the race favourites, Gene McDonnell, who was in third place and about to come past the point at which I was stranded. The horse had been spooked by a helicopter, which had just attended another accident, and jumped out of its field. McDonnell and the horse were killed. It was one of the worst accidents the TT has ever seen. My friends back at the paddock were worried that I had been involved, because I had not come round and there was no radio contact. Christine was stood near to Gene's girlfriend and saw her break down in hysterics on hearing the news. Christine was obviously very upset but my reaction was a simple 'That's awful'. It wasn't an option to let danger into your head. All I was concerned about was winning the TT, so it was straight out for the next race, almost without a second thought.

That race was the Formula 2 and, again, I had a decent chance of a good finish. I was on the same bike as the favourite, Brian Reid, and had the same engine, which was tuned by the same guy, Arnie Fletcher. There was just one problem. Someone forgot to mix the fuel with oil, as is necessary for a two-stroke engine. So I seized up by the time I had travelled 200 yards to the bottom of Bray Hill. Not surprisingly, nobody has admitted to the mistake to this day, and I was livid. My big TT debut was effectively over, because I hated riding production road bikes and didn't stand a chance in the next two races.

But the TT experience worked wonders because, back on the mainland, I broke four laps records in four successive weekends at Donington, Aberdare, Scarborough and, finally, Snetterton, where I was beaten in one race by Grand Prix rider, Andy Watts. At the next meeting, at Mallory, he crashed, damaged the nerves in his arm and never raced again. He had been due to ride in the British Grand Prix for a German guy called Dr Joe Ehrlich who, when he realised that Watts was out of action, asked me to take his place. 'Yes! This is it. This is the big time,' I thought. I had heard all the stories that Ehrlich was a bit of a weirdo and very strict with his riders. But there was no way I was going to pass up this chance, as I was in the best form of my life.

The usual crew set off for Silverstone in our van and we had reached Holmes Chapel on the M6 when the front windscreen suddenly shattered, for no apparent reason. I smashed a small hole in the window with my elbow, so that I could see where I was going, and swerved onto the hard shoulder. There was no point trying to fix it there and then, because we needed to be at Silverstone that evening. So we smashed the rest of the glass out and I carried on driving in the pouring rain, wearing my racing helmet and sat next to my two cousins, who were also wearing spare helmets. The other two were crouched behind the partition, trying to keep warm. We looked a really professional outfit as we rolled up at Silverstone and asked for our passes!

The first job was to introduce my team to Dr Ehrlich. 'Oh, Mr Fogarty!' he said, 'I am sorry but you vill be using my mechanics.' That annoyed me, for a start, and was a real blow for the rest of the lads. Even so, I was desperate to ride, so didn't kick up a fuss. When I sat on his bike, I started to move the bars so that I was comfortable. Ehrlich wasn't happy.

'Mr Fogarty! Zees is not the way to ride zees bike. You tuck zee elbows in to reduce wind resistance.'

'Eh? I like the bars out here. This is how I ride,' I explained.

It was clear this was going to be a stormy relationship and, after the first session, I hated the bike.

'The front end is chattering everywhere,' I complained.

'Zees is how Andy Watts liked it,' barked Ehrlich.

I trudged back to my mates muttering, 'I'm not riding that heap of shit. I don't like the guy anyway, he's a twat.'

Some bloke overheard all this and promised that he could pull a few strings and get me into the race, riding my own bike, which we had brought down as a precaution. I sent Chris over to tell Ehrlich. 'Carl says you can stuff your ride,' he reported bluntly. In the meantime, I was in the office begging for a ride in Sunday's race.

'Come on, please. I have already done one practice day, you've got to let me in,' I pleaded.

'You're not really experienced enough, but we can squeeze you in as the last entry. But you'd better not get in anyone's way or cause any crashes,' said one of the organisers.

I quickly had to switch numbers back to my own bike before the final day's qualifying, in which I knocked two seconds off my quickest time on the other bike. I qualified in 26th position out of a field of around 40, which was pretty good.

Come race day, the heavens opened, which played right into my hands. I was as nervous as hell because I was lining up against guys who were my heroes like the Venezuelan, Carlos Lavado. I couldn't believe it when he winked at me when we were lining up. I was so wrapped up in the event that I hadn't even thought of spraying anything on my visor, or taping it to stop it misting up. I couldn't see a thing, and was so busy trying to open my visor as the race started that I cut straight through the rest of the field. I was riding by sheer instinct and, with three laps still to go, Niall Mackenzie came past me into the points in 10th place – and he was already being tipped for a 500cc ride the following year.

To me, that was a brilliant achievement and again, I expected full recognition in the motorbike press. There was the odd mention, but the reaction was nearly as disappointing as when, earlier in the season at Brands Hatch, I finished second in an international race. My local paper, the *Lancashire Evening Telegraph*, ignored that fact but did an article on another Blackburn rider, Geoff Fowler, coming fourth in the same race.

Even so, I was full of it. It seemed like I couldn't do anything wrong and I was tapped up by Chas Mortimer, who wanted me to ride Grand Prix for his Armstrong team, the biggest and best in the UK. I met him in a pub with dad and we agreed to have further discussions about me turning professional. Meanwhile, the next race was at my favourite circuit, Oulton Park, and I was expected to win my first round in the British championship. So I decided to go to Oulton for a day's extra practice on the Tuesday before the race.

It was Tuesday, 19 August, to be exact – and that number's jinx was to strike again on a fateful day for my career . . .

CHAPTER FOUR

Nineteen

The accident happened after just a couple of practice laps. We had put some old slick tyres on, which I had found in the garage and which probably hadn't been used for about three years, so their grip must have been pretty poor. I was coming out of a fast right-handed double apex corner, a long sweeping bend, and probably travelling at around 100mph. I lost the rear end and knew straight away that I was in big trouble. The track sloped away as you exited the corner and that made the drop from the high side even greater. I remember nothing about landing; I just closed my eyes and hoped for the best. When I opened them again, my right leg was definitely not the right shape.

My first instinct was survival. I dragged myself off the track and into the gravel, in case anyone else rode round the corner and smashed into me. When I reached the gravel, staring at this thing that used to be my leg, I was more confused than worried. I could see the new angle of the bone through my leathers. Modern leathers are reinforced to improve protection but the things that I was wearing were so flimsy they were almost see-through, although I did not realise that the bone had broken through the skin.

It slowly started to sink in that my leg was broken but I could not work out exactly where, because the pain had not kicked in and I was still trying to get acquainted with the new outline of my leg. Another rider stopped, and then quickly rode off to fetch help. When the ambulance arrived, I was starting to feel dizzy and sick through the pain, but they clamped some gas and air over my nose and mouth and I drifted in and out of consciousness at the track's medical centre.

At Crewe Hospital, I was still just about aware of what was happening and was told that I had a compound fracture of the femur, the biggest bone in the body. By this time my dad had heard the news and had driven straight down from Blackburn. My girlfriend, Christine, had also arrived. Everyone looked so anxious. And, when I overheard one doctor say that he didn't think I would walk on the leg again that year, my spirits sank even lower. One minute I had the world at my feet, the next I was in this mess. I was put under general anaesthetic before the job of repairing the break got underway that night. A pin was inserted through my shinbone so that the femur could be kept stable in constant traction. When I came round, I was flat on my back, with my leg straight up in the air and tied to weights on either side to keep it still. I could see the pin through my shin and thought, 'What the hell's going on here?'

For a few days, the leg was the least of my problems. My body had reacted to the hammering it had received and, in protest, had decided to stop me having a shit. This is not an unusual thing for riders to suffer after the shock of a bad fall. My good mate Jamie Whitham had similar problems after his fireball crash at Brno in the Czech Republic in 1999. Unluckily for him, his bladder also shut down and he had to have a catheter tube inserted. Now that's a pain that I just cannot bear to imagine. But my own little, growing problem was refusing to go away, no matter how hard I squeezed or how many prunes I ate on top of all the other fruit.

After day five, it felt like I was five months pregnant and, when the doctors finally offered an artificial solution, I jumped at the chance – despite the obvious drawbacks. While having tablets shoved up my arse was bad enough, I wasn't prepared for what came next. There was a loud rumble before my bowels became an instant food blender. Before I could do anything, the bedpan was full to overflowing and I was almost drowning in the stuff. When two attractive nurses started to wipe my arse, I just wanted to die. It was so embarrassing.

After a week or so, I had recovered enough to be moved to Ward 5 of Blackburn Royal Infirmary where I spent another seven weeks – a shy young man in a strange place, sharing his pain with a bunch of old blokes who were constantly wheezing and coughing. I had a steady stream of visitors, and was kept stocked up with cans of Moosehead lager to help me get off to sleep. Nobody told me that I wasn't supposed to drink while I was pumped full of antibiotics and I think it must have played a major part in the later problems with the leg.

When the time came to leave hospital, it felt kind of strange. The ward had become my new home and the move back to my real home signalled the start of a long hard drag back to fitness, during a winter spent largely watching racing videos. I didn't seem to get a lot of medical support or guidance, just the occasional session with a physio to try and regain full movement of the knee joint. I was too lazy and too stupid to realise that I needed to be out exercising or riding a bicycle. I was just desperate to start riding again, and to pick up where I had left off before the accident – as the rider everyone else had to beat.

The aim for the 1987 season was to compete in the European championship, so we bought two new 250cc Hondas, helped again by Dave Orton. Nobody knew much about the bikes and, as it turned out, we should have played safe and stuck with the Yamaha. The first race was in Jerez and I fully expected to get back on a bike and blow everyone away again, without having done any preparation or testing.

We travelled to Spain early, via the ferry to Santander, to take part in an unofficial practice day and, after a few laps, I didn't feel too bad. Then two guys, who I had been blitzing the previous year, Nigel Bosworth and Rob Orme, flew past me with their bikes on their sides. I knew straight away that I no longer had the confidence to ride a bike at that angle. I was okay with left-hand corners but did not have enough mobility in my right leg to take right-hand corners properly. I tried taping foam onto the seat, to make it more comfortable, but failed to qualify by four seconds. I was devastated and it crossed my mind that I was washed up at the age of 21. Something had to be done.

I visited orthopaedic specialist Nigel Cobb, the guy who rebuilt Barry Sheene's leg, in Northampton. He told me that, instead of knitting cleanly back together, the break had slipped a bit and was preventing full mobility. The only solution was to break the leg again, so that it had a chance of healing properly. There was no way I was going to go through all that again, so I ignored his advice and tried riding a cycle with a block attached to the pedal to try and force my leg to bend further.

The next round of the European championship was at Donington, and Dave Orton turned up to see how his investment was faring.

'How are we doing champ?' he asked.

'Sorry, Dave, I failed to qualify,' I admitted.

He looked stunned. It was now clear that the European champion-ship was a waste of time and we decided to return to smaller British races, in a bid to rebuild my confidence and regain fitness. The next race was at Scarborough on an anti-clockwise road circuit with slower corners, which was easier on my leg and I won both the 250cc and 350cc races there.

But that weekend was more significant for another reason. I was in a packed pub called The Cask during the races, when a girl who looked like a cross between Pamela Anderson and Madonna made eye contact from the other side of the room. That was as far as it got, though. She was gorgeous, but I didn't think much more of it. The day I got back home, the phone went. It was a female voice.

'Do you remember a girl in Scarborough wearing a tight pink top?' the voice asked.

'Yeah! I think so,' I replied, not wanting to commit myself at that stage.

'Well, that girl was me,' she said. 'My name is Alison.'

Bloody hell! I nearly fainted. I didn't have a clue what to say. It was very easy to talk to her, though, and over the next few weeks we spoke loads of times on the phone. I had already started rowing with Christine and we were probably starting to drift apart. And I was by now a lot more confident with girls, and much more aware when they were showing an interest in me. Alison was determined to continue her interest!

My first race in Ireland was the popular North West 200, against the likes of Irish hero Joey Dunlop. In England, I had almost been forgotten after missing the end of the previous season. I was a nobody again. In Ireland, it was incredible how many people were showing an interest. I was signing loads of autographs and even a couple of small television companies wanted interviews.

The races turned out to be huge confidence builders, not because I started winning again, but because I crashed in both 250 races. The first fall was at a slow corner, but the second was much more dramatic. I flew over the front of the bike like Superman and landed on my right leg. I stood up gingerly and put some light pressure on my foot, to check nothing was broken. Dad was furious because the bike was mangled. 'You can't keep crashing on these circuits and getting away with it, boy,' he warned. But I was happy just to be walking, despite the huge swelling on my knee, and I felt a lot happier approaching the TT.

That week in the Isle of Man also proved to be important, because I spent two full weeks on a bike and my leg was feeling a lot more comfortable. I rode well to finish fourth in the 250cc and found that I could pass most people at the corners but, because our bikes were so bad, they would come back at me on the straights. Back on the short circuits of the mainland, the results started to pick up and I was feeling something like my old self. Yet there were still two or three corners on each track where my foot would scrape the surface, because I couldn't pull my leg far enough back out of the way.

Returning to Scarborough, I had my first ever ride on a superbike, an awful 750cc Yamaha. Someone had tuned the engine a little bit, but otherwise it was just a standard bike – the chassis and shock hadn't even been changed. The result was not spectacular, but the difference was huge. For the first time in ages, I felt comfortable riding a bike. And when I went back to 250cc races in a series called the Super 2, for bikes up to 350cc, this was lodged in the back of my mind, despite the fact my mind was on other things.

It was no surprise when Alison turned up, because it had become clear from our phone conversations that something was bound to happen sooner or later. My only problem was that Christine was at the meeting and she had already spotted Alison and me chatting a few times. During a break in qualifying, I noticed Alison in the crowd so I told Christine that I was going to watch another race and went up to Alison instead.

Suddenly from the corner of my eye, I was aware that Christine was heading for us with a face like thunder. 'Shit!' I whispered. 'Christine's coming. Pretend I'm not talking to you,' as I edged further along the barrier looking as guilty as sin. Christine parked herself slap-bang in the middle of the two of us and, to avoid a scene, I trudged back down to the paddock. I was now on dodgy ground, though. It was clear to Christine that Alison was a rival.

Alison arranged to meet me at the British Grand Prix at Donington, while Christine was in London trying to trace her real dad. During that time I fell head over heels and could not get enough of her. We even shagged in the toilet of our caravan, and then spent the night before practice in a motel. It was no wonder I didn't even qualify. I was shagged out. It was blatant, and pissing everyone off big style. My mum and dad were both annoyed, although they were not the types to confront me about it, and my sister could also see what was happening. I have never confronted her, but I know that it was my sister who grassed me up to Christine during the following week.

On the Friday night, I turned up at Christine's house as though nothing had happened. Christine was dressed up and ready to go out, so there were no immediate signs that anything was wrong. She let me inside and closed the door. By this stage I was beginning to sense that something was the matter. It might have been the steam coming out of her ears.

'You were seeing someone else at Donington,' she blurted.

'What the fuck are you talking about? No I wasn't.'

'Don't lie to me Carl,' she shouted. 'Someone has told me all about it. I cannot believe you'd do that to me. You disgust me. Get out of my house now, I'm going out with my mates.'

I was halfway through saying 'You've got the wrong end of the stick, what have I done wrong?' when an iron flew past my chin and clattered into the radiator behind.

'Yeah, all right, but it meant nothing,' I sheepishly admitted.

'Oh! It meant nothing, did it? I've probably got AIDS from that slapper,' she screeched while I was being pushed out of the door.

'No, you won't get AIDS . . .' My words were met by a slammed door.

Dumped. I was devastated.

Two weeks later, I saw Christine out with another bloke at a night-club called Lydia's. It did my head in and I made a right fool of myself.

'Please come back, please,' I pleaded, trying pathetically to kiss her.

'It's all over Carl. I don't want to see you any more. You blew it. I want to be friends because I've known you for ages, but that's as far as it goes now,' she insisted.

I moped around for a couple of weeks, by which time it was all pretty much forgotten and I was on the look-out for something new. It was around that time when one-night stands seemed easier than proper girlfriends. It tended to happen in places like Ireland or at the TT, when you would cop off without really knowing their names. If I was away with my cousins, especially Chris, who is a fairly good-looking bloke, one of us would always score – usually him! And, if I hadn't struck lucky, it was just as good watching him messing around in the back of the van.

Despite having failed to qualify for the British Grand Prix, I won the first of a five-round British championship, at Mallory Park. Then there were two more victories at Scarborough before the next round of the British championship at Silverstone, on 19 September.

Yes, that's right, the 19th. You can guess the rest. All my major crashes up to that point had featured that number and, for years after Silverstone, the tension was unbearable whenever I had to race on that date. It's for that reason that I have never ridden a number 19 bike, as I am very superstitious. For obvious reasons I would never carry number 13 on the bike. But there is also another number, 22, which I would not ride under any circumstances. Two of Dave Orton's previous riders, John Williams at Dundrod and John Newbold at the North West 200, were killed riding bikes which carried the number 22. Dave specifically asked me never to ride another, as he felt the number was jinxed.

It was pouring down at Silverstone and I was lying third, but starting to catch the second placed guy. Coming up to the first turn I slid off in a fairly routine wet weather fall. It appeared so harmless that I tried to stand up, until I noticed that the leg was pointing in the wrong direction again. My tibia had snapped like a twig at the point where the pin was inserted following my first accident. The area around that hole had become infected, weakening the bone. I tried to remember the lessons from the previous year, to try and control the pain by relaxing and taking deep breaths. It didn't work.

At Northampton Hospital, the doctors first tried to knock a steel pin down the bone from top to bottom, with the aim of getting me back on my feet and riding again within a few weeks, which seemed crazy. Despite drips pumping me with antibiotics in both arms, my body rejected the pin and they had to take it out when I fell ill. When I came round from that operation, all their metalwork was on the outside of my leg as the surgeons had built a huge frame to hold the shin stable. They had also scraped away the infected bone, and that seemed to do the trick.

Alison had heard that I had been injured and travelled from Nottingham to visit me – with her brother! I was stuck away on my own in a small side room next to the main ward, with my leg in traction following the operation, and to say I was surprised to see her was an understatement. To say I was pleasantly surprised by what happened next was an even bigger understatement.

The conversation was a bit boring because her brother was in the room, so Alison asked him if we could have a few minutes alone. I presumed she had something important to tell me. But it's rude to talk with your mouth full! For no sooner had the door closed, than her head was under the sheets and she was giving me a good noshing. Nurses were walking past the window and had a perfect view into the room. I caught the eye of one young student, who knew exactly what was going on, and looked very embarrassed. That was not something that bothered me at that precise moment. To be honest, I was in agony because my infected leg had just snapped in half. But, if this was my reward for being brave, I wanted someone to break my other leg. It lasted for about 10 minutes and all the time her brother was waiting patiently in the corridor. She didn't hang around for long and I only ever saw her one more time, when she set more new standards.

The scaffolding on the leg stayed on for more than three months and, when people saw me walking towards them, they turned green and ran in the opposite direction. It weighed a ton and, after the soreness subsided, I became an expert at accidentally banging into people on purpose!

Ironically, it was removed a few days before I bumped into Michaela Bond . . .

CHAPTER FIVE

World Champion

It was early December 1987 and I was out for a night on the town with a few mates to cheer myself up. The pins had only recently been removed and the leg was still sore.

We were in a pub called The Woodlands when there was a tap on my shoulder. I had never seen the girl before in my life. 'Might be my lucky night,' I thought.

'Do you remember Michaela Bond? She used to be a good friend of your sister. She says you are a tight git and she wants you to buy her a drink,' said the girl.

'Yeah, I remember her. Why? Who are you?' I asked, still playing it cool.

'My name's Louise Southworth. I'm a dentist and Michaela works for me. She's sat over there,' Louise gestured.

Sure enough, Michaela was sat in the corner of the pub with a few colleagues on the dental practice's Christmas party. I hadn't seen Michaela for six years and she looked a lot different. Her clothes were a bit scruffy and she was wearing a silly hat. This was not how I had imagined she would turn out. But I still fancied having a go at chatting her up.

I wandered over with the drinks and said, 'I thought you were dead.' Okay, it was not a great chat-up line, but it broke the ice perfectly. It took us straight back to the time when, as kids, I loved to wind her up. But it was obvious she had changed. The new Michaela was very confident and very brash. 'You used to pick on me, you bastard,' she said. 'I never really liked you.'

We soon got chatting about more important matters.

'Have you got a boyfriend?' I asked.

'Well, I'm kind of seeing someone, but we're not getting on that well.'

'Do you want to go out tomorrow dinnertime, then?'

'Yeah, okay,' she replied. Bingo!

The surgery where Michaela worked was in Langham Road, near the town centre, and I turned up in my mum's Ford Escort Cabriolet, looking the business. All her work-mates were staring out the window as she came out, still wearing her nurse's uniform, which was quite a turn on. 'If she lost a few pounds she'd be bloody gorgeous,' I thought. After a few drinks, she had to go back to work so we arranged to meet up in town that evening.

I was a bit nervous because I had known her so long, but never in a sexual way. Michaela wore another wacky outfit, a big fluffy jumper and another 'trendy' hat. She looked weird, but not weird enough to stop me fancying her something rotten by the end of the night.

She shared her bedsit, which was close to the surgery, with another girl and two blokes. We ended up there and I thought, 'Surely she's not going to let me shag her on the first date?' I wanted to, very badly, and we drunkenly fell into bed, laughing and giggling, and fumbling around. If I was being honest, the sex was not memorable. My leg was still sore, which limited the number of positions available for a start. There seemed to be a lot of messing around for the length of time it eventually lasted. She says it was 30 seconds!

For the first few weeks, it was as though nothing much had changed since when we were kids. Our relationship was built around putting each other down, but now there was a physical attraction as well. I seemed to sleep at her bedsit for the next few weeks. Mum still did all my washing, ironing and cooking, but, even if I had been out with my mates, I ended up at Michaela's with my supper – curried beef, chips and beansprouts, never anything different.

Neither of us thought it was going to turn into anything long term and I couldn't have been the best of company, because the injury was really getting me down. I didn't have all that much money or prospects and I had serious doubts whether I was cut out for a career in the sport. It seemed to be one hard knock after another and the rewards were small. If dad hadn't kept me on the work's payroll during both winters of recovery, I would probably have looked seriously for another job.

Michaela was starting to grow on me, though, and she was beginning to look really good again. Then I fell ill with jaundice and could hardly leave the house during Christmas and into the New Year. Michaela spent a lot of time with me; we stopped all the pretend bickering and probably got to know each other a lot better. As that year went on, I guess I must have been falling in love with her. After a few months, we moved in together and she was suddenly a part of everything I did. We rented a refurbished one-bedroom flat above one of the betting shops owned by my mate John Jefferson's dad in a part of Blackburn called Bastwell – not the best area of town, to say the least. There was a toilet, shower, living room and kitchen, and it seemed like paradise because it was my first place away from home, our first place together and only cost £40 a week. Looking back, though, it was a shithole.

Two things were in the back of my mind as I battled for fitness in the run-up to the 1988 season. Firstly, there was a lot more money in riding bigger bikes. So my dad, and even some sponsors like Dave Orton, were pushing me in that direction. On top of that, there has always been more prestige attached to bigger bikes. Secondly, I now knew that the bigger bikes were more comfortable for my leg. Yet, still, I was strangely reluctant to abandon the 250cc class. Maybe it was my old insecurity rearing its ugly head. Or perhaps I had my heart set on becoming the 250cc world champion. If it hadn't been for the injuries, I think I could have achieved that.

After all the problems we'd had with the two 250ccs the previous year, Honda gave us a good deal on a RC30 750cc Honda, my first superbike, which didn't arrive until after the season had started. So I had to start the season on 250s, which was good in a way because I needed to ease my way back into things and the 250s were familiar territory, where I could regain my confidence and rediscover the winning touch at places like Scarborough.

And that's not all that I rediscovered there. I had almost forgotten that Alison was still lurking in the background!

This time she turned up with a boyfriend in tow. She looked as fit as ever but I couldn't quite work out the deal with the boyfriend. She seemed to be able to get away with far too much, without him minding what was going on. Alison was wearing a short skirt and another tight jumper, obviously with nothing on underneath. I had also forgotten what great tits she had. She was flirting as usual, grabbing my leg, and I responded by pinching her arse.

All the time her boyfriend, a smallish bloke who raced single cylinder bikes, was watching and laughing along. I couldn't see what Alison saw in him, but it didn't bother me that she was with someone, as I was with Michaela by then. 'Carl, we've nowhere to stay tonight,' she suddenly piped up. Not being too slow on the uptake, I suggested, 'Why don't you come and stay with us in our caravan.' So, after a few more beers, we all piled into the back of the van and went back to the circuit, where the caravan was parked.

Her hands were all over me, even on the way back with her boyfriend in the same van. My mechanic Tony Holmes and his girlfriend were sleeping at one end of the caravan and, at the other end, was a bed that slept three. 'You might as well get in here with me,' I suggested, without even trying to sound innocent! Her boyfriend sparked out as soon as his head hit the pillow, which left Alison in the middle and me on the other side. We were both wide awake.

I cannot quite believe it to this day but, as he was snoring next to us, I was shafting away while she stroked his hair. My mechanic got out of his bed at one point to see what on earth was happening, because the caravan was rocking like a cradle. It was too good to be true and probably didn't last for more than a few minutes. It took a lot, lot longer to sink in.

My theory is that her boyfriend must have been the type who got his kicks knowing that someone else was doing the business with his girlfriend. In the morning, it was as though nothing had happened. Her boyfriend was first to get up because he had an early practice. Alison and I stayed in bed, and it's not rocket science to work out what happened next.

That was the last I ever saw of her. The stories on the grapevine were that she soon finished with that guy and was respectably married a couple of years later. Only a year before, she had been urging me to marry her. No thank you! However gorgeous she was, I would never have trusted her for a minute, because sex was not a bit of fun, it was an obsession. And I would have been knackered!

While it was obvious that my leg had healed better this time, and that I hadn't lost any more movement, I could still not get my toe to the end of the footrest on a 250cc. And, especially on tight corners, I was scraping half my boot away on the ground. When the RC30 eventually arrived, there was a mad dash to convert it from a bike ready for road use, by stripping off all the shit like indicators and lights, and to tune the engine in time for the North West 200. The tuner was Tony Scott, in nearby Leyland, who probably built his reputation on the back of my success. For some reason, he insisted that he would not touch the bike until it had 1,000 miles on the clock. So I ended up riding it around the roads of Blackburn for 1,000 miles before Tony would strip the engine down and rebuild it. There was just one snag. I didn't have a road licence!

As soon as I sat on the RC30, it felt right. It was sitting in your favourite armchair compared to the 250cc bikes, as there was so much more space between the seat and the footrest. I came fifth in the North West 200 against established international riders like Roger Marshall, Steve Henshaw, Andy McGladdery, Trevor Nation and Kenny Irons, who was to die later in the year. The 250cc race at the same meeting was one of the best I've ever been involved in. I was neck and neck with five or six very fast Irish lads for the whole race and led entering the final corner. I pushed too hard and ran wide, allowing Steven Cull to dive inside me while the others crossed the line at virtually the same time. They were both great results, considering I was probably only riding at 80 per cent and with the doctors' warnings, that my leg would break if I crashed again, ringing in my ears.

This was a big boost ahead of the TT, which doubled up as the first round of the TT Formula One World championship, a series created in 1977 to compensate the Isle of Man for losing Grand Prix status because of the obvious dangers. When that status was first taken away, the TT was classed as a one-race 'world championship', which meant very little. But the series, based in Britain, expanded to feature other road circuits like the Ulster GP track at Dundrod, and European venues like Vila Real in Portugal, Kouvola in Finland and Pergusa in Sicily, circuits that were also considered too dangerous to host major events. It would be wrong to suggest that it was a very prestigious championship.

The World Superbike championship had just started and was stealing what little limelight existed for the bigger production bikes. And, even though Formula One was living on borrowed time, manufacturers still sold bikes on the back of TT successes, so they certainly thought it was a big event. I finished fourth, which meant 13 points towards the world championship, and was very satisfied.

I was still riding within myself and we were still learning about the bike. For instance, we didn't know any better than to race using the road suspension, and it wasn't until we returned to the mainland that we tested a Proflex racing suspension unit. We were also racing with Metzeler tyres for the first time, for the simple reason that they were free. The company was an established producer of treaded road tyres, but had only just started to make slick racing tyres. As a result, their performance was a bit hit and miss and caused a few problems.

But none of those frights compared with one morning at breakfast during the TT. I had noticed that one of the waitresses in our hotel had taken a shine to me. She was very young, perhaps only about 16 or 17, and we went out for a few drinks after she finished work on the Monday evening. We ended up in a club and then back in my room. Michaela flew out the next day and I was a nervous wreck for the rest of the meeting. Because the girl worked a breakfast shift I didn't dare leave the table when Michaela was there, in case the waitress decided to spill the beans. But I still had to live with my guilty conscience.

It eventually got the better of me and I told Michaela, many years later, mind you. I was expecting a roasting but she took it very calmly. 'It's okay,' she said, 'I've been unfaithful, too. When you were in Scarborough with that girl Alison, I went back to Oxford and saw my old boyfriend. But it just proved that I didn't want to be with him anymore.' We were both young when it had all happened and our relationship was not too serious at that stage. And at least we had been honest.

Following the Isle of Man meeting, and completely out of the blue, I was sent an entry form for the next round of TT Formula One World championship, in Assen, Holland, a circuit that I would grow to love. There had been no definite decision, but it had almost become accepted that I was now switching classes to concentrate on superbikes. My mechanic, Tony Holmes, could not travel to Holland, as he probably had to sign on the dole. And my cousins had drifted away during my injuries, as I had never returned to work at the warehouse and they had found other interests. So Gary Dickinson took time off work to travel with me but the extent of his bike knowledge, at that time, was limited to changing a wheel or a sprocket. He had not even passed his driving test but took the wheel in Belgium, as I needed a break, and drove through the border into Holland. Dave Tate came along for the ride, but he did more damage than good to the bike.

This was Blackburn's version of the Ant Hill Mob. But the back-up team's ability was not as important for racing superbikes, as the engines tended to be reliable for about 1,000 miles. We stopped off in Amsterdam for a spot of window shopping, where Gary tried unsuccessfully to get a wank for a fiver, and slept next to the canal in the van.

The Assen race had attracted a lot of good riders, who didn't mind racing on this fast flowing track but were not so keen on the other more dangerous circuits in the F1 series. We were nearly caught out before the race because we had stuffed a washer into the exhaust to limit the noise level, as they were strict about things like that in Holland. One of the scrutineers spotted us taking it out after the inspection but decided to turn a blind eye. Joey Dunlop was the man to beat and I finished one place behind him in ninth. To me, it was not a bad result in my first race abroad, and kept me in the points, but the folks back home had expected better.

In England, I was slowly losing credibility because the TT Formula One was seen as a championship for road racing specialists, and not very competitive. It was the other British riders, not racing abroad, who were making the headlines, like Brian Morrison, Darren Dixon, Jamie Whitham, Andy McGladdery and Mark Phillips. That did not bother me, though, as superbikes were a challenge and the comfort was still a novelty.

In one of my first races on the RC30 in England, at Cadwell Park, I witnessed the freak death of Kenny Irons, a hot favourite to win domestic titles having raced in Grands Prix the previous year with Suzuki, before unluckily losing his place. I was on the second row of the grid and was entering the back straight of the warm-up lap, when Keith Huewen's engine cut out in front of me. I had to swerve quickly to avoid him and looked back to see Irons run into Huewen, who is now a Sky Sports commentator. Irons slid harmlessly down the sloping back straight. Another rider, also called Mark Phillips, but not the one in contention for the championship, panicked and fell off. His bike also slid down the straight and smashed into Irons, killing him. This was all televised live on the BBC, but it was the first death that Michaela had experienced at a racetrack and she seemed to cope very well.

The next world championship venue, Vila Real, was exactly the type of dangerous road circuit that put other riders off the Formula One World championship. For instance, the F1 series leader, Roger Burnett, chose to travel to Austria for the World Superbike round, instead. The circuit was really slippery and riders had to cross over a rickety bridge, which had a 100ft drop on either side. A lot of the road surface was covered by tramlines – and it took days to reach. It was a particularly bad journey for dad who suffered travel sickness and had to bang on the back of the van every few miles of windy Portuguese country road, so that we could stop for him to throw up.

It was the middle of the summer and bloody hot, although it poured down for race day. But I was as comfortable in the wet on a 750cc as I had been on a 250cc and was in fourth place when the race was stopped and restarted. This time I got in front until water seeped into the electrics and the bike cut out. Luckily, Dunlop also had trouble and again I didn't lose too much ground in the points table.

Before the next round in Finland, I rode one of my last ever races on a 250cc bike at Knockhill, where I was also an unimpressive sixth in the superbike race, but still riding within my limits as the F1 world championship had now taken on greater importance. The trip to Finland involved four ferry journeys, including a 15-hour crossing on a massive cruise ship which had a nightclub, and a mate of my dad, Lou Durkin, helped out with the driving in between ferry trips. That meant a lot of time kicking my heels and it was hard work fighting off the temptations provided by the gorgeous Scandinavian women.

The Finnish people were like the Irish, very hospitable and always willing to please. And a fair crowd of around 15,000 turned up to watch us race around an industrial estate, where every corner was a right angle and you had to dodge the manhole covers in the middle of the road. This time, the lack of a proper back-up team cost us dearly. At least one fuel stop was needed for a Formula One race but the Ant Hill Mob put more fuel over me than in the tank. So I had to make a second unscheduled stop which dropped me down to fourth, behind a quick Finnish rider called Jari Suhonen, with the Swede Anders Andersson, who was to become my main suspension man in 1995, in second place. Joey Dunlop, now leading a series which probably only featured six or seven riders who took part in every round, was third and his brother, Robert, fifth.

The big race for the Dunlop brothers was the Ulster Grand Prix on the fast Dundrod circuit, in front of up to 60,000 fans cheering on their local hero, Joey. But there was also a strong contingent of British riders. The wet weather of race day played into my hands and, from a terrible qualifying position of 21st, I was in the lead by the end of the first lap after a flying start. From that position there was no turning back and I won my first ever world championship race by 16 seconds. Michaela had not travelled with me but managed to tune the car radio to an Irish station, which was covering the race live, and so heard all the action from a shop car park in Bolton. Joey was only seventh and, from nowhere, I was second in the world championship and just five and a half points behind him with two rounds remaining.

The battle for the title had captured the imagination of the lads back home. From a situation at the start of the season, when even I wasn't planning any further ahead than the next race, we had assembled a crew of about 10 for the expedition to the next round, in Pergusa, Sicily. I had not bothered to ask Dave Tate to come to Ulster, as he had been stirring trouble with Lou in Finland. But the owner of a club in Blackburn, Reg Gorton, agreed to drive three others down in his Jaguar, while the rest piled into the van. We headed for Genoa to pick up the ferry for Sicily but had to catch the boat without the Jag, which did not turn up in Sicily until a day after we had arrived.

'What took you lot so long?' I asked.

'It's been a nightmare,' Reg explained. 'That dickhead put us on the wrong boat . . . to Sardinia!'

It turned out they had had to drive across the whole of Sardinia in order to catch another ferry to Sicily.

The weather was steaming hot and most of us slept outside, under an awning that we attached to the van. Joey had parked next to us and was sharing a tent, which seems strange now as there is no way you would share anything with a rival in today's cut-throat world of racing. There was time to acclimatise to the heat, though, as we had a couple of days to kill before the race. My main problem was that I was still a steak and chips man and had not discovered Italian food. But I found a bar that served thin slices of beef, chips or *patate fritte* and gravy, so I was happy.

The Blackburn lads were also enjoying the trip until one of them, Paul Russell, took my scooter out around the circuit in the evening as the light was fading. He was not that used to riding bikes, so the rest of us sat on the pit wall to see how he was getting on. When he came round the corner, I realised that the circuit officials had put up some temporary railings across the track to stop people riding round at night. They were a grey-silvery colour and were hard to make out against the track.

I started to panic. 'He hasn't seen the fucking railings,' I shouted. Everyone screamed at Paul to try and alert him. But he only spotted the railings when he was a foot away from crashing into them, travelling flat out at 30mph. He slammed on the brakes and the bike almost stood up, vertically. Paul was thrown over the bars, through the railings and landed on his face on the other side.

The first thing he did, for some reason, was take his false teeth out and put them in his pocket. I have never seen blood like it. He had shaved all the skin off his cheek and around his eye. It was a right mess. When we reached him, because he was concussed, he was fumbling around saying 'I've lost my false teeth', so we wasted time looking for those. We rushed him to hospital, where he was cleaned and bandaged up. When it finally scabbed over, he looked as though he had a horrible birthmark across one half of his face. But, because he didn't pick at the scab for the next few months, it healed perfectly.

It cheered everyone up when I took pole position from the local hotshot, Gianluca Galasso, riding a factory Bimota – the same bike that my future team boss, Davide Tardozzi, was leading the World Superbike championship on. Joey crashed in practice but, after our lads looked after him in hospital, he was fit to ride in the race. He suffered more bad luck when his bike would not start for the race but, by this time, I was locked in a real battle for the lead with Galasso, unaware of Joey's problems.

Although the track was bumpy and patchy, I had adapted to it and we also worked out that this was one of the few Formula One races where you could risk making it to the finish without a refuelling stop. We were wrong. With a lap and half remaining, and having built up a fair lead, the engine started to cut out, so I pulled into the pits. The crowd was whistling and I was screaming, 'I need more fuel.'

My uncle Brian sprinted over and shouted, 'You're winning with one lap to go. You can make it.'

'Well, bloody well push me back out then.'

I dropped the clutch as they pushed like mad and the engine fired. I completed the lap to take the chequered flag and the Blackburn crew went mad. This was Mafia country, though, and I couldn't help worrying that someone was going to take a pot shot at me on the podium for beating the local favourite!

With just Donington to go, I had a lead of 15 points. From starting the season with serious doubts about my career, I was one race away from a world championship at the age of 23. Yet my attitude was 'The least I can get is second place', while everyone else was insisting 'Don't be so stupid. All you have to do is follow Joey round to win it.' I was due to race in Scarborough before Donington, but pulled out to be on the safe side. So everything was in place. There was quite a lot of media attention and I featured on the front of the programme for the meeting.

None of the British championship riders said anything to my face, but I could tell that their attitude was 'I cannot believe he is going to be a world champion. I can beat him easily.' The facts of the matter were, though, that they had not taken part and could only guess at what might have been. I felt that I proved my point, finishing fifth in the race, with Joey out of harm's way in 11th, and ahead of most of the British guys. The only British riders in front were Grand Prix rider Niall Mackenzie, Roger Burnett from World Superbikes and the top British rider that year, Brian Morrison. I actually thought I was going to finish fourth, until Andersson came past when I pulled in for fuel.

When I pulled into the pits, the T-shirts were ready with 'Carl Fogarty: World F1 Champion' already printed up. But, even after winning the world title, I couldn't escape a bollocking. My Metzeler tyres had been poor in practice so, at the last minute before the race, I switched them to some that Michelin had given me and blacked the Michelin logo out with a marker pen, because I had an agreement with Metzeler. Both companies were pissed off, but I couldn't have cared less. It was straight back to Blackburn, with Joey and his Irish mates, for a party at a pub called The Barge – and a lot of beer. I featured on the front page of my local paper the next day and even regional TV caught up. It was only then that I was starting to become a bit more relaxed and confident in front of the microphone and TV cameras.

There was still one race remaining, the Neil Robinson Memorial Trophy at Kirkistown and I was desperate not to spend the winter on crutches again. Even so, in horrible conditions, I beat the British F1 riders to finally earn their respect. Joey, who was one of the three big names in Northern Irish sport along with George Best and Alex Higgins, owned his own pub, The Railway. And he was keen to show us some typical Irish hospitality to repay us for the party in Blackburn. I couldn't believe that the two huge Isle of Man TT trophies, the Senior and F1, were on the piano in his pub. I was dreaming of getting my hands on these things, while other people were banging into them and spilling beer. Then he brought out some poteen – Irish potato wine. It was about 90 per cent proof and I had one sip and was knocked out. I fell asleep and came round at five in the morning when Joey and his mate carried me into the van. I could smell the stuff on my breath for three days.

That win in Kirkistown really meant a lot to me because, deep down, I knew that I hadn't really pushed myself all year. Having suffered so much bad luck in the previous two years, this season had been a big leap forward. So, with proper organisation and a proper team behind me for 1989, I didn't expect any contest. I was confident of winning everything in sight.

A couple of months later, the title also earned a trip for dad and me to the Federation of International Motorcycling Awards in Rio de Janeiro for a glittering presentation night for all the world champions – although the 500cc Grand Prix champion, Eddie Lawson, didn't turn up. It was a new experience for me to have exotic dancers shaking their stuff all around as I went up to collect my trophy. Even though the TT Formula One World championship didn't have the highest of profiles within the sport, my own profile was growing. That meant that my bargaining position had improved for the following season.

Honda wanted me to retain the championship and their Chiswick-based importers, Honda Britain, gave me two RC30s for 1989. But it was a year too early for them to run a proper team. Dave Orton continued to help, for his final year, by providing a converted horsebox, which served as a big motorhome with a living area and storage space for the bikes. Metzeler, despite the incident with the marker pen, and Shell also upped their sponsorship. Having briefly returned to work at the warehouse, I packed that up to concentrate full time on racing and turned professional in February, gambling on picking up enough prize money to make a living. We were all set up; it was just a pity that the race organisation wasn't as good.

At one stage, it looked as though the series was going to lose world championship status, as Assen almost opted to stage a Superbike round instead. That would have meant the number of races dipping below the minimum six rounds. In the long run, it was obvious there was not enough room for two Superbike championships, but I decided to stay with Formula One and defend my title. To go to World Superbikes, which was only in its second year, would have cost way too much.

On the face of it, there was not much difference between the two classes, Formula One and Superbikes. But, while you started off with the same production bikes for both, they were very different. In F1 you could do whatever you wanted to the bike, even changing the frame. With Superbikes, the rules were a lot tighter. Four-cylinder bikes up to 750cc, three-cylinder bikes up to 900cc and twin-cylinder bikes up to 1000cc were all allowed, but there was very little that could be done by way of modification. The aim of Superbikes was to produce a competition that the biking public could identify with, because the bikes that were being raced were similar to production models on open sale.

The size of the crowds turning up for the World Superbike championship events these days proves that the idea was a success. But the rules meant that, whenever I rode in a British superbike race that year, I had to take off the £20,000 carburettors that Honda had provided for F1 races and replace them with standard road bike carburettors. It was all very messy and confusing.

The ACU were way behind the rest of the world, partly because Norton had made a comeback, which brought in crowds keen to see a bit of nostalgia. So the ACU did not want to invent rules that would stop the Nortons racing. But that bike was like nothing else, so was not allowed in superbike races. It had a rotary Wankel engine, which some argued was 580cc, while others insisted it was 1300cc. Whatever the capacity, these machines were incredibly fast in a straight line, even though their riders, Trevor Nation and Steve Spray, were fairly average.

Before starting the defence of my world crown, I was involved in the Eurochallenge series between European riders and Brits, staged at Brands Hatch and Donington. I was fifth in that series, ahead of the lads who had been beating me in England the previous year, but behind a new rider, Terry Rymer, who had burst onto the scene. He was a mouthy Londoner and not someone I ever got on with too well. But he was a bit too tall to get into a fight with, and probably too big to be a great rider. His Yamaha was not as fast as my bike, but handled better in the corners. And my motto has always been, 'Give me a bike that works and not one that is fast.' Rymer went on to have a good season and won a World Superbike race. I also rode in my first ever World Superbike race, at Donington, finishing seventh before brake problems in the second race left me in 13th place. It was not as daunting an experience as it might have been, because I had raced all the other riders in the Eurolantic series at that same meeting.

Back in England, I was pushing that bit harder because the doctors had given my leg the all-clear. So I was pretty confident for the first round of the TT Formula One World championship in Sugo, Japan – the first time I had raced so far away from home. And I had the shock of my life. The Japs were on very good machinery and, to make matters worse, I missed the only dry part of practice. Having qualified 30th, I pulled it round in the race to finish 13th and collect a couple of points.

Next stop was Mallory and then onto the Isle of Man – and a completely new and disturbing experience in racing . . .

CHAPTER SIX

Fearless

Some of the lads who had made the trip from Blackburn to help out and support me stayed at a small guest house run by the parents of an Isle of Man rider, Phil Hogg. He was one of the favourites to win the production class and had previously won the Manx Grand Prix. I had got to know him quite well that year and had a few beers with him at the hotel on the Wednesday evening, the night before final practice for the Supersport 600. On the Friday morning, at the age of 23, he crashed and died.

Even at such an early stage in my career, I had been around a fair amount of tragedy. Gary Dickinson's dad had died on the Isle of Man and there had been the Gene McDonnell incident with the horse. I had seen my dad fracture his skull, and read and heard about any number of other deaths. Yet none of this had affected me.

That attitude might appear cold and cynical to some people, but it's just a fact of biking life. Death can be around every corner. And there are only two ways to react – to let it eat at you and allow the images to haunt you, or to get back on the bike and concentrate on racing. I have never had a problem with the dangers of my sport, and I'm typical of all the other riders. Racers are a different breed, they can block things out of their mind very quickly – they have to.

For some reason, Phil's death was totally different. Maybe it was because we had such a good laugh on the Wednesday night. Maybe it was because I was due to ride in the 600cc race later that Friday. I genuinely don't know the answer. But, for the first time, a death had really got to me. I freaked out and pulled out of the race, and wanted to go straight home. That night, I kept myself to myself in my room. First, my dad came up to me and said, 'You've got to race. You've

77

got to just get on with it and forget what has happened.' Then Michaela tried to reason with me. Initially, I dug my heels in and insisted I wouldn't race.

It wasn't until someone passed on a message from Phil's dad that I began to see that my actions wouldn't change what had happened. He said, 'It's what Phil would have wanted. Go out and do your thing.' So I raced on the Saturday morning in the TT Formula One World championship race and came fourth. It was pretty much as though nothing had happened. In fact, I had reportedly collided with a slower rider in Parliament Square. To this day I cannot remember hitting anyone. I think I just went past him very close and he panicked and fell over. The next day, though, I was called before an ACU meeting and told to calm it down. So it was clear that my riding style had not been affected.

And my attitude to the danger of the sport hasn't changed much to this day. I have never been worried or obsessed about death in any way. I have never once thought, 'God, that could happen to me.' The way I tend to think is, 'So and so has been injured – he'll ride again. Or he's been injured, but he won't ride again.' I can brush it aside that easily. People who know me realise that it is just my way of dealing with things.

Where I differ from many other riders is in the amount of life insurance that I pay. A lot of them pay up to £20,000 or £30,000 a year, whereas I pay about £4,000. I know that Michaela and the kids would live comfortably off the money we have already put away in investment plans and pensions. It seems stupid taking out such a hideous amount of money to cover something that I would see no benefit from while, for a much smaller figure, there would still be more than enough paid out from the insurance.

Phil's death probably rammed it home that it's inevitable that riders are going to die at the Isle of Man TT. Over the years, the event has given motorbike racing a bad name. It's an understatement to say the meeting is dangerous. If you fall off at the TT once, it could be the last time you do anything. Having said that, nobody has to do the TT, as it's no longer part of any world championship. It's like the Grand National in horse racing, it's something different – a challenge with obvious dangers and risks. But riding a 37-mile circuit over mountains and through tiny villages, at touching distance from the spectators and occasionally actually touching the kerbs, is a fantastic feeling –

especially if you win. And, ever since I was a kid, I had wanted to win the TT. It has a tremendous history and was the event that my dad raced in more than any other. At that age I didn't even understand the dangers; they only sunk in as the years went by.

But nothing can be done to make it safer, except to knock down everyone's back gardens and all the stone walls on the Isle of Man. Road racing is dangerous, it's another harsh fact of life on two wheels. Riding a bike for pleasure on the roads is also dangerous. Personally, I don't see the point in it. Ever since I was 17 and first sat behind the wheel of a car, I have never liked riding bikes on the road. When I am travelling somewhere, I want to wear a T-shirt and have a few mates in the back of a car with the music blaring out. On a bike you get pissed wet through, covered in oil and shit, and you have to wear leathers and a helmet.

If I had my way, I wouldn't want my daughters Danielle and Claudia anywhere near the roads on a motorbike. They have a little quad bike, which they love riding in the fields, and that's fine. But girls don't seem to have any sense on a bike, even when they get older. So the chances are that they would fall off and injure themselves at some point, and I really don't want that to happen.

In 1989 a total of five riders died at the Isle of Man TT, including big names such as Phil Mellor and Steve Henshaw. I have known other riders, probably better than I knew Phil Hogg, who were to lose their lives there in later years. Mick Lofthouse, who lived near Blackburn, was killed during practice in 1996 at Milntown, when he was blinded by the sun and clipped one of the kerbs. He was the favourite to win two races that year, and had only rung me the week before to ask if he could borrow some racing gloves.

Mick's was one of the few funerals that I've attended. I hate them so much that I really have to know a person well to go. In 1999, another Lancashire rider, Simon Beck, who helped me out at a few meetings around 1992 and was a former winner of the Manx Grand Prix, died on the island. But the death of a rider has never affected me as badly as Phil's did.

Even so, it didn't stop me winning my first race there the following week, in the 750cc Production class. For this race, you rode bikes exactly as they were sold over the counter, with just the lights taped up. Two of the fastest guys that year were Dave Leach and Steve Hislop. We were still setting off in pairs in those days, and I started with Leach, 10 seconds behind Hislop. In a four-lap race, Hislop stopped three times to refuel, I stopped twice and Leach once.

It turned out that me and Dave were just behind Hislop on the last lap, although we had a 10-second advantage from the start. All the way from Union Mills, through the fast sections of Glen Helen, the humpback Ballaugh Bridge, and on towards Ramsey, I was simply trying to hang on to these idiots. But, having reached the mountain still in contention, the other two were now in my territory. The surface is smoother and you can see the bends, so this 10-mile section was more suited to my short circuit style than these road specialists. I passed them immediately and, although Leach came back alongside me with the last few corners to go, I held him off through Signpost Corner and the three Governor's corners with some mad riding. People said I was short circuit-scraping – throwing the bike on its side, braking as late as possible and running out onto the kerbs – but they were exaggerating as you simply cannot get away with that on roads. But, by Governor's Bridge, the front wheel was hopping because I was braking so hard and I hung on to win by 1.8 seconds.

That result proved that I had finally become a fast rider on the circuit, a proper TT racer. Hislop was particularly pissed off, because he won a record three TTs that year and became the first guy to lap at over 120mph. But I had stolen his thunder. It made up for the fact that I didn't finish the senior race because of an oil pipe leak. After I won, dad bought the bike back off Honda and sold it to a millionaire owner of a local discount shoe factory, Dale Winfield, who wanted it for his private collection to go alongside the 1988 bike that I had won the F1 world title on.

I was the only rider to compete in every round of the Formula One world championship that year. Following the Isle of Man TT, I won easily in Assen, where Hislop had a bad result, but he pipped me in Portugal. That result was reversed in Finland. With just the Ulster Grand Prix remaining, sixth place would be enough to clinch the title, whatever Hislop did. I was leading by 20 seconds when I pulled in for fuel, but Hislop gambled on using one tank for the whole race. By the time I came out of the pits, he had passed me but, despite a close finish, I had clinched the world championship for the second year running. It was great to win the title in 1988, but this year hadn't meant as much to me. I had wanted to win, if only to prove the previous year wasn't a fluke. But now I had bigger things on my mind, like 500cc Grands Prix or the World Superbike championship.

There were other highlights in the year, like a clean sweep of seven wins at Scarborough and a few wins in the British Superbike championship, although I did not compete often enough to mount a serious challenge on the title. I beat Niall Mackenzie in three races at the King of Donington meeting, which was a real feather in my cap as he was the best rider in Britain at the time, although not that used to riding bigger bikes. I also won the Stars of Darley and, in the final race of the year, I almost beat Ron Haslam on his 500cc Suzuki at Kirkistown, which was a bit embarrassing for him. I was all over him in the corners, but he nearly blew me off my bike when he flew past on the straights!

But the real experience of the season was my first visit to the Suzuka 8 hours in Japan, the biking equivalent of Le Mans where a team of riders take turns on the bike. This is the biggest race of the year for the Japanese and I was riding for a semi-supported factory team called the Takada Racing Project. My team-mate for this race was Steve Hislop and he took his mechanic, Anthony Bass, along. This was the first time I really got to know Tony, more commonly known as Slick, who was to become my chief mechanic for six years. There are different stories as to how Tony got that nickname. I always thought that it was because he was covered in oil. Others say that it's because he's so quick at his work – or fast with women . . .

I didn't relish taking Tony Holmes on such a long trip, so I asked a lad that I had started to mate around with, Tony Hudson, who worked in a bike shop in Preston, if he fancied it. He'd have been mad to turn it down because the Japanese flew us all out a few days early and treated us like kings, all expenses paid.

We were provided with two interpreters and our every wish was their command. If we wanted to go to McDonald's, we were taken to McDonald's. If we wanted to go jet skiing on a lake, we went there (and nearly killed each other). We were all given spending money, which was a bit like letting monkeys loose with hand grenades, as we immediately disappeared to the hotel bar to get drunk. We clearly weren't taking the trip quite as seriously as the Japanese, but we had to attend one formal dinner at a posh restaurant with the team owner, Mr Kiyokazu Takada.

As Steve made polite conversation, Slick tried to make me laugh by pulling stupid faces, because I was sat opposite Mr Takada. We were like a couple of naughty boys back at school, acting the goat by bowing stupidly when the food arrived. Then the waiter brought some soup full of noodles. It was a bad move. Mr Takada picked up his spoon and noisily slurped a huge mouthful down. I burst out laughing, which set Slick and Tony Hudson off. All this time, Hislop was trying to keep a straight face. But we had obviously offended Mr Takada. He threw his spoon into the bowl and didn't eat another thing all evening.

When I eventually stopped giggling, I was blushing badly and the rest of the meal was hard work. We were effectively sent up to our rooms early but, when the team bosses had gone home thinking their riders were safely tucked up in bed, we all came back down and set off for some karaoke bars. Me and Slick sang Beatles songs so much, and so badly, that one owner gave us a pot of money to shut up and leave. It was the first time that I had been with a mechanic who knew how to have a good time, but also put the hours in on the bike.

When the race came around, we were all feeling pretty good after a few days' holiday and arrived at Suzuka tanned and raring to go. We were up against the likes of Wayne Gardner, riding a full-blown factory RVF Honda, which was a lot better than our bike, and other stars like Kevin Schwantz, Rob Phillis and Mick Doohan. So it was a good chance for me to make a bit of a name for myself. They were the hottest conditions that I have ever raced in but we managed to qualify around 16th, which was not bad considering the standard of the opposition. It was also the first time I had been involved in a running start, where you dash across the track to where your partner is holding the bike, hit the start button and you're away. I got a flyer and was soon up to seventh. Steve was probably crapping himself in the pits, knowing that he wouldn't be able to keep us up there when I came in after around 50 minutes, the equivalent of a full tank of fuel. I had been lapping around a second and a half quicker than him – and this was his bike, set up by his mechanic!

He need not have worried because, with a couple of laps of my stint remaining, I went down going into turn one. The front end rolled and tucked underneath and the bike slid off into the gravel. It was a twisted bent mess with water spurting out everywhere, but when I hit the start button it fired up again, so I rode it back to the pits. Slick was moaning, 'What a fucking mess. What the hell are we going to do with this?' Meanwhile, I was busy apologising to everyone. But, because it was an endurance race, we had to try and get back out there. I swear we spent 50 minutes trying to fix the thing, even fitting new radiators. Why we didn't jack it in right away, I'll never know.

Eventually, it was fit to ride again, but even then, with a couple of hours to go, Steve had to kick an engine bolt back into place after it had worked loose as he was riding. We finished 33rd but, because we had made such an effort to finish, the Japanese treated us like heroes and sprayed us with champagne. It was probably the only time I have enjoyed racing in Japan. The culture is different, the people are hard work, the food is difficult and the climate is awful. It's fair to say it's not my favourite place.

I had made a lot of progress as a privateer during 1989 and my results had been good enough to attract offers from two teams. First, Norton invited me down to their factory with suspension guru Ron Williams, who knew the team manager, Barry Symmonds, very well. He had a reputation as a very serious and professional person who never smiled, a bit like a few football managers, so I was very nervous. I had no idea they were going to make me an offer, but Symmonds came out with it there and then. The package was £25,000 for the year plus a £10,000 bonus if I won the British championship, as well as another £20,000 if I won the TT F1 world championship. That was a good deal because the Nortons had been faster than any other bike in 1989, and looked cool with their all-black John Player Special sponsorship. I had been edgy enough just looking round the factory, but I shit myself when they started talking figures. So I mumbled that I would go home and think about it. The story made the front page of the *Motor Cycle News* under the headline 'Fogarty signs for Norton'. But they had jumped the gun.

Honda Britain were re-launching a team for 1990 after an absence of three or four years, to be managed by former racer, Neil Tuxworth. I had never met Neil but knew of him from my dad's racing days. At a meeting in Blackburn, he also made me an offer, which was nowhere near as good as Norton's. Honda's offer was £15,000 up front plus a few bonuses and a company car. More important than the money, Honda were a much bigger company and were also offering the chance to take part in a few World Superbike rounds outside Britain, although their priority was for me to retain the TT F1 world championship. This was too good an opportunity to miss and the decision didn't take long to make.

The money, which was not to be sniffed at in those days, allowed Michaela and me to move out of our hovel of a flat and into a detached house on Columbia Way, on a fairly new estate in an area of Blackburn called Lammack. With a bit of help from my dad, we could comfortably afford it. That was the first time I had any money of my own to speak of. So it blows wide open the theory that a load of people try to trot out, for some reason, that Michaela is only with me because I'm rich and famous. When I first started seeing her, I was relatively unknown and didn't have what you could call very good prospects. Sure, my dad was quite wealthy through his own business, but I was no spoilt brat and I was always prepared to earn my keep.

Things were just starting to take off and we were very happy. Sure, as with any couple, there was the odd argument, particularly if she hadn't made my tea, or if I forgot to pick her up from work and she had to walk home! In particular, there was one huge scrap before I was due at a Honda photocall at Alexandra Palace and I had to turn up with a deep gouge down my face, which was still visible on some of the publicity shots. It's fair to say that, when we fight, the walls shake.

Michaela instantly made friends with Andrea Cooke, the girlfriend of my new Honda team-mate, Jamie Whitham. He was one of three young British riders around at the time, along with myself and Rymer, who had the chance to go on to bigger and better things. I had met Jamie before, as he'd ridden a Suzuki in the British Superbike championship in the previous two years, but didn't really know him too well. He turned out to be one of my best friends in racing. Jamie is daft and is always cracking jokes. But he's also very intelligent, which adds to his sense of humour. And he coped well with my moods, by acting stupid and taking the piss, which I probably deserved.

Jamie had told Honda that he no longer wanted to ride on the roads. Instead, he wanted to concentrate on the short circuits of the British championship. That left me to concentrate on the TT F1 world championship. As it happened, only five circuits applied to stage F1 races and the series was downgraded from a world championship to a new title of FIM Cup. As soon as that happened, it was clear the World Superbike championship or, even better, the 500cc Grand Prix circuit, was the way forward for me. For the immediate future, though, these were not options and, as a factory rider, the pressure was on to retain my F1 title.

I asked Neil if I could have Slick as my mechanic, as I knew from the previous year's trip to Suzuka that we could work well together.

But, during that year, when Honda were providing bikes for Steve Hislop to ride while Slick was his mechanic, various parts had gone missing. I knew that it wasn't Slick, but all kinds of people were in and out of the depots and garages. So it could have been anyone. There was no way, though, that they would take him on and I was told that a guy called Dennis Willey would be my mechanic for the year. He was a good mechanic, quiet but pretty good to get on with. All the others on the team seemed to be Neil's mates. It's now the same with the Castrol Honda team. There are so many people on board from Neil's hometown of Louth in Lincolnshire that they might as well call it Team Louth Honda.

Jamie was not to have a good year. I beat him in every race and he began crashing more and more as the season went on. But, the more he crashed, the more his confidence dipped and the more Neil Tuxworth would sulk. When I crashed, the bike would slide off the track with nothing more than a few scratches. When Jamie crashed, the bike would dig in, flip over and be smashed to pieces. Neil would moan 'He's cost me £100,000 in damages this year.' It was not all Jamie's fault, though. The RC30 was as fast as anything out there in 1989 and 1990, but very difficult to ride. It didn't suit my style but I was able to ride round the problems with the front end of the bike, by holding it up with my knee. Jamie couldn't do that and, whenever he tried to get anywhere near me, he came off.

Don't get me wrong, he is a very good rider. But he was never quite good enough when it came to the world stage. At the end of the day, one rider will always ride better than another. In 1990, I rode better than Jamie and have done ever since. That, and the fact that I wanted to win more, is why I'm a world champion. He has had good results on some circuits but, to challenge for world championships, you have to finish in the top four or five on circuits that you don't like. But Jamie would really struggle at places like Phillip Island in Australia, Sugo and Misano. He has a weird style, hanging way off the bike, and that limits how fast he can go. He has also always been a big crasher and I watched his latest, the fireball at the Czech Grand Prix at Brno in 1999, from a beach bar in Ibiza. I thought, 'What a surprise, Jamie's crashed again.' Half an hour later, I heard he had been badly hurt and I contacted him as soon as I returned home.

My success has perhaps niggled him because, if I had not been around, he would have been Britain's best rider over the last 10 years.

That's not my fault, though. And he was annoyed about some comments I made in a recent magazine interview, when I was asked why he hadn't had a factory ride in the 1999 World Superbike championship. I said that his results hadn't been good enough and that, unless you were consistently in the top three, no job was guaranteed. You can be lucky, sure, like Vito Guareschi and Gregorio Lavilla, who kept their World Superbike rides for 2000 despite poor results the previous year. But, having finished eighth in the championship for two consecutive years, Jamie's chances were always going to be slim. He's a nice guy, but nice guys don't necessarily win anything. The truth hurts, and I am always honest. And I thought it was better coming from me than someone he didn't know.

Obviously he didn't see it like that and was upset with the way I had said it. We had already become a bit distant, as I also think that he has found it hard to accept my status in the sport. But we still meet up for dinner, and I've enjoyed seeing a lot more of him in 2000, as he's back in the Supersport series.

The tone was set for both our friendship and Jamie's season at our first race of 1990 in Daytona. From the word go, we got on like a house on fire. We rented two hire cars and I was pulled over by a traffic cop within an hour of leaving the airport, after treating a 'Stop' sign as a 'Give Way'. I was handed a fine after producing my passport and driving licence but I screwed it up, threw it in the back and ignored the penalty. It was only when I returned the following year that I started to worry whether the unpaid fine would show up on my passport record.

The aim of the week, though, was to destroy the hire cars by playing dodgems. If Jamie stopped at a red light, I would deliberately smash into him. 'Hey man! That guy's just run in the back of you,' shouted the stunned bloke in the next lane. 'Yeah, I know,' Jamie replied calmly, rubbing his neck from the whiplash. 'That's Daytona for ya,' yelled the Yank as he sped off. Yet there was hardly a mark on the cars when we returned them, as the bumpers were so big and sturdy.

Daytona is a huge event in the American calendar. It is similar to the TT because the tradition of the event attracts a lot of the top foreign riders. And, also like the TT, it's a dangerous circuit. The slope of banking is not really a problem, except that it causes tyres to blow out more than usual. The danger is the concrete wall around the track. If you hit that wall at speed, and at Daytona you're flat out most of

My dad, with his arm in a sling after breaking his collarbone in a racing accident, holds me in the backyard of our first house at Lindley Street.

Check out the Disney T-shirt in this class photo at Feniscowles Junior School, aged 10. I'm fourth in from the left on the back row.

Standing in front of Italian legend Giacomo Agostini at the Isle of Man TT, aged five.

Riding schoolboy
motocross in 1982.

One of my sponsors, Dav
Orton (right), helps celebra
my first ever TT win in th
750cc production class in 198

The metal frame used to
stabilise my leg after the second
bad break in 1987.

On my way to the F1 TT
title in 1990. You can
see the determination to
win in my eyes.

The V for victory after securing my first world title, the Formula One TT championship at Donington in 1988. Amongst those helping me celebrate the moment are Reg Gorton (fourth from left), Paul Russell, still sporting the scars from his crash in Sicily, 'Taste' (fifth from right and partly hidden), Lou Durkin (thumbs up), my cousin Chris (third from right), and someone I wish I'd never set eyes on, my uncle Brian (second right).

Crashing out of the British Grand Prix at Donington in 1992 after hitting some coolant from the bike of John Kocinski. I shaved the skin off my toes and had to kick the bike away with my free foot to prevent more serious injury.

My gran Vera cooks up another of her massive meals during a dinner break while working for my dad.

The night of my double win at Misano in 1999, with our good friends Graham and Louise and Geoff and Mandy. Louise is with son Matthew, while Danielle and Claudia are either side.

Breaking my wrist at Hockenheim in 1994 after flying over the front of the bike. When I looked up from the gravel (inset) the first person I could see in the crowd was Michaela. It was probably the first and last time she ever watched me from anywhere but the pit lane.

A very emotional moment after clinching my first World Superbike title at Phillip Island in 1994. I had to push the television crews out the way so that I could hug Michaela.

Above: Ducati chief Gianfranco Castiglioni helps celebrate Ducati's 100th superbike win at the alzburgring in Austria in 1995. Anthony Gobert was second and Troy Corser third. During the second race there had been a huge brawl between track marshals and my Ducati team.

elow: The lap of honour after clinching the 1995 world title at Assen. I had asked the fan to tie the flag around my neck but he thought I meant jump on the back. It earned me a warning from the FIM because I wasn't insured to carry a passenger.

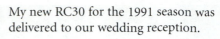
My new RC30 for the 1991 season was delivered to our wedding reception.

Danielle tries one of my helmets on for size in the back of our motorhome on the way back from Hockenheim in 1993.

Photographer Annabel Williams took this family photo.

The media frenzy on the grid before a race. As usual, Michaela is holding my umbrella.

A record crowd of 120,000 turned up at Brands Hatch in 1999 – but the races did not go to plan.

Deep in thought in the pit garage during a qualifying session.

Hannah Walsh, the daughter of our friends Graham and Louise, who died in a tragic accident in our swimming pool.

the time, you're in serious trouble. Before our race, we watched that happen to an Irish lad, Gary Cowan. He was a good 250cc rider, signed by Kenny Roberts to ride in his Marlboro Yamaha team in America, and a tip to be a future world champion. He was paralysed in that crash and would never race again.

Despite this, I still probably didn't appreciate the dangers of the track at that age and led our race at one point. Then, having stopped for fuel, I was desperately trying to catch up again when I tangled with a slower rider and crashed out entering the first turn, one of the slowest corners. Luckily, I was sliding onto the safety of the in-field run-off. I escaped with a few cuts and bruises, but didn't expect the reception when I limped back into the pits. Neil Tuxworth was not one to rant and rave. Whenever something was bothering him, he would bottle it up like a spoilt child. And the fact that both of us had crashed out when we had a chance of winning was really bothering him. He did not speak to us all the way back to England.

All in all, though, I've always got on very well with Neil and we have had some laughs. That's mainly because he cannot have a conversation without talking about tits and fannies. He is also quite tight. In my experience he doesn't buy anything himself. I have lost count of the number of cans of pop I have bought for him in Japan because he does not want to break into a yen note. He collects anything, and never leaves any tips. So you can imagine what he was like as a team manager. There was one set of tyres for practice and maybe, if you did well, he'd give you a new set for the race. So, even though we were factory riders, he was not exactly throwing money at us.

That seemed to change at the first World Superbike round of the year at Jerez. Our eyes lit up when Jamie and me travelled business class, along with a load of top officials from the Chiswick headquarters of Honda Britain, who were attending a meeting out there. I hadn't even had a chance to get used to the fact that I could turn up for a meeting in a car, and not have to worry about transporting the bikes in the horsebox. We were also booked into a top hotel in Spain and were beginning to think that this lifestyle was just a taste of things to come for the year. You can imagine Neil's reaction when he discovered that it was all a big cock up and that we were supposed to be on budget packages, and that he would have to foot the bill.

We were expecting to blitz the World Superbike riders, like reigning champion Fred Merkel on a factory Honda, Raymond Roche on a

Ducati, Fabrizio Pirovano, and the British pair of Rob McElnea and Terry Rymer on the Loctite Yamahas. But we had the shock of our lives at Jerez. Not only did the bikes, delivered by a Ready Rent-a-Van hired in Louth, arrive too late for unofficial practice, we found the competition really tough. Jerez was one of the many tracks where the front handling problems of the Honda were horrendous. I finished 14th and crashed out of the second race after tangling with Pirovano for eighth place.

The second round of the World Superbikes at Donington went a lot better with two sixth places, the best results of the British riders. Then, after a couple of decent results at Sugo and in the North West 200, I turned my attentions to the TT.

This was my burning ambition for the season. I was desperate to win at least one of the two big races, the Senior or the Formula One. I now knew what I was doing, having learned the ropes the previous year. After his performance the previous year, when he won three TTs and smashed the lap record, everyone was still talking about Steve Hislop, who had joined me as my team-mate for the meeting because Jamie didn't want to race on the roads. Steve was a decent guy, quite quiet, although if you did get him talking, it would always be about himself. But I hardly spoke to him in the build-up to the races. I wanted to hate him because I was so determined to win. This was probably the first time that I had tried to psyche out an opponent. I told everyone, 'There's no way Steve Hislop is going to beat me this year.' Jamie had come over to the island with his mates to go trail bike riding. I think even he got sick of me saying, 'I'm the best, I'm going to beat Hislop.' Whenever he was asked for a prediction, he replied, 'Foggy is going to win, definitely. The way he is talking, he has got to win.'

After the first Monday practice for the Formula One race, Steve started to complain that I was faster. 'Carl is riding stupidly. He's dangerous. The weather wasn't good enough to ride like that.' I thought to myself, 'You were the one riding the kerbs last year, Steve.'

By the time the race arrived, I think I had pretty well done his head in. My only worry was that I would pull a muscle in my arm during practice from heaving the bike round the corners. For the first year, riders set off on their own at 10-second intervals. He was number six and I was 20 seconds behind, riding number eight. The fact that I was behind Steve also unnerved him. By lap two I had caught him and we were level going down the long and bumpy Sulby Straight, despite the fact that I had to keep popping my loose rev counter back into place. His bike was quicker, but I was determined not to lose. Approaching the tight right-hand Sulby Bridge corner, it was a case of 'Who's going to brake first?' Then. . . 'Shit! I've got to brake now.' I somehow got round the corner but he ran wide and had to work the bike back round to face in the right direction. I was away and he retired on the next lap, claiming there was a problem with the brakes. When I asked his mechanic about the problem, he just shrugged, as if to say, 'There was nothing wrong with his brakes.'

It was, without doubt, the biggest win of my career so far. I was on a massive high.

There was a five-day gap before the Senior race, during which I finished second in the Supersport 400 behind Dave Leach. I had a lot of respect for Dave at the TT, but felt that I would have won the race if we had set off as pair, instead of me starting 10 seconds in front. I had beaten Steve again, and that niggled him even more. I also rode in the 600 race, which I didn't enjoy, especially when the bike spewed out oil approaching Brandish, one of the fastest parts of the circuit. With the back wheel sliding round, it was a miracle that I kept the bike upright to avoid hitting the banking head on. This was just one more warning of the fine line between escape and disaster.

The weather was poor for the Senior race and the start was put back a few hours. I panicked over the tyres as it could have been snowing on the other side of the island on a day like that. Having seen that Steve had chosen cut slicks, I went for the same and set off like a bat out of hell. I could have come off after running wide at the Quarter Bridge roundabout but passed Leach almost straight away before nearly hitting the wall at Union Mills because I was pushing so hard. The first signal told me that I was first equal. I thought, 'Who the hell is with me?' Trevor Nation had stayed with my pace on his Norton. Coming out of Glen Helen, I could see Steve in front. 'Come to daddy!' I reeled him in and went underneath him at the village of Kirkmichael. I had made up about two seconds a mile and was leading by 22 seconds at the end of the first lap, which is some going. Hislop had pulled in at the end of the first lap, claiming that the conditions were too dangerous to race in.

Coming down the mountain at the end of the last lap towards Creg ny Baa with the finish line in sight, the emotion of the moment became overwhelming. I began crying for the first time ever in a race. This was a race that I had seen my dad try and win so many times. It even meant more than the F1 win, earlier in the week. This was the main race, before Formula One was even invented. To hold those massive trophies, which had been around since 1907, was an incredible feeling. The double TT victory still ranks as one of my biggest achievements.

To achieve that success, I had pushed myself to new limits of bravery and skill. I had proved my point and saw no reason to risk my life on the island again. At the end of the week, I confirmed the speculation that I expected it to be my last TT.

I said, 'I'd rather concentrate on one thing in the future. If I do a full season of World Superbike, which looks likely with Honda, there's no way I could do the TT. If I were lucky enough to get a Grand Prix ride, it would be the same. Plus the prize money's not very good. When Joey Dunlop won here five years ago, he got 10 grand plus a lot of start money. But now you only get six grand for winning and it costs the earth in hotels, ferries – you name it. All the expenses have gone up but the prize money's come down. It annoys me a bit.'

I wouldn't have dreamed of shooting my mouth off like that a couple of years earlier. But the world titles and high profile wins at the TT had improved my self-confidence and I was no longer fazed by interviews. Already I was developing a reputation for speaking my mind and slagging everyone off. And, for the first time, it landed me in hot water.

At the end of the week, I received a warning from Honda after a story appeared in *Motor Cycle News*. It quoted me saying that I was a better rider than Terry Rymer and that the only difference between us was that the Yamaha was a better bike than the RC30. I had given the interview after a few beers in a nightclub, celebrating the Senior win. As always, I was just trying to be honest and tell the truth. I felt I was the best rider in Britain, but Rymer was beating me because of the front end handling problems. These seemed worse for a rider who carried a lot of corner speed, as I did. Had Rymer been on a Honda, he wouldn't have been able to see which way I was going!

I suppose it didn't help that I wasn't great at setting the bike up. My approach had always been to try and ride round problems, without worrying about the set-up. It was only after the inconsistency of the 1998 season with Ducati that Davide Tardozzi urged me to pay more attention. He said, 'Stop trying to ride fast laps. Think about where the bike is not quite right, where it is running wide or chattering.' So I improved on that side of things during 1999. I don't think that I was ever hopeless at it, but I could have contributed more. Other riders were just as bad as I was, but tried to hide it by talking a load of crap.

The problems with the bike were not as bad on the road circuits, where you don't lean over as far, and I breezed through the FIM Cup without any competition. I won in Portugal before beating Rymer and Rob McElnea in the British championship at Knockhill.

It was at about this time that news had filtered through that Honda were on the lookout for a rider to replace the injured Pier-Francesco Chili in the British Grand Prix. My name was in the frame but Honda's priority was to retain the F1 TT title. So I had to fly to Finland under protest, pleading with Neil Tuxworth to get me the Grand Prix ride. Phillip McCallen, who had a similar arrangement with Honda as I'd had the previous year, drove my bike out in his van. He eventually turned up, with the van smashed to pieces and having spent a night in a Finnish police station, for running into, and killing, a moose.

The weather was appalling at Kouvola but, in those days, I was almost unbeatable in the wet. Nowadays I'm shit. I have tried to win races but, again, because I lean so far over on short circuits, I usually crash. But I was in a class of my own for that road race and lapped everyone to win the title for the third time, even though it was now just called the FIM Cup and not the TT F1 world championship. But there were hardly any celebrations. That title no longer mattered to me. I was pissed off because I was sure that somebody else would probably have been offered the Grand Prix ride by the time I got back to England.

Neil Tuxworth was waiting at the airport. It puzzled me why he was there. 'I've got some good news for you,' he said. 'Honda want you to ride the NSR500 in the British Grand Prix.'

Yes! This was it – the big time . . .

CHAPTER SEVEN

Big Time

As always with Neil Tuxworth, there had to be a downside. Honda Britain decided to release me from my contract while I was racing for the French-based Roc team in the Grand Prix. It was just his way of saving a few quid and I couldn't have cared less. This was the big chance I had been waiting for. If I went well at Donington, there was a chance that I could secure a ride for the following season.

Before that, though, we had to slip in another Suzuka 8 hours. I was riding for the same Takada team, again with Steve Hislop as my team-mate, but this time Neil also travelled with us, so there wasn't as much mucking about.

During the race exactly the same thing happened as the previous year. I was going well in seventh or eighth – too well. At the second turn, I came off and the bike was mangled again. It took the mechanics 15 minutes to repair, but we were effectively out of the race. Neil had a face like thunder and the rest of the team, apart from Steve, were also sulking, which was pretty pathetic.

Neil made my life hell for the two days travelling home. If I tried to have a laugh that night, or at breakfast the following morning, he would be ready with his little digs, 'Thank God we're getting rid of you now. You can go and crash that 500 bike instead.' These were hurtful things for a rider to hear. As a team manager who used to ride motorbikes, he should have known better. That's exactly the wrong way to treat your riders. He seemed to have forgotten everything I had already won for his team. I was so close to smacking him one and walking out on Honda Britain.

Within a day of getting back to England, Neil was on the phone as if nothing had happened, asking me if I wanted to stay at his parents' farm while I tested for a day at Cadwell Park before the Grand Prix. The idea was to meet the Roc team, run by Serge Rosset and a German called Dietmar Mayer, and sit on the NSR500 before the big day at Donington. There was some oil down on the track, so I took it easy for the first few laps. Even so, the bike felt pretty good, so they asked me to take it up to 12,000 revs in every gear. I couldn't believe how fast it was.

When I came in, one of the mechanics said, 'Hold your hand out!' It was shaking from the adrenaline. I asked for the bars to be moved out a bit, for extra comfort, and broke the lap record when I went out again. Mind you, I have always liked Cadwell and hadn't even experienced the front handling problems with the RC30 at that track. I left Cadwell thinking I was going to win the British Grand Prix that Sunday. But I arrived at Donington thinking someone had swapped bikes!

The same bike was awful to ride, as though the wheels had been put back on out of line. And, while everyone was friendly enough in hospitality, nobody seemed too bothered about my problems with the bike. If it had been my current boss, Davide Tardozzi, he would have bent over backwards to make sure that everything was right for me. I soon got the impression that I was only there to put the bike on the track and keep the French TV sponsors' logo exposed. I felt cramped and uncomfortable, but nobody wanted to help by changing the foot-rest positions or raising the bars. I could out-brake other riders, but couldn't carry any corner speed and felt that I was going to crash at every turn.

Even so, I qualified in 11th and, in the race, worked my way up to seventh. 'These guys are no better than me. They are going well because their bikes are working right,' I thought. 'It might just be me, though. Push it and see.' On the third lap, as soon as I pushed that little bit harder at McLean's Corner, I crashed out. I picked myself up, looked into the crowd and saw the huge disappointment on their faces. One guy offered me a can of beer and said, 'Forget it Foggy, there's always next time.'

It suddenly dawned on me that the crowd had really wanted me to do well. I was the next big prospect, as Niall Mackenzie was the top British rider but he was never going to win anything. I had let a lot of people down as those fans had been starved of success for so long – and deserved better. From that moment on, I wanted to put things right for the fans, as well as myself.

Despite the fall, the Roc team were quite impressed and offered me another ride at the next Grand Prix, at Anderstorp in Sweden. Before the race, I stated publicly what I had privately thought during the Donington race. I might have been up against the likes of Wayne Gardner, Mick Doohan, Eddie Lawson, Wayne Rainey and Kevin Schwantz – proper racing legends, not like the current crop of Grand Prix riders – but I really didn't think they were anything special. 'They are not that good,' I was quoted in the press. 'I was catching most of them up in the corners. The only place I was losing out at Donington was in the middle of the corners, where I was losing the front end every time that I tried to go fast.'

They hated me for saying that. Mayer took great delight in telling me that the others were now taking bets to see who could out-brake me. And Rosset didn't seem interested at all. I was quickly coming to the conclusion that this lot were a bunch of arseholes.

The Swedish circuit suited me more than Donington, but I was still experiencing the problems at the front of the bike. As a result, I qualified around 13th, probably the last of the factory riders. In the race, I had a brilliant start and was fourth at the end of the first lap, learning all the time from the rest of the big name riders. I needed a decent result after what had been said, and my sixth place finish, after a real battle with Jean-Philippe Ruggia and Juan Garriga, was not bad at all, especially as I still felt that I could do a lot better. All of a sudden, the Roc team were a bit more interested.

Chili's injury was taking longer to heal than expected, so I was offered further rides in the Czech Grand Prix at Brno and the Hungarian round at Hungaroring. I said, 'Okay, but on one condition. I want the team to start helping me. I want the bike setting up properly. That means different bars and different footrests.'

I arrived in Czechoslovakia, as it was then, and nothing had changed. I crashed in practice, when I lost the front end, and by this stage I hated riding the thing. I wasn't even given grade A tyres to use, as they were saved for riders with a chance of winning the championship. So, after another good start, I dropped back through the field, after two or three scary moments with the front end, to finish 10th, having been passed by two riders on the last lap because my tyres had deteriorated so much.

Hungary saw my first ever run-in with Mick Doohan. I came in after a quick first practice session, during which I had set the fourth fastest time. Out of the blue, the Aussie stormed into the garage shouting, 'What the fuck do you think you were doing? You mad bastard, you cut me up; you fucking well should have seen me.'

I stopped him in full flow. 'I haven't a clue what you're talking about, so fuck off. I'm not interested.'

Doohan carried on shouting, but some of my mechanics had separated us and shoved him out of the door. Maybe he was a bit touchy because he hadn't won a Grand Prix by then, and saw this new guy on a Honda as a bit of a threat. Since then I have always got on well with Doohan. He seems pretty quiet and laid back. In some ways he is a lot like me, avoiding the publicity and superstar status of an attention seeker like Max Biaggi, preferring to be out of the way and doing his own thing.

In the next session I was quick again, but crashed for what seemed like the 12hundredth time. On the last day, I was third quickest with 10 minutes remaining but dropped back through the field to qualify in eighth or ninth. Even so, I was up with the top four in the race until the rear tyre shredded again and I finished eighth, although I was only something like 23 seconds behind Schwantz in third. Ironically, Doohan had gone on to record his first GP win.

I was pissed off to say the least and felt a million miles from home, with only my dad for company. While I wouldn't have admitted it at the time, I was too young to have been given that chance. The fact that I couldn't set the bike up didn't really help. And the team that I was with had helped even less.

A couple of years down the line, I would have been more prepared. So, when they offered me one more race in Australia, I told them where to go and I was slaughtered in the press. Their line was, 'How does he expect to get a regular 500cc ride if he doesn't want to race in the Australian Grand Prix?'

Maybe I should have gone. But I didn't see the point of travelling all that way to ride a bike that didn't work for me, in a team that didn't help me. It made more sense to return to winning races at places like Oulton Park, my favourite track, where the next British race was being held.

Neil was happy to get me back and, sure enough, I won the Oulton race, which put me back in with a shout of the MCN British Superbike championship. So Neil got me a late entry in the next round at Cadwell, the very next day. For some reason he was not at the meeting, which was also staging the one-off annual King of Cadwell race. It was the biggest race of the day, but I had only been entered in the British championship races. I had won the second and was feeling pretty good, so I said to my mechanic, Dennis, 'I might as well do the King of Cadwell.'

'You know that Neil said you weren't to race in that,' he warned.

'Bugger that, I'm entering anyway.'

Sure enough, I won that race as well, and was headline news in the racing papers. Within a couple of days, a written warning dropped through the letterbox. Neil said that, because he had been disobeyed, we would no longer be able to contest one of the World Superbike championship rounds in France.

As always, it came down to budgets. Taking part in the King of Cadwell could have cost no more than £30 for a tank of fuel but, apparently, it had blown our allowance. He was just sulking again. As it happened, he backed down and let me compete at Le Mans in France. But he stopped Jamie from going, using the excuse that he had been crashing all year.

I was convinced that, having had a few decent results in the Grand Prix, I was ready to win a World Superbike race. Instead, I got the shock of my life. I qualified in 12th and had to be content with trying to beat Rymer, when I was eighth in the second race.

My final race of the year was at Brands Hatch, where I still had a mathematical chance of stealing one of the MCN British F1 championship, if Trevor Nation crashed and I won. But I had missed too many rounds to have a realistic chance. And, always in the back of my mind for the final race of the season, was the dread of spending another winter injured. Sure enough, I lost the front end in one race and crashed out, before finishing third and fourth in the other two. It also proved to be the last time that I raced as Jamie's team-mate, as I think he crashed out in all three and was sacked by Honda. Typically, Neil didn't confront him, but allowed Jamie to find out from one of the mechanics instead.

In December, at the end of another hard season, we went on holiday to Fuerteventura with Jamie and Andrea. The scenery on the journey from the airport was bleak. The island is like a desert and we were on a coach full of Germans driving through the sand dunes when a dot appeared on the horizon. It was our hotel and it was in the middle of nowhere. We would obviously have to make our own fun, if the holiday was to be a success. All the beaches were for nudists, so we found a secluded spot and walked around stark bollock naked, occasionally bumping into some old Germans with shrivelled todgers and tits like Durexes.

We also introduced a system of penalties to spice up the evenings' drinking. Michaela is usually pretty good at Trivial Pursuit but, one night, she got herself into a mess. She seemed to answer all the early questions wrong and the penalty that night was a foul potion of four liqueurs in one glass, which had curdled to make it even more disgusting. It looked and tasted disgusting. Each time she slipped up she had to drink this horrible cocktail. And the more she drank, the more questions she got wrong. She was soon off her trolley and refused to drink any more penalties. So we introduced forfeits. Sure enough, she got the next question wrong and had to perform the forfeit, which was to give me a blowjob under the table. She did, and was sick five minutes later, which I can only presume was down to the drink. I could never get her to play the game again.

Danielle was conceived on that holiday – it might just have been that night – and Michaela found out that she was pregnant on Christmas Day. This was only a month after she had started taking fertility pills.

We had not been taking precautions, yet nothing had been happening so we both had to have tests. I had to wank into a bottle at home with a bit of help from Michaela because I was too busy laughing. Then she rushed it up to the hospital, with the heater on in the car so the sperm didn't die. The results were magnificent! Then they discovered that Michaela was having trouble ovulating and the pills did the trick.

Once news of the pregnancy got out, everyone started telling us that we should get married. After a while, Michaela started agreeing with them. So, when the subject cropped up again when we were tenpin bowling with a few of her mates, I thought it might be the respectable thing to do. 'Okay then,' I agreed. 'But I'm busy with my racing. You sort it out and let me know when it is.'

Okay, it might not have been the most romantic proposal, but it got the job done. Within eight weeks, Michaela had her side of the bargain sorted and the date was set for 16 March.

I was re-signed by Honda for 1991 for £22,000, a company car and a new motocross bike – Neil's way of keeping my salary down. I was promised the top bike, direct from Japan, to race in the World Superbike championship. It was to be exactly the same as the factory bike provided for twice world champion Fred Merkel, a typical surfy Californian – long blond hair, bronzed and a part-time model – who had just lost his title to Raymond Roche. I always got on with Merkel really well, which is unusual for me with Americans.

The Honda Britain team had a new sponsor in Silkolene, a bigger budget and I had a new high-profile team-mate in Niall Mackenzie, who had come straight from 500cc GPs. He was a very quiet guy, who didn't cause any problems and kept himself to himself. It was good motivation as he was possibly regarded as the best rider in Britain, even though I felt that I had proved I was better. Rymer was riding a factory Yamaha again and he was another rival to my status of the best rider in Britain.

To prepare for the battle ahead, I went swimming every day during the winter at a local hotel's fitness centre, feeling like Rocky with a mental picture of Rymer as the opponent.

The TT Formula One championship had been scrapped, so there were no distractions from superbikes. The stage was set to make a big impression on the world stage. I just hadn't bargained for the speed of the Yamahas, Ducatis and Kawasakis! Or the fact that, not only was the Honda still handling badly, it was now one of the slowest bikes and well past its sell-by date. It was to be a very tough year.

I didn't win a single superbike race in Britain during 1991. Whenever I returned from the World Superbike championship, I was up against guys in the new Supersport championship, who were set up for F1 rules. And those open rules were just as much of a joke as ever. Britain remained the only place in the world where the Nortons could race. It just wasn't eligible anywhere else, as it did not relate to a street bike in any way. Suzuki were running a three-year-old bike that was rumoured to be an 850cc, on which Jamie had some incredible results. There were also suggestions that the Yamahas were 1000cc, and I could not touch the Kawasakis of John Reynolds and Brian Morrison, guys who I should have been beating. But my bike just couldn't compete.

The first race of my season was again in Daytona and it was an almost exact repeat of the previous year. I had led at one point, until the officials brought out the pace car after an accident. This car drives round at the front of the field until the wreckage has been cleared, allowing all the other riders to bunch up behind the leader. The

Americans like to use it to liven up a boring race – or to help one of their riders. Despite this, I was still in contention in fourth place with a couple of laps to go. Suddenly there was smoke everywhere and, before I could complete the 'oi' of oil in my mind, I was on my back sliding down the banking before turn one, a very fast part of the track. It was like a toboggan run and I was travelling so fast that the friction almost burnt through my leathers, even though I was trying to lift my back up off the track as I hurtled along.

When I came to a stop, there was not a mark on my front and I ran towards the bike, hoping that it wasn't too badly damaged. When I saw oil pouring out, I knew that my race was over. Back at the pits, I was told that I had been docked a lap for passing another rider when the yellow warning flag was up, preventing overtaking. I didn't bother arguing, because I had crashed out. But I had already had enough of the place and was in no rush to go back. Even after the 1990 race, when me and Jamie both crashed out, we had been told that the Americans would have disqualified us in any case, for using illegal forks and having non-standard fairings, the fibreglass bodywork. It was bullshit. And, by then, I was convinced that you weren't going to win the race unless you were American.

I had been lucky to escape without serious injury in more ways than one, as our wedding was the following weekend. Michaela would have killed me if I'd had to limp down the aisle on crutches. There was no time for a stag do and, to be honest, I'm not really into all that anyway. But on the Friday before the big day, my mechanic Dennis, rang to tell me that my new Honda was in the country. And Rev Phillip Webb, who was due to marry us, had already suggested that I bring it along if possible.

There was just time. I would be able to get it to the reception if we moved quickly. One call to the team boss, Neil Tuxworth, and it was all sorted. The bike was driven up to Blackburn in a van on the day of the wedding, at the United Reformed Church, and was waiting for us at the Dunkenhalgh Hotel when we arrived for the reception. It was on nearly all the pictures and, whenever there was a gap in the speeches, I couldn't stop myself nipping outside to sit on it.

Gary Dickinson's best man speech was hilarious, because he was as nervous as hell. He had it all carefully written out but muddled up all his pages. So, when he started to lose track of where he was supposed to be, he lost the plot altogether. At one point he tried to tell the story of the night that I had met Michaela again in town, as he was with me at the time. But, instead of saying that we had bumped into her, he said, 'Me and Carl both banged her in town.' The whole room was rolling around laughing.

The father of the bride speech was just as good. Alan, a former traffic cop, started by saying he couldn't ever remember seeing so many people that should have arrows on their pyjamas! Let's just say that there were times during his career when he came across some of the Fogarty brothers. So you can imagine his face when I first turned up on his doorstep with his daughter!

Michaela looked absolutely stunning and I just knew that we were meant to be together. Quite a few other riders were there, such as Steve Hislop, Robert Dunlop and Jamie Whitham. The ushers were Paul Kay, another long-standing friend, and my cousin, Chris. It was great having all my mates in one place and all looking pretty smart, apart from my dad who was wearing the wrong waistcoat.

And I guess I must also have been sinking a few beers on the sly as, when it came to the business end of the night, my engine backfired. I wasn't in the best of moods, anyway, because some tosser had filled our bed with biscuit crumbs. 'Bloody childish,' I moaned. 'I'm going to have the bastard that's done this,' as I cleaned the bed and Michaela tried the Jacuzzi out for size.

I jumped in for a glass of champagne but I was more interested in getting to bed – for some sleep. She did me proud, though, when her friends asked the inevitable questions about how I had performed that night. 'Oh, it was fantastic. Just as I imagined,' she said.

There was no honeymoon as it was straight into the World Superbike championship at Donington, a race that provided the first signs of the struggles ahead for that year. This was what I had prepared for all winter, yet somehow I didn't feel up for it. I was blowing hot and cold, probably through a lack of confidence. I retired in the first race, when the gears broke, but finished ninth behind Niall and Merkel in the second. So, for once, I couldn't really blame the bike. The outlook was no better after the second round, at the Spanish circuit of Jarama. Two Spanish riders on Hondas, Juan Lopez Mella and Daniel Amatriain were third and fourth, and Merkel beat me in both races, while I was breaking my back just to finish ninth and eighth. It seemed that my bike was even worse than the previous year.

I couldn't even claim any satisfaction when we murdered the Yanks in a special challenge series at Mallory and Brands. It was embarrassing. We turned up to be told that it was open rules. So the American riders, who included people like Scott Russell, Freddie Spencer and Miguel DuHamel, were in the same boat as me – on superbikes against British riders on all kinds of different bikes. There was no contest.

At Mallory, a local rider called Ray Stringer won all three races. It was not surprising, because he was riding a 1000cc Yamaha – a missile – while I had to weave all over the track just to try and hold people up, which prompted a complaint from Ron Haslam. 'I've got to do that because my bike is so slow,' I grunted back at him. I think I pissed a lot of people off that weekend.

That continued at Brands Hatch, where I clashed with Scott Russell for the first time. I had held him up for around five laps and, when the race was over, he flicked the finger at me. I thought it was only fair to return the gesture. This was to develop into a classic rivalry. The Americans didn't win one race in the challenge series and the British lads loved it. But I didn't feel like joining in the podium celebrations, so I stomped off back to the caravan on my own.

Worse was to follow at the British championship round at Donington. I was sixth in the F1 race and seventh in a 600cc race. Having started at the back of the grid, I didn't think that was too bad a result. My dad soon put the matter straight. 'You've just finished seventh in a British 600 Supersport race. What do you think you are doing?' He was right. What was I doing taking part in the race in the first place? What made it worse was the fact that Niall won the main race on his new bike. I started to have big self-doubts. Maybe I had lost my edge, or was it that Danielle was due in a few months? Whatever the reason, I was suffering a crisis of confidence. Thankfully, the TT was around the corner.

Neil Tuxworth had approached me early on in the year at the Superbike Show in London. 'Look Carl, it's Yamaha's 30th anniversary at the TT this year,' he said. 'We have to spoil their party. Honda want to send two special bikes over. I know you said you didn't want to do it again, but it's a great chance for you to ride the RVF.' It did seem too good an opportunity to miss.

But now I had other responsibilities. I knew that Michaela was not keen on me going back to the island. She was obviously as much aware of the dangers as anyone was. And the fact that she was pregnant might also have been preying on her mind. But there was never any suggestion of her trying to persuade me not to go. In the end, the fact that I was doing so badly in superbikes probably helped me make up my mind.

When the meeting arrived, I was a totally different person to the fired-up, aggressive and cocky rider that had competed the previous year. Instead of trying to hate everything that Steve Hislop did, this year I was happy for him to collect me from the airport. And we stayed in a cottage next door to his girlfriend, Leslie Henthorn, a former Miss Isle of Man winner and Miss World contestant. The owner of the cottage was an Australian girl, who was away during the meeting, and I don't think we were perfect houseguests.

First, our Chihuahua, Arai, pissed all over the cream-coloured carpet when we left him alone. It got worse. Michaela ran a bath, which seemed to take ages to fill to the top. She had stayed upstairs while it was running and it wasn't until I returned home that we noticed the water pouring into the kitchen, as the overflow pipe of the bath was not connected to anything. We received a call from Leslie a few weeks later, saying that when her next door neighbour returned home and sat in the bath, it sank through the rotten floorboards and the kitchen ceiling!

As a result of this new attitude towards Steve, I was far too laid back. I had also missed out on the usual road circuit build up, at meetings like the North West 200. And when I sat on the RVF for the first time, it was like a live wire and I couldn't stop it jumping all over the place. I brought it back to the pits, my face as white as a sheet after a hairy ride.

'I don't like this thing at all. What do you think, Steve?' I asked.

'Mine seemed to be handling fine, actually.'

'Bloody typical!' I groaned. 'I get the one you can't ride.'

Maybe it's part of my mental approach to racing, to always think that the other person's bike is better. That way, I have even more incentive to ride at my peak. I thought that Steve's bike was quicker at the TT the previous year, and I don't even think my bike was the best out there during the 1999 championship win. The speed trap times proved my point. The Hondas and Kawasakis were always quicker. It's not a frame of mind that I've deliberately set out to develop, but it does seem to help me focus.

It also worked on this occasion. After the next practice session for the Formula One race, I was faster than Steve. But, because I would miss the Senior race on the Friday, in order to fly out to the States for the World Superbike championship, I had to share the bike during practice with Joey Dunlop, who was to take my place. That didn't help, as I needed as much time as possible on the RVF. By the final practice session, I was slower than Steve, although he'd set an unofficial lap record of an average 124mph and I was only seven seconds slower overall. But I wasn't up for the race. I had scared myself too many times in the build-up and, at the kind of speeds we were forcing each other to ride at, someone was going to get hurt.

Others sensed the same thing. The head of the Honda Racing Corporation, Koichi Oguma, was on the island and had watched us push each other to the limits in practice on the Thursday before the race. All he was bothered about was spoiling the Yamaha party. And that wouldn't happen if we were both lying in a ditch. So, Oguma and Neil Tuxworth locked the two of us in a room and told us to come up with a team plan for the race. The door closed. I turned to Steve.

'There's no way I'm going to let you win,' I started.

'And there's no way I'm going to let you win,' replied Steve.

There was nothing more to be said. When Neil and Oguma returned, I told them, 'Thanks for the concern, but we both want to win the race. It's not in my nature to fix a race and Steve is here all week. You can't expect him to watch me take all the glory in one race.' They were obviously frustrated, but there wasn't much they could do. Or so I thought.

It has been said that it was a classic race. I disagree. People forget that my race was effectively over after the first five miles. On the first lap, before Ballacraine, the bike mysteriously cut out and I lost around three seconds. At the first timing point at Glen Helen, I was five seconds behind Steve. By Ramsey, I had pulled that gap back to one second. But, as I went over the mountain, it cut out again and I lost more time.

On the second lap, at Ballaugh Bridge, I had to pull in as the engine had stopped completely, as though it had run out of fuel. Just as I came to a halt, it fired back up. By now, Steve, who had started 30 seconds behind me, was just in front and we diced it out for a while. I passed him over the mountain but, as we were exiting Brandish, the thing suddenly cut out again. I anxiously looked over my shoulder to see Steve miss me by inches, because I had slowed so quickly. He must have been wondering what the hell I was up to. I tried to make signs that it was cutting out, but we were still racing and the gestures were pointless. We both pulled in for fuel at the same time, when I told him the problem. He thought I had just missed a gear. I also told the mechanics about the problems, but nobody seemed all that interested.

I was all set to pull out again when Neil ordered the mechanics to hold me back for a few seconds. 'I don't want those two together on the road,' he said. When we pulled out again, the bike continued to misfire at the end of long straights, and the race was over for me. That settled me down a bit and I finally got my head into TT gear. I started to enjoy riding the RVF and could just about see Steve in the distance. On the fifth lap, there were no problems and, as I came down the mountain before the start of the final lap, I slowed down and thought, 'Right, I am going to smash this lap record to pieces.'

It had been a big thing all week whether either of us could go through the 125mph barrier, the average speed of a lap. I was certain that I could do it and I flew through the start-finish. People said that they had never seen anyone ride so quickly down Bray Hill. 'This is going to be so fast!' I said to myself. Then, on the run down to Ballacraine, it completely cut out again. From a speed of 170mph, I was down to 5mph within seconds. Although it fired up again, I was totally pissed off. So I gave up and rode it back to finish second. The press reports paid very little attention to the problems I had suffered.

To this day, I have not been given a satisfactory explanation as to what was wrong with the bike. A mechanic said that a small wire kept coming loose, but I wasn't convinced. I'm not saying that I would have won necessarily, as I wasn't in the right frame of mind. But it would have been a lot closer. After that, as far as I was concerned, I didn't expect to be returning to the TT again.

Back with the World Superbike championship, at Brainerd, Minnesota, it was the same old story. We looked like a club outfit compared to the other teams out there. The bikes were dog slow and I finished 11th in both races. But that round proved to be a turning point in my season. Niall was behind me in both races, and it was as much as he could take. He spent the whole week on the phone, and it was obvious he was trying to sort out another ride. Having ridden in GPs, Niall was used to having money thrown at him and not having to make savings all the time.

After one more British championship round at Brands, he quit the team. I was glad in a way, because the team wasn't big enough for both of us. It wasn't a personality thing, just that there were not enough funds. I was given his newer bike and his mechanic, Nick Lee, starting working for me alongside Dennis Willey, who was rapidly losing interest. Suddenly, the expectations were back on my shoulders, which was good for motivation. It showed straight away, as I was second at Cadwell next time out before travelling to Japan again for the 8 hours race.

I hated every second I was out there. Suzuka is owned by Honda, who were desperate for revenge after Yamaha's victory the previous year. Wayne Gardner and Mick Doohan were given brand new RVFs to ride, while me and Steve Hislop were on the 1989 models that I had ridden at the TT. It seemed that everyone else was riding the very latest machinery. But that wasn't the problem. It was Neil again. After crashing in the previous two years, his attitude was, 'You just keep it upright and don't do anything to ruin our chances.' It was all 'Steve, Steve, Steve'. Even my own mechanic spent more time with Steve than with me. I was made to feel like a spare part.

So it was no great surprise when he was quicker than I was in practice. It showed how badly my confidence had been affected, because Steve was not a short circuit rider. He started the race, because my final practice times had been set in the wet and, I have to admit, he rode really well in poor conditions. All the time, though, as I waited for my turn, I had to listen to Neil in the garage saying, 'Look at these short circuit wankers, crashing everywhere. There, another one's gone.'

Whatever he was trying to achieve, it didn't work and, instead, placed even more pressure on me. Everyone was waiting for me to crash. I hated him for making me feel like that. So I rode like a snail, but did what they wanted and stayed upright. We stayed out of trouble as others continued to fall and we finished third behind the factory Yamaha of Doug Chandler and Kevin Magee. It meant absolutely nothing to me, because I had played no part in it. While the others went out for a few beers, I went back to the hotel alone.

Results started to pick up in the world championship because, after Suzuka, I had set myself new targets of beating the other Honda riders, like Merkel and the Spanish lad Amatriain. My best results of the year were a pair of fourths at Anderstorp, despite the fact that Dennis was really pissing me off now. He was building a home with his girlfriend and didn't want to make the long trips abroad. And he didn't believe me when I complained about the bike. I think he'd lost confidence in me and would say things like, 'Look at Doug Polen. He can ride a bike!' before looking at me for a response.

He knew it wasn't in my nature to even think that I could be second best to the other riders like Polen, Rob Phillis and Raymond Roche. I knew that, on a decent bike, I would beat them. So it was a relief that he didn't travel to the next round in Sugo, where I was promised some factory assistance.

When we arrived at the garage, I got excited when there was a new bike waiting. But it wasn't for me. All I got from the Japanese factory was a new exhaust system, similar to a Ducati's. Still, I did receive a camera for finishing eighth in the second race, in a line with the fifth, sixth and seventh placed riders. Scott Russell, in fifth place, won a big Woofer stereo. If I had known that was up for grabs, I would have T-boned the lot of them off the track at the last corner!

That trip to the Far East typified the highs and lows of the year. It had been an emotional trip to the airport. Michaela was by now heavily pregnant and, although the doctors thought they would be able to delay the birth until I returned after the races in Japan and then Malaysia, there was obviously a chance that I would not be around for the birth. Michaela drove me to the airport in floods of tears, which wasn't helped by Bryan Adams singing, 'Everything I do, I do it for you' on the radio.

Having left Japan to travel straight to Malaysia, we stayed in a magnificent hotel in Kuala Lumpur, but had to share three to a room because Neil said it was too expensive. I was on the provisional second row of the grid but he wouldn't allow me a new set of tyres for the final session, so I slipped to the third row. So I was quite chuffed with eighth and seventh places when I arrived back in England on Tuesday, 3 September.

The plane landed at Heathrow in the morning, so I immediately rang home. My mum answered.

'I'm in London now, just about to catch the flight up to Manchester. Will someone come and pick me up at the airport?' I asked her.

'Okay *dad*,' she replied.

'What do you mean "Dad"?'

'Congratulations. You're the father of a beautiful little girl. Michaela had the baby last night while you were on the plane,' she said.

There had been nothing the doctors could do to keep Danielle inside any longer. When I came off the phone, my smile stretched from ear to ear. I wanted to shout out to everyone in the middle of the airport.

I had already said my goodbyes to the Honda mechanics but I went rushing back to where I had left them. 'I'm a daddy, I'm a daddy,' I beamed. They immediately warned me that all the hard work was about to start. I naively shrugged it off. How wrong can you be!

My dad dropped me off at home and I rushed in, splashed some water on my face and left for the hospital still wearing my Honda team shirt that I had travelled in from Malaysia. On the way to the hospital I bought a huge bunch of flowers and a bottle of champagne and waltzed into the ward like I owned the place, wearing a pair of Starsky and Hutch-style sunglasses. Everybody was staring at me as if I was a right idiot. Michaela was absolutely shattered. She took one look at me as she was rocking the baby and shouted, 'Where have you been? Here, you can have her. I've had to look after her all night.' She shoved Danielle into my arms and the swagger drained out of me straight away.

As with all new parents, we both learned how to cope soon enough. You have to. You also have to make sacrifices, too. We couldn't just pop out for a drink whenever we wanted to, as we had been used to before. My main contribution, apart from the usual nappy changing and getting up in the middle of the night, was helping out with the tea more often. Cooking wasn't, and still isn't, my strong point. But I was a dab hand at grilled chops, chips and baked beans. It was quite crafty, I suppose, because Michaela soon got sick of this every other night and was happy to get back to cooking duties. I did try other things and developed my own special recipe for chilli, putting just about everything in it like baked beans, kidney beans and peas. For the first few attempts it was clear that something wasn't right, but we couldn't work out what it was. Then Michaela spotted that I wasn't draining the juice from the can of kidney beans. For some reason she does all the cooking now.

Fatherhood can often affect a rider but, despite all these new pressures, results remained pretty consistent and I finished seventh in the world championship won by Polen – ahead of former world champion, Merkel, on the same bike. All things considered, I was pleased because it could have been a lot worse.

There was just one race remaining, a big international meeting at Kirkistown. And, at long last, I won on the 750 – but only at a price. I beat the British champion Rob McElnea in one race, was second to him in the other but, in the final race of the year, it was almost inevitable that I would crash. I was leading and tipped off coming out of the chicane, breaking small bones in my ankle and hand. The freezing cold made the pain 10 times worse and the Irish doctors were ultra-cautious, putting big pots on both my arm and leg. It looked as though it was going to be another winter of hospital visits and recovery. But, back in England, there was less concern and the doctors cut the pots off straight away, because the fractures were only hairline and would heal easily enough.

In any case, broken bones were to prove to be the least of my problems that winter . . .

CHAPTER EIGHT

The Privateer

Honda Britain's experiment in World Superbikes in 1991 had proved too costly, so Neil Tuxworth told me that they would not be competing the following year. The only thing the team could offer me was a ride in the British championships. I told him that I would rather ride a moped. On that RC30, I would have been struggling to finish in the top six. So I was on the hunt for a new ride.

There had already been some interest. An Italian businessman, who only revealed himself as Mr Bogo, had contacted me. He'd been impressed with my riding over the previous few years and wanted to run me in World Superbikes on a Ducati, with big sponsorship from Agip. Obviously, I wanted to stay in the world championships, so I didn't even consider approaching the big names like Kawasaki or Yamaha for a ride in the UK. Bogo's offer sounded too good to turn down. Roger Burnett, who had recently retired from racing and was trying to set up his own promotions company, acted as a go-between. He said, 'It sounds really good. This guy will pay you around £50,000.' There was no reason to doubt him.

But the deal dragged on over a couple of months. I was starting to get pretty anxious.

'Look Roger, when will we see some money in the bank?' I asked after the New Year had passed.

'Bogo assures me that everything will be ready soon,' Roger promised.

Even so, I became more and more concerned and went to my former backer, Dave Orton, for some advice. He said that we needed to meet this guy face to face.

Dave used his own plane to fly me, dad and Roger to a meeting in

Geneva. Bogo said that he would be flying in from Italy in his own helicopter. We waited for him in a private airport lounge that had been set aside and he eventually appeared, all of a sudden, as though he had just stepped out of a taxi round the corner. Despite this, the meeting was all very reassuring and Bogo continued to make the right noises. He promised that he had already ordered the bikes and that he was simply waiting for the money from Agip before it was all systems go. I must have still been wet behind the ears, because all this sounded great to me and I was already thinking about where we could buy a new house! Then again, I wasn't used to people messing me about.

Another month went by, and the excuses continued to flow from Italy. It hit me before any of the others.

'I think he's leading us on here,' I told dad.

'Don't be daft,' he replied. 'He sounds genuine enough to me.'

But it soon got to the point of 'Put up or shut up'. Did Bogo have the bikes or didn't he? By then, he was not even answering the phone. It was a disaster and I was really upset.

The season was only a few weeks away and I didn't have a ride. Panic stations set in. Dad started to ring round everyone, as did Roger. Kawasaki said that they already had their riders in Brian Morrison and John Reynolds, but if they had known I was available they would have grabbed me like a shot. Very flattering. But no use at all. Then I rang Neil Tuxworth. 'I've just gone and signed Simon Crafar,' he said. 'There's nothing much I can do, except sort a bike out for you for some of the road circuits.'

It was an unbelievable situation. I knew how good I could be on a superbike – I just needed a bloody bike.

Roger finally managed to sort one ride out, but that was in the World Endurance championship for Kawasaki France. Ironically, I was to team up with Terry Rymer and would be paid £3,000 per race, plus another £10,000 if I won the race. Terry, who was always more into the money side of things, managed to negotiate a better deal. It was not bad money, but it wasn't a steady wage. And it was not superbikes. The World Endurance ride would do as a fall back, but there was only one other thing for it.

I would have to spend the money that I had made riding for Honda and buy my own bike. And it had to be a Ducati.

There were two Ducati importers in England: Northampton-based

Moto Cinelli, who I was to deal with a lot as my career progressed, and a Manchester-based company called Sports Motorcycles, who had sponsored my dad and Mike Hailwood. Sports Motorcycles promised to help me out throughout the season if I bought the bike from them. It cost around £25,000 – and that was without any extras like wheels! I also had to buy a truck, as well as employ Roger's old mechanic, Doug Holtom. I had tried to tempt Slick to join me, but he had already been fixed up with Terry Rymer, although that team soon folded.

It was like turning back the clock to 1989 when I was a semi-professional. I did have sponsors, like Putoline Oil, but the whole package probably cost me around £45,000. So we weren't exactly flush. And, when Doug went out in the first few weeks buying things from Roger like a new compressor and benches, I immediately began to wonder what I had taken on. I had always known Doug, while he was working for Roger, but it's funny how quickly relationships can change when people start working for you.

At the time, the move to being a privateer didn't seem that much of a gamble. I hadn't taken much notice of how much I had earned in the past. So now, when dad said 'Sign a cheque', I just signed it. And I always knew that I could sell the bike and truck at the end of the year to get a chunk of it back. I actually felt under less pressure than riding for a factory, because now I was just riding for myself. And I was confident that, on the right machine, I was as good as the rest of the World Superbike riders.

It was still a complete step into the unknown, though. I didn't even have time to test the bike before the first race in the British championship, at Thruxton, from where Doug and the boys would take the bike on to the first World Superbike round in Spain at Albacete. My first time on the Ducati was on the morning of the Thruxton race, in torrential rain. I slid off, without doing any damage, but the organisers kept postponing the start time because of the conditions. There was no sign of the rain stopping and spectators started to pack up and go home. I didn't see any point in hanging around, so set off on the long drive home, only to hear the result of the race on the car radio!

Having flown to Spain with dad, I finally had the chance to put the Ducati through its paces. Although I didn't feel as though I was riding all that quickly, the practice lap times were good. It felt completely different to the Honda, much slower going through the revs, up to a maximum of around 11,500, compared to the 13 or 14,000 of the RC30. This bike was smooth. But the weather for race day was poor and, after a cautious ride in the first race for a 12th place finish, I gambled badly on intermediates for the second. In the wet first part of the race I was almost leading but the track dried out, my tyres were destroyed and those riders who had gambled on slicks charged through to leave me in 10th.

In the weeks before the next WSB round at Donington, I was second in two British championship races behind John Reynolds and was slowly remembering what it was like to go into a corner without feeling that I was going to lose the front end. It wasn't all plain sailing, though. Doug was trying to dictate things more than he should have been. We were paying him £350 a week, which was an obscene amount in those days. A lot of today's mechanics aren't paid that much. But everything had been so rushed that he had us over a barrel, because he seemed to be the only person who knew much about the bike, having spent a lot of time with Sports Motorcycles during the winter. They were also slow in delivering their promises of financial help, so the whole venture was starting to cost me a fortune. At that stage, the plan was to race the bike for a few more rounds and then concentrate on the World Endurance championship for which I already had a guaranteed ride.

Donington changed all that. I was one of the quickest in the first practice session, despite the fact that the bike was misfiring. In the next session, I fell off when it jumped into neutral. Yet I was still fifth or sixth fastest. 'Bloody hell,' I thought, 'I haven't even got going yet. All I need is a bit of luck with the bike.' The guy from Dunlop, Phil Plater, noticed my times and offered me some better quality tyres that Doug Polen, the reigning world champion, was using. 'They should help you,' he said. Sure enough, I set the fastest time straight away. I couldn't believe it, although the second group of riders still had to go out for their final session.

I was sharing a garage with Terry Rymer, who had also taken a step backwards, leaving Yamaha to set up his own Kawasaki team with Mobil 1 sponsorship. It was the first time I had really spent much time with him and we started to get on a lot better. He was in the second group, so I challenged him. 'Right Terry. Go out and beat that.' He didn't, but surely Polen would go faster? I paced nervously up and down the pit lane, staring at all the garage monitors to keep a check on things until the very last rider returned.

Pole position was safe. It might even have been the first time that I had qualified on the first two rows. Suddenly, the whole world was my friend again. I wanted to stop and talk to everyone in the paddock. For the first time since 1990, I felt I could hold my head up high. A privateer in pole position – it was almost too much to take in.

Having pulled comfortably away from the pack in the first race, I built a three seconds lead coming into Goddards, a hideously tight left-hand corner which is bumpy in the middle. I was later told that the angle at which I was leaning the bike over appeared to defy gravity. And it must have been that bit too much, because I slid off in the most pathetically slow crash imaginable. But the engine was still running, so there was still a hope of rejoining the race. I heaved the bike up and was about to jump back on when I noticed that the footrest had been knocked off. I slumped over the bike and burst into tears. I was crying my eyes out. Having worked so hard to bounce back from the disappointments of 1991, this was another massive kick in the teeth. Back in the paddock, I shut myself away in the caravan with Michaela, who was just as devastated. It was an all-time low and I felt like jacking it all in.

The last thing I needed was for dad to storm in and start playing Holy Hell with me for coming off. 'What were you playing at? You wouldn't get Wayne Rainey doing something like that.' It was completely out of character and brought out Michaela's protective streak.

'I can't believe you've actually said that, George. You, of all people, should know better. He was riding his heart out, out there. Do you think he meant to fall off? Don't talk to him like that!'

Shortly before the second race, he came back sheepishly. 'I didn't mean what I said before,' he said. 'You know we're all behind you. Go out and do your best son.'

My best was good enough. After a poor start to the second race, I began to pick riders off left, right and centre and again pulled away comfortably. The win was there for the taking – until the bike started to jump out of gear with a couple of laps to go. 'Please God, no! This surely can't happen,' I thought. The problem made me push even harder and I set the new fastest lap on the way to winning my first World Superbike race – the biggest win of my life up to that point.

From being inconsolable a few hours earlier, I was ecstatic but, at the same time, emotionally drained. There were more tears all the way round the lap of honour. I felt that I could stick my finger up at all the doubters, who thought that I had moaned about the Honda too much in 1991.

No one had given me a chance of winning at Donington as a privateer. So it was a case of, 'Fucking right! I've shown you now that I'm the best rider in Britain and capable of beating the best in the world. I've proved it, now that I've got a bike that is working for me and doing what I want it to.' The Ducati was by no means the fastest thing out there, but it didn't need to be at Donington, as there are no long straights and winning is all about carrying corner speed.

My financial plight had obviously touched the British fans. A van driver handed over a £20 note after I had signed an autograph saying, 'Go and treat yourself to a few beers, you've deserved it.' A policeman sent £50 through the post, urging me to carry on despite the costs. And a businessman gave me a £5,000 cheque in return for me carrying his sticker on the bike. He was a very quiet, strange chap, who started to tag along for a couple of meetings after that and became a bit of a pain in the arse. But he was getting so much publicity through me that he sent me another cheque for £15,000, although that bounced and we never heard from him again. But, with all this faith in me, there was no way that I could turn my back on World Superbikes.

Ducati were also impressed. They gave me a spare engine for the rest of the season, which meant a lot on a shoestring budget. It wasn't a factory engine, like those of their other riders, Doug Polen, Giancarlo Falappa and Raymond Roche, but it was good to have as back-up. Phil Plater at Dunlop also pulled a few strings to guarantee free tyres for the season. So I was on a massive high before the first round of the World Endurance championship at Le Mans – my first 24-hour race.

Everyone expected sparks to fly between Rymer and me. But, now that the initial rivalry was out of the way, things were fine. Any bad feeling had probably been down to me being ultra-competitive when he first appeared on the scene. The third member of our team was a Belgian called Michel Simeon.

My inexperience was obvious at the start when, after sprinting across the track, I forgot to hit the start button and was left standing by the other 60 bikes. But the Kawasaki was not a bad bike to ride and, by the end of my first 50-minute stint, I was almost riding like it was a short circuit race. Before handing over to Terry during the refuel stop, I had made it back up to second place behind another Kawasaki team featuring Alex Vieira and Steve Hislop. The next mistake I made was continually tucking into the incredible Kawasaki France hospitality during my rest periods, so I felt a bit sick.

And then, at around 4am, I made the biggest mistake of all. Each of the riders has their own space in one of the massive trucks, with a sink and somewhere to lie down. After one of my stints, I put my head down and the next thing I knew, one of the mechanics was hammering on my door 'Carl, Carl! Just 10 laps to go!' But I'm not one of those people who can have a nap and wake up straight away. If I fall asleep, I'm out for the count. So I didn't know what day it was. Having fumbled around for some coffee and orange juice, I managed to heave myself into my leathers and jumped back onto the bike. One of my eyes is lazy at the best of times, and riding at night made that problem worse. So, for the first couple of laps, I was on autopilot and almost fell off twice.

When the sun started to rise, I got my second wind and, having eaten a lot of chocolate and energy food, I was focused back on the race, which we were leading comfortably by three laps. The other Kawasaki team had broken down with a snapped camchain, and our team bosses were worried that the same thing would happen to us. So we knocked off the gas and lapped at around 10 seconds slower. Sure enough, the Kawasaki, which was a pretty good bike to ride, started to rattle badly. It didn't look good. We needed a plan.

It's not unusual during a 24-hour race for the crowd, which was massive at Le Mans as many had camped overnight, to invade the track before the race has finished. With the bike on its last legs, this didn't seem a bad option. Nearly the whole of our crew, as well as the two other riders, sat on the pit wall and egged the facing crowd to come onto the track. And, when they did, there was no option but for the marshals to bring out the chequered flag with an hour still remaining. We had won at the first time of asking. I didn't care that we received some stick in the press for our unsporting methods! It was just a fantastic new feeling. To spend so long on the bike, and win a race that I thought was never going to end, was brilliant. Imagine how gutted riders are when they race for 20 hours and then break down! It all seemed pretty straightforward to me.

'Hey Steve! We're going to piss this championship,' I told Hislop, cockily.

'It's not as easy as all that,' he warned.

Our team packed up and drove for an hour or so, to spend the night in Paris before a morning flight back to England. I went straight to bed at 7pm, but felt really weird. Every time I tried to close my eyes, it felt as though I was still riding the bike through a dark tunnel, with lights shining brightly. All of a sudden, I would come to a hairpin bend and wake up with a start. It felt as though I was hallucinating for more than an hour, before I finally drifted off. Even though I felt like a zombie back at home for a day or two, it soon wore off as I was still on a massive high.

The win at Le Mans had eased money pressures a bit, but the next races in Britain seemed heaven sent for me to earn some more cash. Donington and Brands staged two £5,000 Dash For Cash shoot-outs – where the winner takes all the prize money on successive days. As far as I was concerned, the money was mine. Nobody would be able to get near me in this form. It was a different story when the clutch went on the first lap and I dropped back through the field. My race looked doomed but, amazingly, the problem cured itself and I soon had leader John Reynolds in my sights after riding, head down, like a madman. When Reynolds broke down, the £5,000 was in my pocket. I could do no wrong. Even so, I wasn't too confident about repeating the result at Brands, a circuit that I had never enjoyed. Until, that is, I claimed pole position. This time, though, the Ducati showed its unreliability. As I slowed down to take my position at the front of the grid, the fuel pump broke and the bike cut out. While the other riders flew off, I had to push my bike off the track. Five grand down the drain, just like that.

There were more teething troubles in the next WSB round at Hock-enheim, as the engine blew in practice and I was brought back down to earth in the races, where it was obvious my bike couldn't live with the best on the faster circuits. It was a similar story at Spa-Francorchamps in Belgium, where I qualified on the second row. When the green light showed, the bike was revving like mad but I was stood still. As I had let the clutch out, it had sheared through the sprockets because someone had not inserted the metal collars that the sprockets sit on. All this time, Sports Motorcycles were promising support and spare parts, which I wrongly assumed would be free, in return for me carrying their stickers on the bike. So, imagine my shock when a bill of around £10,000 for these parts landed through my door after the Spa round. Needless to say, that was the last time we had anything to do with them. We'd had nothing but reliability problems with the bike, in any case.

I was not prepared to ride the Ducati at the TT, because it was so unreliable. But I needed the cash and, in the end, I was relieved when Yamaha offered me a ride, on good money. I also wanted to put the record straight after the problems I suffered in 1991. The Yamaha guys, Andy Smith and Jeff Turner, were good to deal with and my team-mate was Mark Farmer, who died at the TT a couple of years later in 1994. Their normal rider, Rob McElnea, didn't want to race on road circuits. I had always wanted to ride this bike and, while it was not as fast as the RVF or the RC30 Hondas, I could really push it through the corners. I was leading the F1 race by more than 30 seconds and was really pleased that I was going to break Honda's 10-year dominance of the race for Yamaha.

Then, at the top of Snaefell mountain at The Bungalow on the second last lap, the gearbox went and I had to coast down the mountain with my hand on the clutch in case it locked up. In fact, I almost crashed at the bottom when I instinctively tried to change gear. I was devastated, more for Yamaha and Dunlop than for myself. When the engine blew in the Supersport 400 race, the pressure was on me for the Senior race at the end of the meeting.

Steve Hislop, who was riding a Norton, was also without a win and desperate for success. And our battle was probably one of the best races that has ever been seen on the island. It reminded everyone of the days when Mike Hailwood and Giacomo Agostini were up against each other at their peak. I was riding number 4, while Steve was 19, so we were miles apart on the circuit as the starting order is decided by the number on your bike.

But the lead changed after every lap and I was riding so hard that the bike was falling apart around me. None of the clocks were working, the front fork seal had gone, the rear brake arm was bent up, the rear shock was broken – the bike was an absolute mess. I was nine seconds behind at the start of the final lap, which was a lot to make up. To make matters worse, the exhaust blew coming over the mountain as I made that final push. After I had finished, I could hear the commentary over the tannoy, '. . . And here comes Hislop, he wins by four seconds . . .'

To pull back five seconds was amazing and, in doing so, I had set a new lap record of 123.61mph – the average speed over the 18 minutes

18.8 seconds it took to complete the lap. Okay, Steve had won the race, but I had always wanted to be the fastest man around the Isle of Man TT circuit. To me, on this occasion, that was better than race victory.

'Congratulations,' I told Steve, 'but I've got the new lap record,' who obviously didn't believe me. 'I broke your lap record on the last lap,' I insisted.

I could tell that he was a bit pissed off. Don't forget that the Norton was between 10 and 15mph faster than my bike, not to mention its better acceleration. And Rob McElnea had said that you only had to shake my bike for bits to fall off after the race. I still maintain that no other rider on this planet could have matched what I did on that lap on that day. Not bad for my last ever lap around the circuit!

The record stood for seven years until beaten by Jim Moodie in 1999. Ironically, his mechanic was my best man, Gary Dickinson. Moodie lapped in 18 minutes 11.4 seconds, at an average speed of 124.45mph from a standing start. But I was not sorry to see the back of the TT.

Nowadays it only survives on riders who specialise in that sort of thing and who don't do very well on the short circuits, because it doesn't guarantee a world or even a British championship ride, as it did in the 1980s. I was the last of the big name riders to go there and also win a world championship in the same year. Nobody has done it since, and nobody will do it again.

And no other rider had to put up with the journey that I had for the next two rounds of the World Superbike championship in Spain and Austria. It was not until I was halfway through Spain, after a ferry trip from Portsmouth to Santander, driving our massive Chevrolet motorhome which was pulling a caravan, that I wondered what the hell I was doing.

The caravan was for dad to stay in because he insisted on travelling with us. We had Danielle in with us, sleeping in a do-it-yourself cot that I had knocked together to fit into the bath. Mum had seen sense and flown to the Spanish round at Jarama, where I was fifth in the first race and lost the front end in the second race when I was in second place behind Doug Polen. She then flew home, while the rest of us – plus caravan – set off for the next round at the Osterreichring in Austria.

When a fuse blew on the way there, causing us to stop for a good few hours, my patience snapped and dad took the brunt. 'Why the frigging hell don't you stop in a hotel like everyone else, so we don't have to lug that thing all over Europe?' I shouted at him. That delay, though, was nothing compared to the trip home from Austria, where I finished sixth and seventh.

Having reached Germany late at night, I was grabbing a few hours shut-eye in the back of the motorhome, while dad was at the wheel with Michaela navigating. I was woken up by a loud crash and scraping noise. The powerful eight-cylinder motorhome had been too much for the flimsy caravan and had pulled the connecting A-frame almost clean off. There was no way we could continue and we parked up at the side of the road for the rest of the night.

In the morning, I'd had enough. I wanted to leave the caravan there and tell the insurance company that it had been nicked and burnt out. We tried some local garages and, after eight hours at the side of the road, someone turned up to weld a couple of plates and a new ball-coupling joint onto the caravan, which was enough for us to be able to tow it back to England. Back home, I felt ill through exhaustion and did not speak to dad for a couple of days. Needless to say, we didn't take the caravan with us ever again.

The remainder of the World Superbikes season was a story of inconsistency. I was always a regular pain in the arse for the factory riders at the twisty circuits like Assen, where I was fourth and second and the top points scorer on the day. At quicker circuits, like Mugello, I could pass the likes of Raymond Roche and Rob Phillis almost at will around the corners, only to see them breeze back past me down the straights on their faster bikes.

The penultimate round at Monza typified my bike's unreliability, as I broke down in both races. We were learning all the time, though, and the factory Ducati team that was run by Franco Uncini, as well as Amatriain's outfit backed by Marlboro, were very helpful with advice. Even so, although I hadn't competed in every round, I still managed to finish ninth, which was enough to impress the Ducati top dogs.

Between WSB races, the World Endurance championship continued at Spa in Belgium. This was the only time when I ever felt that I had cheated death – and I didn't even fall off my bike.

I had qualified in pole, which earned me a £1,000 bonus. Rymer thought the cash went to the team and was annoyed when he put his invoice in at the end of the year and found out that it had gone to the individual rider with the fastest lap. We led the race, but were being pushed hard by the Suzuki team. We were faster on the track but the Suzuki boys were quicker in the pits and kept pegging back our lead, although they could not pass us. My race wasn't going well, as I had leaned over too close to one of the little poles that carry the square reflectors for night riding. It caught my little finger and cracked the bone, so I was in agony for a few laps.

To make matters worse, when I was due to take over from the third rider, Jehan d'Orgeix, one of the mechanics pulled the nozzle out of the fuel tank and sprayed petrol straight into my eyes. 'Fucking hell. I can't see a bloody thing. Jehan will have to get back on,' I shouted. But, just as he was about to set off about 30 seconds later, my vision started returning and, because he was the slowest in our team, I almost dragged him off the bike.

Then, all I remember is coming out of the fast Blanchimont corner at top speed and realising that the bike was starting to slide. It just about registered that the oil flags were out and an ambulance was parked at the side of the track, tending to the Suzuki rider, Herve Moineau. His engine had blown, dumping a load of oil on the surface. I hit the oil and was out of control. At that instant, I knew that if the bike went from under me, there was no way I could avoid smashing straight into the ambulance. There was no grass or gravel to slow me down. It would have been helmet against solid metal at 120mph and only one outcome – certain death. The bike twitched but incredibly I stayed on, missing the ambulance by the skin of my teeth.

When I returned to the pits, I was as white as a sheet. I sat in a corner on my own, trying to take in what had just happened. One of the mechanics asked, 'What's up?'

'You will never know just how close I have just come to losing my life,' I replied.

Everyone else forgot all about it straight away because I hadn't even fallen off. But it had scared me rigid and stuck with me for a few weeks.

Despite my close shave we won the race comfortably making it two out of two in the World Endurance championship, with the Suzuka 8 hours to come. I didn't even get a chance to ride the bike in the race, which was fortunate because the weather was so hot as to make riding unbearable. The bike was fast, but bulky and difficult to handle, and I had a big crash in practice, when the fairing caught the track and threw me off. So Terry set the fastest qualifying lap and started the race for the only time that year, but crashed twice within the first hour to put us out of the race.

I was watching the monitor for the first fall and said to myself, 'Leave the bike, don't even try to pick it up.' It was hideously hot and the race was inevitably going to be won by Grand Prix hot-shots, who had no chance of affecting our championship standings.

We expected Terry to hand straight over after his fall, but he carried on only to come off on the very next lap. 'Give up,' I whispered to myself. 'Do not press the frigging start button.' By now I was just thinking about the cool swimming pool at the hotel around the corner from the circuit.

When Terry finally conceded defeat and placed the bike up against the bales, the rest of the team were gutted. I had to pretend I was too. After a couple of less than impressive 'Shit, damns' I ran out of the back of the garage rubbing my hands together and shouted, 'Yes!'

I bumped into the Australian, Rob Phillis, who had just finished his stint and looked absolutely knackered.

'We broke down, Rob. Just off for a swim,' I said gleefully.

'Jeez mate, I wish I was in your shoes,' he replied.

Back in the cooler temperatures of the British climate, I was selected, along with Jamie Whitham, as one of two local riders allowed to take part in the British Grand Prix. I was offered a ride on a Harris Yamaha by Stuart Medd, whose company, Medd Brothers, were running two bikes for Kevin Mitchell that year. Stuart was a really nice guy who had put a lot of money into racing over the years, but didn't enjoy the returns that he deserved.

Of course, I still felt that I had a point to prove in Grand Prix racing after the episode in 1990. Everyone had always said that it was difficult switching to 500cc, but I found the Yamaha easy to ride and qualified on the second row ahead of Niall Mackenzie, Doug Chandler and Alex Criville, which was embarrassing for them. I don't think that, to this day, any other privateer has put a bike on the second row of the British Grand Prix.

Their attitude was, 'He's only doing well because it's his local circuit.' But my bike was nowhere near as fast as the big-bang engines ridden by Gardner, Lawson, Rainey, Schwantz and Doohan. Even so, I was up in fifth with four or five laps to go and winding down, because nobody was pushing me from behind.

The next thing I knew, I was on my arse going into Redgate. The bike fell onto my foot, pressing it into the track and shaving some skin off my toes as I skidded along. I had to kick the bike off with my free leg to prevent more damage. Only then did I see Kevin Schwantz standing waving a flag that he had snatched from a marshal, while Doug Chandler picked himself up out of the dirt.

We had all touched some coolant, which had spilled out of John Kocinski's bike when his engine had blown a couple of laps earlier. The coolant had dried quickly, making it difficult to notice. I was in tears again as I trudged back to the pits. Aussie rider and race winner Wayne Gardner was also whining about the way I passed him on the first lap.

'You were going too slow, what do you want me to do?' I said.

'It was the first bloody lap, mate, how could I have been going too slow?'

He didn't take too kindly to me telling a live television interview that it was a typical reaction, as he was always moaning. 'I'm glad he won, as he's one of my heroes,' I said. 'It's just a pity he's obnoxious off the track.'

The papers recognised my achievements with headlines like 'Wild Carl'. And that's probably what a French marshal also thought of me at the next round of the World Endurance championship at the Paul Ricard circuit in Bol d'Or. I was trying to drive into the paddock, and had the right pass, but there was just no way that this jobsworth was going to allow me through. Stopping and trying to argue with him would only have made matters worse, so I edged the car forward while trying to convince him that I had the right pass. The idiot just stood in front of the car, shuffling back as I was moving forward.

I must have reached a speed that he couldn't match. So the car sort of scooped him up and he rolled off the side of the bonnet and onto the floor. I thought, 'Oh fuck. What have I done here!' I panicked and shot off through the paddock, hoping that nobody had seen what had happened.

No such luck. The police became involved and I had to explain to the Team Kawasaki France manager, Christian Bourgeois, what had happened. The gate-man was limping around like I had driven a tank over his leg, but there was nothing wrong with him. I had seen him walking normally just a few minutes before I was questioned. It resulted in a £100 fine and a warning about my future conduct from race officials.

Worse than that, I had to apologise to the little bastard. 'I am very sorry and nothing like this will ever happen again,' I told him, before going out, pulling a massive wheelie at the end of the warm-up lap, and winning the race. Well, I'm telling him now that I wasn't sorry and, if I do ever see him again, I'll finish the job off good and proper.

We had won all three 24-hour races without any problems, although the team told me that it would be better for the bike if I didn't do wheelies before the race! Normally, during a 24-hour race, you at least fall off once, or have to push the bike back to the pits. For us, it had been a piece of cake and I don't think any other rider has won three consecutive 24-hour races at their first attempt. However, it hadn't been quite enough to clinch the championship and Kawasaki France, who hadn't really wanted to travel for the final two rounds in Australia and Malaysia, decided that they wanted to play safe.

Before those rounds, though, I raced for a Singapore businessman, David Wong, in the Malaysian national championship, with a view to him providing sponsorship in 1993. There were about five people watching but the racing was heavily sponsored even though there were only about nine riders on the grid, including a couple of fast Aussies. I think I lapped the fastest Malaysian after about five laps and won. Wong knew how much money I had spent during the season, so offered to buy the Ducati off me when I returned to Malaysia for one final race in December. His only condition was that I would return the following year to race it for him.

Back in England, the Ducati in question was becoming more and more unreliable and I was getting fed up with it. So I asked Kawasaki if they would take their superbike in their freight to the next World Endurance round in Australia, so that I could also compete in the World Superbike round the following day. The freight was already paid for because I had finished in the top 10 the previous year, so it didn't cost them anything. It also meant that I could ditch Doug, which I had wanted to do for some time. Even the little things about him, like his catchphrase, 'Let's get organised' were starting to bug me.

I did have some extra freight of my own for the journey, though. Michaela had brought Danielle to all of the races in Europe that year but this was the first long haul trip she attempted, as her mum was now living Down Under. It was a big mistake because that flight is no fun with a 13-month-old baby.

It was windy and freezing for the penultimate World Endurance race at Phillip Island, run half in daylight and half in the dark. As many as 20 marshals were taken to hospital suffering from hypothermia – in Australia of all places! Phillip Island is bleak enough at the best of times, without the wind blowing bits of rubbish and twigs all over the track. When I finished my first stint, I pleaded with officials to at least cut the race down to six hours. You feel the cold more in an endurance race because you are not going as fast as in a superbike race. Yet we won by three laps and our main rival, Michele Graziano, was only third. That meant Terry and me were World Endurance champions. On the rostrum, there was only one thing in my mind, and that was a nice warm fire back at the hotel.

The World Superbikes race, which was probably more important for me as I was still angling for a contract for the following year, was something of an anti-climax. I was absolutely knackered from the day before and chose too soft a tyre for the first race, when I was seventh. Then, in the break before race two, something occurred to me. Terry had exactly the same number of points as me in the individual Endurance championship, as we had ridden every race together. But, if I were to injure myself in the second WSB race, I might be unable to ride in the final World Endurance race of the season, the following weekend at Johor in Malaysia. That would mean Terry would go on to be the individual world champion. I wasn't prepared to let that happen. It also started to drizzle just before the second race, which made me even more miserable. I just wasn't up for it at all and I wasn't going to impress anyone riding that Kawasaki, which was fast but difficult to handle. So I thought, 'Fuck this' and I pulled in at the first opportunity. 'The engine is back-firing, I can't ride like this,' I told the team when I retired from the race. Nobody realised nothing was wrong with the bike.

While I went off to race in Malaysia, Michaela stayed in Australia to spend a week with her mum near Brisbane. She has only seen her once since that occasion, when I clinched my first World Superbike title in 1994 at Phillip Island when she visited us for a few days. Since then, there has been a bit of a fall-out. I think they have always been a bit distant. Even when Michaela moved down to Oxford, her mum ended up moving even further south. So, when she finished with her boyfriend, Michaela decided to return to Blackburn. It's not for the lack of trying on Michaela's part, as we have offered to pay for her mum to come and see us in England, but she hasn't bothered for some reason.

After the final World Endurance race in Johor, which turned out to be as much of a cakewalk as the rest of the championship, I returned home briefly to meet up with Michaela and Danielle. Then it was back to the Far East as me and Jamie Whitham had been invited to ride Yamahas in the Macau Grand Prix by a businessman called John Stratton. It was a GP, but not part of the world championship.

Macau is an island near Hong Kong, where the Chinese go to gamble and throw themselves off the bridge when they lose! It has a dodgy closed-road street circuit, with a terrible surface. We were there basically for a holiday and our plan was not to go out and kill each other trying to win, so we agreed to try and win one of the races each. I qualified in pole, but our plan went out of the window when Japanese star Toshihiko Honma started riding like a madman.

In the first race, Honma and Jamie were swapping the lead while I sat in behind, wearing a dark visor which became smudged by flies. The track was dangerous enough, without having to struggle to see what was happening ahead of me. But they both made mistakes and I slipped through, posting the fastest lap of the race. Jamie tried to out-brake me at one corner, but crashed into the bales and bounced back into the middle of the track. I was half an inch off hitting him. The overall result was decided on times and I managed to build an eight-second lead over Honma in the last three laps.

All I had to do in the second race was sit in behind and make sure that the gap didn't approach eight seconds. But the bike was running rich and I kept losing a few hundred yards on the fast coastal section, before pulling it back on the top twisty part of the circuit. I held on, though, to finish third in that race and first overall. Technically, that makes me the only rider ever to have won a World Superbike race, a Grand Prix, a TT F1 race and a World Endurance race!

I returned to England to be punished for going too fast – in my car. I had reached 10 points for a variety of speeding offences and was passing through possibly the worst place on earth for traffic police – Dumfries. I was doing 93mph on the A75 near Annan, on my way to catch a ferry from Stranraer to Northern Ireland for the North West 200 earlier in the year, where I rode Simon Crafar's Honda RC30 and came fourth.

You could murder someone up there and get away with it, but if you are caught speeding they throw the book at you. So, in November, I travelled up to plead my case and told them all about my charity work and how I needed to be able to drive. 'We do not allow speeding in this district,' said the beak. Bang. Six points. Banned for six months. No arguments. Bastards.

I decided to drive home anyway but, when I got back to Blackburn, the local paper already had their billboards out, 'Blackburn bike ace banned for six months'. I tried to hide my face for those final few miles until I could park up at home in safety. It was just at the start of winter when I really needed my car and I was totally gutted.

My last race of the year was back in Malaysia, the final of the three races for David Wong. I took a couple of lads from Oxford Products, who had run a Ducati team in England that year, out there with me to look after the Ducati before I sold it to David. When they started to set the bike up one of them said, 'There's a part missing off the bike.' I was sure that it had been in working order the last time I had ridden it.

Within a couple of hours, a fax arrived from Doug Holtom in England. It said that he didn't trust us to pay him the money that he felt I owed him, and he had taken the part until he got his cash. He could kiss goodbye to his money. I had fully intended to pay him but, instead, I decided to buy the part from Ducati Australia at a good price. The bike had problems cutting out in the torrential rain but Wong stuck to his word and bought it, which was a load off my mind.

It had been an incredible season, probably the one that helped me reach where I am today. I had been Ready Rent-a-Rider, on a Ducati in World Superbikes, a Yamaha at the TT and in a Grand Prix, and a Kawasaki in World Endurance. For much of the year, everything that I had touched turned to gold and the financial gamble had paid off, as I was easily in pocket. Surely the offers would come flooding in for 1993.

They did – but nothing was ever that simple . . .

CHAPTER NINE

Luck of the Irish

The fiasco at the start of 1992 with the mysterious Mr Bogo had taught me a lesson about placing my trust in strangers. And that experience probably prevented me from getting in over my head with the business-man who invited us to Macau, John Stratton.

Before that trip, Stratton had contacted us through former racer Mick Grant, a good friend of Jamie's. Stratton's plan was to run a couple of Harris Yamahas in a Grand Prix team run by Mick. After a successful first meeting, at Grant's house, we met Stratton alone, at a hotel near Brighouse on the M62, when he produced a couple of thick contracts. He wanted us to sign there and then.

'It all sounds really good, but I want to show the contract to a couple of people before I sign anything,' I told him.

'What do you mean? The contract's fine, you can see for yourself,' he argued. 'No, I'm not signing anything yet,' I insisted.

Jamie agreed with me and Stratton's mood changed quickly, as though we had insulted him.

'Fine, if you want to be funny about it,' he snapped.

The next day he was back on the phone, as nice as pie, wanting to know what alterations were needed. But Mick insisted that nothing would be signed until there was money in our accounts, as a gesture of good faith.

In the meantime, Stratton had arranged for us to take part in the Macau Grand Prix, on a couple of bikes that were sprayed in hideous colours and displayed the logo of a credit card that nobody had ever heard of. The bikes were leased from Padgett's, a big family run racing bike shop based in Batley. The warning bells started to ring loudly when we arrived in the Far East and the bikes hadn't been paid for.

129

They refused to let us use them until the money showed up. The money never did arrive, but in the end Padgett's, knowing we would be stuck out in Macau without a ride, agreed to let us use them anyway. That was the last anyone ever heard of Stratton and we will probably never know the full truth of it. Fortunately, though, this all happened before Christmas and there was plenty of time to look elsewhere.

Ducati had obviously shown a big interest at the end of 1992, but nothing was ever put in writing and, although the lure of Stratton's GP ride was tempting, I had never been put in a position where I had to turn Ducati down. There was some talk in the press that Garry Taylor wanted me for his Lucky Strike Suzuki team. I now think that was just his way of signing Doug Chandler at a cheaper price.

It was also difficult to convince non-English sponsors to employ an English rider. The Grand Prix circuit was, and always has been, very political and it's not always the best rider that is given the opportunity. There were a lot of offers to stay and race in Britain, but that was never going to be a serious option. Kawasaki France also wanted me back for World Endurance but, again, that was not a road that I wanted to go down.

But in January I was still without a confirmed ride for 1993 and was worried that there might be a repeat of the previous year's last-minute panic. I needn't have bothered, as Ducati were notorious for leaving things like that until the last minute.

I received the first call, from Davide Tardozzi, my current boss. He had retired as a rider at the end of the previous season and was set to run a factory Ducati team in World Superbikes. The Belgian rider, Stephane Mertens, was to be my team-mate. I named my price at £50,000, but Davide knocked me down to £40,000, and insisted that I used their mechanics. I didn't want to commit myself and said that I would call him back to confirm.

The very same day, former world champion Raymond Roche called. Throughout 1992 he had been telling me that he wanted me for his factory Ducati team that he was planning to set up. But it never went any further than that. This time he meant business.

'What are you doing for a ride this year?' he asked in his pigeon English.

'Nothing has been sorted yet, but I've just spoken to Davide Tar-dozzi,' I told him.

'Ah yes. He is also running a team. But I have the official factory team with Giancarlo Falappa. I need an answer, as I am here at the factory now with Claudio Castiglioni.'

Castiglioni was the owner of the Cagiva Group, which in turn owned Ducati, and he had run Eddie Lawson's team in GPs. When I told him that I wanted to sign, we started to talk money. I knew that Davide had knocked me down from £50,000, but thought it was worth another try. I could hear Roche consulting with Castiglioni on a three-way line before agreeing. Encouraged by that I thought I would try my luck a bit further. 'I also want my own mechanic, an English guy called Slick. And . . . what about expenses?' I asked, timidly.

There was more discussion before Roche came back. 'We will pay you £55,000 and you sort out your own hotels. You can have your mechanic as long as he is not a troublemaker. Fly here tomorrow to sign.'

Bingo! I was more than happy, until Roche later told me that I should have started the bargaining at £100,000 and I might have been paid £80,000!

I was shitting myself when I arrived in Italy but didn't sign the contract until I'd had a chance to chat with Raymond over dinner. I trusted him and he assured me that it was the same deal that he had signed the previous year. 'With the Castiglionis, contracts mean nothing. When you are with the family, it is their word that counts. Sign it and shut up,' he grinned. It was time to put pen to paper.

The money didn't matter, but it was handy. We had only just moved house, having bought Verecroft, where I lived as a teenager, off dad, while he used our old house as part exchange on a new one for him and mum. So the new deal allowed us to spend money on it. But the main thing was to have my foot in the door with a major factory team, whether it was in World Superbikes or Grand Prix. The big money would eventually come with success.

It was to be a big year for the WSB series in its battle to become established on the world scene. The top three riders from 1992 were no longer in action. Roche had retired and Rob Phillis's contract with Kawasaki was not renewed, as they felt that he was too long in the tooth. Instead, they went for Scott Russell and Aaron Slight. The third big name, Doug Polen, had returned to race in America. He was the loudest of loud Americans. He could frighten the life out of you with one 'Hey Carl', if you were doing something like cleaning the motorhome windows with your back to him and didn't spot him approaching. In Britain, the profile of the series was boosted when the Sky Sports channel abandoned their coverage of the Grand Prix series to concentrate on World Superbikes.

Raymond had promised to ride one more race, at Daytona, before packing it in. When he returned home to Cannes, in the south of France, he found Slick sat in a van on his driveway.

'Who are you?' he asked.

'I'm Tony Bass – Slick – here to start work,' he answered.

'You are here two weeks early,' said Roche.

He had given Slick completely the wrong date. It was a sign of the disorganised way that Raymond would run things in his first year as a manager, and Slick had to sweep the floor in the workshop for a couple of weeks to kill time.

I enjoyed riding for Raymond, as he was laid back and one of the lads, similar to Davide Tardozzi, but not as motivated and efficient. He was also very helpful in setting up the bike and knew what made a rider tick, having won the World Endurance title and the World Superbike title in 1990, not to mention some great results in GPs.

The first test on the famous red factory 888 was at the Paul Ricard circuit in France. I didn't sleep a wink the night before, as I didn't want to show myself up. 'I hope I can still ride a bike. I hope I haven't lost it,' I fretted. The bike didn't seem too much different from the one I rode the previous year. But it was a lot more powerful, and that was the thing that had stopped me challenging the factory guys in 1992.

The nerves still hadn't gone in time for the first round at a cold and wet Brands Hatch, although I led the first race on the opening lap. But, coming into the final corner, I had conflicting advice running through my head. Roger Burnett had warned me not to use the inside line, while another rider told me exactly the opposite. I was so confused that I stuck to the middle of the track, slammed on the brakes and almost took my team-mate, Falappa, out as I fell off. I seemed to gather speed as I slid into the gravel, crashed into the bike and smashed into the tyre wall, damaging ligaments in my right shoulder and almost dislocating the joint. Funnily enough, after a skiing accident this year, the doctors took X-rays of my left shoulder but were puzzled by the size of the gap in my right shoulder socket. It was probably caused by that crash.

The pain was unbearable, but it was difficult explaining that I couldn't take part in the second race when no bones had been broken. It wasn't a great first impression for my new team, but Roche just said, 'We fix you and you win the next round.'

Meanwhile, Falappa won both races at Brands, while I moped around with my shoulder in a strap, feeling pretty sorry for myself. And that's rare for me, as nobody could call me soft. The only thing I ever moan about is the number of colds that I catch. If there's a bug going round, I'll catch it. This all probably dates back to when I broke my nose as a 15-year-old, mucking around in Blackburn town centre chasing one of my mates.

He was a bit too quick for me and, when he changed direction quickly, I carried on and smacked straight into a concrete post on the multi-storey car park. There were little birdies flying round my head. Ever since then I have had sinus trouble, not particularly during the racing season, but definitely during the winter.

Confidence was restored with a couple of decent results at Hockenheim. After the race, Slick spewed his guts up out of the window of the motorhome all the way from Germany to Dover, as he had worked his balls off that weekend in hot conditions. The boss of the UK importer for Ducati, Hoss Elm, had also asked me to ride a bike in a couple of British rounds but he didn't enjoy the first meeting, at Oulton Park, where I didn't finish either race. It was the first time he had been in charge of a team and didn't really know what was happening. He would ask some stupid questions like, on a wet circuit, 'Do you not think you should be using slick tyres, Carl?'

'No, Hoss, it's pouring down!' you would reply.

Being a successful businessman, he was used to things going his way. I didn't even see him after the races, as he'd sulked off home.

His mood changed at the North West 200, in what was to be my last ever road race. Dad had once finished second here and I had been trying to win for years, but had never found success – or much luck. For some reason or another, I always seemed to break down and not finish. So, when someone asked me how I thought I would do in that year's race, I said, 'Oh, it'll probably be the same old story. I'll be leading until one lap from the finish and then something will go wrong with the bike.'

The bloke replied, 'What you need, is the luck of the Irish. Wear something green and you'll win the race, to be sure.'

It was worth a try, so I asked Michaela if she had packed anything green. She pulled out a Benetton vest, which I wore the next day for the races. Sure enough, I won both and set a new lap record.

Ever since then, the green vest has been an essential part of my kit. Of the 59 World Superbike races I had won by the end of 1999, 57 were in that vest. For the other two wins, I had left it behind but still managed to wear something green. The first time was in Indonesia when I had packed it, but left it in the team hotel, which was half an hour away from the track. There was no time to send anyone back to fetch it from my room. So my boss at that time, Virginio Ferrari, went to a nearby supermarket and bought the nearest thing to a green T-shirt that he could find and cut the arms off, so that it would still feel like I was wearing my special vest. Sure enough, I won the first race. The other time, I borrowed something green from Kawasaki.

People might not think so, but racers do occasionally wash their kit and the green vest has shrunk severely over the years. So, now, when I take my leathers off, people see this skimpy little number that finishes half way up my stomach. It must look odd, but I don't care what people think as long as I think that it will bring me luck. In 1999, I wore the same pair of underpants for every race, because I started the season with a double win in them. Believe me, I washed those after every round.

I took some photographs of my North West 200 win to show Raymond, who hadn't even known I was taking part. 'You crazy Englishman,' he laughed. 'Now you concentrate only on the world championship. Now you win for me.'

I did just that at the very next round, at Albacete. It was there that Raymond noticed that I was trying to ride the Ducati like the Honda. He said, 'You don't need to use all the gears all the time. Last year I won here using just four of the six gears. Use first gear wherever you can.' The advice helped a lot and I won both races, my first win on a factory Ducati and my first double win. The results gave me a lot of confidence and I felt that I no longer had to prove myself to Ducati.

My team-mate, Giancarlo Falappa, was leading the championship going into his home round at Misano. The first time I set eyes on Falappa in the paddock he frightened the life out of me, as he looked a bit of a thug, like an English football hooligan. Danielle was also scared stiff of him and would start screaming every time he came over to say hello. It was very embarrassing because he was a genuinely nice guy, very softly spoken and we never had a falling out. But he wasn't someone I would share information with or go to for advice, or even socialise with. The Italians tend to go out later in the evening and have wine with their meal, whereas we prefer an early evening Chinese and a few beers. His bike set up was strange, more like a motocross bike than a superbike. But I felt that his was that little bit better than mine, and that he was receiving more help from the team.

The Misano round proved to be a case in point. Falappa's bike was fitted with an experimental gear change device, a button on the handlebars. Normally, you change gear by pressing the gear lever without shutting off. It cuts the engine out for something like a 1,000th of a second. That lever is on the left-hand side of the bike. So it's harder to change gears smoothly at Misano, which is all left-hand corners, as you're constantly leaning over to that side. It was soon obvious that the device gave Falappa an advantage, as he was pulling away at the long corners and won both races. If a team-mate was given preferential treatment now, I would be ranting and raving. But, because he was leading the championship, it seemed fair enough.

Falappa retained that lead in Austria but, in the Czech Republic, my season went up a gear. I won the first race comfortably and that got to Falappa, who crashed out in the second, leaving Scott Russell leading the championship with me tucked nicely in behind.

But the World Superbike battle was put on ice when I was handed another wild card ride at the British Grand Prix, on the same Cagiva that Doug Chandler and Matt Mladin were riding in the world championship. It was obviously my first time on the bike and, in general, 500cc bikes needed much more time to set up properly. 500s are a lot lighter and therefore more powerful than superbikes. I was not confident with tyre choice or gearing, but finished the first day having set the second fastest time. 'I can go a lot faster tomorrow,' I thought, as the British press started to whip up a feeling that I was going to win a home Grand Prix.

I crashed in the Saturday morning session, which knocked my confidence and affected the bike. It meant that I had to use the second bike, which wasn't as good, for final qualifying and I was edged off the front row right at the death. More importantly, I had missed valuable track time when I could get to know the bike. Still, fifth fastest for the British Grand Prix, was good going. And, when Mick Doohan took out Alexandre Barros and Kevin Schwantz on the second lap, I dived inside Luca Cadalora and into second place. The 23,000 fans inside Donington went absolutely mental. For a couple of laps I made ground on leader Wayne Rainey, before the problems set in. The rear tyre was too soft, I always seemed to be in the wrong gear in the corners and, when Cadalora inevitably came back past me, I was seen on TV to be adjusting the front brake.

By then, Niall Mackenzie was closing in and threatening my first GP podium finish. With two laps to go, it started to cut out but I felt I had done enough to hold him off when, coming out of the hairpin with two corners remaining, it died on me. With the line in sight, Mackenzie came screaming past. I had run out of fuel. It was probably my style, whipping up the throttle as I changed down gears, which had used up more fuel than normal. And I am convinced that, if things hadn't gone against me during the whole weekend, I would have won the British Grand Prix on that day. It took me some time to come to terms with that.

Superbikes welcomed me back with open arms. My performance at Donington had proved that their top riders could mix it with the GP boys. And I carried on where I left off in Brno. I had a double win in Sweden and Russell's face on the podium was a picture. He didn't take too kindly to me saying it looked like a 'slapped arse' and, from then on, we were locked in a war of words. Russell thought the twin-cylinder Ducati had an advantage, as these bikes could accelerate out of corners better than four-cylinder machines like his Kawasaki, which were marginally quicker down the straights.

Two more wins in Malaysia at Shah Alam and the points difference was down to five. And that was wiped out after the first race in Sugo in Japan, where I completed five wins in succession. The championship lead only lasted for two hours when, after being annoyed by a Japanese back-marker while I was leading the second race, I tried too hard to push past him and a high side threw me right over the bars and onto my coccyx, the bone at the base of the spine. Now that was painful! Russell won the race to regain the lead, while Roche tried to kill the guilty Japanese rider.

Raymond almost killed me in Japan as well – with laughter. A lot of Japanese hotels have shallow communal hot and cold pools, segregated for men and women. We went down to try the men's pools, but Raymond stopped me before we left the changing room. 'Watch this, I will have a laugh,' he said. He took off his towel and walked straight into the women's section, pretending it was a simple mistake.

He is not a man lacking in confidence – or inches – and it only took a couple of seconds before the roomful of Japanese women were screaming the house down.

Any man who had made a genuine mistake would have covered his dick up and crept out. But Raymond flung his arms out shouting 'Sorry! I am very sorry. So sorry, ladies,' while he backed out of the room, still on full display. I was almost wetting myself on the other side of the door with Slick. The women complained to the hotel management, but Raymond was an expert at talking his way out of trouble.

I was sharing a room with Falappa in Japan. His season was turning into a disaster and he was crashing more often than not. He was a rider who didn't seem to know his own limits and would try to pass in places you don't normally try to pass. He was probably one of the hardest riders I've ever raced – but dangerously hard. He was a crashing machine and the crashes were often big, breaking lots of bones.

Falappa had fallen twice in the previous round in Malaysia and was murder to share a room with, as he was still in a lot of pain. The night before the Sugo races, he was up every hour for a hot water bottle, an ice pack or some painkillers. That's typical of Italians. To make matters worse, he crashed again in the first race in Japan. It left him black and blue and in a bad way.

Yet he still managed to get friendly with a fit local interpreter, and invited her back to our room. 'Carl, do you mind leaving us alone for an hour,' he whispered. I was also in agony after my fall, but did the decent thing. While killing time in the hotel foyer, I bumped into Roche.

'What are you doing down here?' he asked.

'Giancarlo's trying to shag that interpreter up there,' I told him.

'Ah, come with me then,' said Roche. 'We will have some fun.'

He led me out into the grounds of the hotel and we climbed up onto the roof of a shed, from where we could clamber onto the row of balconies. We scrambled along until we reached our room.

There was only a fine mesh covering over the window, and a gap between the two curtains. It was enough for us to see Falappa and the Japanese girl sat on the bed. He was whispering something close up and then moved in for the kill. While they were kissing, we were pissing ourselves outside, but trying to keep quiet. His hand slipped up her skirt, but it was obvious she wasn't all that keen and she pushed it back down. So he tried for her tits, but got the same reaction. Then he unzipped his flies and got his cock out, and tried to guide her hand onto it. Again, she was having none of it. By now, we were in hysterics outside. These fumblings seemed to go on for ages until she made her escape.

Falappa pulled himself together and was about to leave the room. We needed to get back to the foyer, and quickly. 'Don't tell him what we've seen,' whispered Raymond, 'he'll be very mad.' We clambered off the balcony and back onto the shed roof. And, as if my aching coccyx wasn't enough to contend with, I slipped off the roof and into a bunch of nettles, or their Japanese equivalents.

We wandered casually back into the hotel, Raymond acting as if nothing had happened, me rubbing my sting. Giancarlo was waiting and I asked, 'Well, did you get anywhere?'

'Oh yes, Carl. I shag her,' he boasted.

We knew different!

Back in Europe, I struggled to make any ground on Russell in the championship, despite a double win in Assen. But, whenever I won a race, Russell seemed to be behind me in second place. At that stage, he had just three race wins to my 10 and yet he led the championship by seven points. That lead was stretched to nine in the appalling weather of Monza, where I took a pair of fourth places compared to his second and fifth.

This meeting again proved that I was no longer fast in the wet. I was totally demoralised but had Donington to look forward to, where I was expected to blitz the opposition. Perhaps I was over-confident. On a freezing cold day, when Russell's Dunlops seemed to be working better than our Michelin tyres, I was closing in on his lead when a crash deposited oil all over the track at the Melbourne Loop. The race was stopped with Russell leading by around a second, which meant that I had to beat him by more than that margin in the restart. Coming out of the Esses, on the last lap, I was one second in the lead. But I was too cautious round the final corners and, as I crossed the line, I turned round to see him right behind me. The crowd, not realising that I needed to win by more than that first race margin, thought I was the winner. But I had my doubts. And when Slick held up two fingers to signify second, I was devastated. 'Not on my home track,' I thought.

There was still a chance to make up for it in the second race, though.

And I was pulling away from the rest when I had a massive crash, pushing too hard through Craner Curves. Russell won, to stretch his lead to 32 points and the championship was all but over. I threw in the towel. There was no way I could pull back that points difference with just two rounds (four races) remaining. In those days, there were only 20 points for a win and, more importantly, there were not enough talented riders, with the exception of Aaron Slight on occasions and Falappa when he felt like it, to stop Russell from finishing second.

Strange as it seems, in view of our recent history, Slight and his wife Megan came to stay at our house in the gap between the next round in Portugal, as I had arranged to keep his motorhome in winter storage in a nearby village, called Hoghton. We got on well during that year, as he was in the same team as Russell but didn't like him too much, either. I spent a lot of time in Aaron's motorhome during the season, taking the piss out of the American over a brew. Maybe Slight was being a bit two-faced, as I think he actually got on with Russell quite well.

For me, there was no doubt. I found Russell arrogant and mouthy. But I probably needed to hate him as well, because he wanted to win as badly as I did. It was the same with Terry Rymer in 1989. The rivalry intensified my aggression and made me a better and more focused rider. There were never any clashes, as such, because most of the bad feeling was conducted through the press. But you only have to look at pictures of us on the same podium to realise there wasn't a lot of love lost between us.

I crashed yet again in Portugal, which I didn't think mattered too much at the time – until Russell broke down for the first time in the year. If I had won the race, the gap would have been down to 12 points with three races remaining. Still, there was nothing that could be done about it, and I was already resigned to finishing second in the championship.

Normal service was resumed for race two when I won, beating Russell into second. My hand gestures made it quite clear that I was the number one and that he was a wanker. A couple of viewers later complained to Ducati about such obscenities on live television, and I was given a bit of a bollocking. But Roche was equally pumped up. 'You are unbelievable,' he said. 'You crash in the first race and win the second. Unbelievable!'

Pumped up from my win he was in a typically naughty mood. He had just bought some golf clubs while in Estoril. So, as we were packing up, he took out his Big Bertha driver and smashed an apple into the garage. It splattered everywhere, into the engine, my ear, even inside my leathers. Not content with that, he then teed a golf ball up outside the garage and smashed it one, over the track and the facing grand-stand. It landed where hundreds of spectators were still filtering out of the stand. It must have nearly killed someone.

Trailing by 29 points going into the final round in Mexico, it's perhaps a good job that my title challenge was effectively over because the race organisation was appalling. During practice, there were people playing football at the side of the track and dogs wandering all round the circuit. To cap it all, when Russell was at full pelt down the fastest straight, a truck pulled out right in front of him. He managed to miss it, but that was the last straw.

We had been saying all during practice that the officials had to sort it out, or we wouldn't ride. Russell and I drove round the circuit in a car to see if there had been any improvement on the Saturday before final qualifying. I remember thinking, 'This is a joke. I really don't want to race here. I'm too far behind in the championship and I hate the place, anyway.'

Scott, who had nothing much to gain by riding, was pointing every small detail out in a bid to get the race cancelled. But he was right. I couldn't just think about myself – I had to think about all the other riders. If anything had happened it would have been down to me, so we decided to pull out of the race. To fill in the time, we arranged a football match – The Rest of the World versus Italy on a pitch at the circuit. How they staged the World Cup out there, I'll never know. The air is so thin and the smog so thick that I was out of breath after five minutes. Still, I scored a hat-trick and we were leading 4–1 until Slick gave away two penalties when the proper ref turned up. The final score was 5–5 and I sulked for ages!

We bumped into Russell and his team later that night, celebrating their world championship at the Hard Rock Café in Mexico City. I had a quiet meal with Slick on a separate table and, when we went to pay, the waiter told us that Russell had already settled up. That pissed me off as well. I did not want his charity just because he had beaten me to the title.

It was a strange way to end a strange championship. I had won 11 races to Scott Russell's five – and he won the championship quite easily. Perhaps the most important statistic was that he had been second 12 times to my two. It was clear that my inability to finish high in the points when I hadn't won races had cost me dear.

That was perhaps the only time in my career when some people regarded me as a crasher, maybe because I was pushing too hard in order to impress the new team or even because I lacked a bit of experience. And it came on the back of the couple of high-profile falls in 1992, before my first WSB win at Donington, and in the British Grand Prix. So it was perhaps not the frequency of falls, but the profile of the races, which made people think I was a crasher.

I actually think that my record for crashing is very good. It's a fact that some riders fall off more than others. Some get away with it, some don't. Look at Mick Doohan, for instance. He hardly ever fell off but, when he did, he suffered terrible injuries. There was the crash at Assen in 1992, which cost him the world title. And I saw him in America, after the massive fall in the Spanish Grand Prix at Jerez in 1999, when I was sure he'd never race again. That was a guy who'd had too many bad injuries. In a way, I was relieved to hear that he'd retired at the end of that year.

In contrast to Doohan, Jamie Whitham had always been a frequent crasher. But, until Brno in 1999, when he broke his pelvis in three or four places, and another fall in 1989 when his ankle was badly broken, he didn't suffer many serious injuries. Steve Hislop is another guy who has never hurt himself badly. So I suppose I should count myself lucky as, although my injuries will no doubt continue to give me problems later on in life, I'm still in one piece.

During that summer I decided it was about time to try and obtain a road licence for riding a bike. It had never really been a problem, until I needed to run in the new Honda in 1988. But I had to turn down one personal appearance in Newcastle, where the organisers wanted me to ride through the city centre, because it would have been illegal, as I had never taken my test. You don't need a normal licence to take part in road races. The local press found out that I had applied for my test and, suddenly, the pressure was on for my big day. I would look a right idiot if I failed.

I had actually taken the first part three years earlier, and that was a piece of cake. But, during training for the second part, I had a few problems adjusting to the brakes, as I wasn't used to riding so slowly. The instructor insisted that I should brake with four fingers, whereas

I only use two in races. He also told me to cover my back brakes with my foot, but my toes always rested on the edge of the footrest when racing. It was pouring down on the day of the test and the examiner had to follow in his car, because his bike would not start, which made me even more nervous. He pretended he didn't know me, which was good, although he did ask me how my racing was going – after informing me that I had passed.

Towards the end of the year, we sold Verecroft and bought a near-derelict Grade II listed farmhouse called Chapel's Farm, in a village outside Blackburn called Tockholes. We made around £35,000 on the £100,000 that I had paid dad just over a year before for Verecroft. He was a bit annoyed about that, but we had done a lot of work on the house.

We had seen the Tockholes house just before travelling to Mexico and the price had dropped from £200,000 to £160,000. No one had lived there for five years and, though the structure was sound, the inside was a shell. But we fell in love with it. It was ideal. The stone walls gave it character, it was out of the way and had five acres of land, in which we could keep a horse for Michaela and buy some other animals.

I was on the phone all the time I was out in Mexico and made a final offer of £140,000. We also had our eye on another house in Langho, which footballer Kevin Gallacher eventually bought. When I mentioned this, the owners finally accepted our offer. To celebrate, I went out into Mexico City and bought a saddle for the horse, having borrowed $100 from Kawasaki manager Peter Doyle, as I had forgotten to take any cash. He keeps reminding me that I haven't paid him back.

For once, I thought there would be no doubt where I would be racing the following year. The figures were soon agreed with Raymond and I was left to concentrate on the house move. But Honda had decided to make a comeback, sponsored by Castrol, and Neil Tuxworth had tentatively approached me a couple of times before the end of the season. I didn't think much more of it until he rang again and made their plans seem very professional.

I heard enough to persuade me to set up a meeting, at an M62 service station, with Neil and the boss of Honda Britain, Bob McMillan. With a Ducati deal already agreed but not signed, Honda were going to have to almost double Ducati's offer to have any chance of prising me away. These were not figures that Neil was used to dealing with and he knocked me back. But I was bothered. I wasn't keen to leave Ducati at that stage of my career anyway. Honda eventually signed Aaron Slight, for one year, and Doug Polen, on a two-year deal.

When our house was sold, we stayed at dad's new house for a few months until Chapel's Farm was ready. That was hard work, but I spent nearly every day of the winter up at Tockholes and absolutely loved every minute. It kept me busy and fit, plus we had financial security with the Ducati contract in the bag. There was also the small matter that Michaela was pregnant again with Claudia. My life seemed all in order – until the animals started to arrive . . .

CHAPTER TEN

'Where's Michaela?'

Bridget and Arai, a Great Dane and Chihauhau, were already on the scene and causing havoc around the house. Bridget, however, was living on borrowed time. She was so thick and clumsy and used to shit four or five times a day, which was just too much for any man to cope with. In fact, the only purpose she seemed to serve in life was providing something for the Chihauhau to hump. Arai, named after the make of helmet, was not only a bit too small to shag a Great Dane he was also a bit confused. So he basically tried to hump anything he could reach – her leg if she was standing up or the back of her head when she was lying down.

While the dogs were running wild outside, work was progressing well inside the house. I couldn't even tear myself away from the renovations during a 10-day holiday at an all-inclusive resort in Jamaica. I was on the phone all the time to check on progress back home where dad was helping to lay the drains and a drive.

Michaela's dad, Alan, also leant a hand on occasions and there were times when sparks flew. My dad tends to rush in headfirst, do it his way and then have to repair it later. Alan is a perfectionist who likes to take his time. During one operation, to level the stable floor, Alan could see that the floor was sloping and needed more stone at one end before the concrete was laid. But my dad was having none of it and they almost came to blows with planks of wood. It took one of our other friends to separate them before Michaela stormed outside and sent them both home!

The first occupant of that stable, when it was eventually finished, was a horse called Cassie. She was trouble from the start. She was bought locally, from a couple that promised she was bomb-proof. We were told that nothing could scare this horse. If a truck drove by, sounding its air horn, this horse would not bat an eyelid. So we were told.

I was bored one day, just after we had moved in, when Michaela suggested I should take the horse out for a ride to see what she was like. I didn't bother wearing a riding hat as they make you look a right idiot. Everything was going smoothly until a car came into view further down the road. Cassie stopped and started backing up. Then she started to spin round and reared up. I gripped the reins tightly and closed my eyes as the driver slammed on the brakes and screeched to a stop. He apologised but I told him that it wasn't his fault. She seemed to settle down and we continued for a while along the road, before turning off down a public footpath through an area called Rocky Brook. I could now pick up a bit of speed and was galloping through the woods feeling like John Wayne. Some of the walkers, who had to dive out of the way, were not too chuffed, though. 'You shouldn't be in here on that thing,' one shouted as we thundered past. This was more like it.

On the way home, exactly the same thing happened. When Cassie spotted another car, she backed up, span round again and pulled another wheelie. This time the car nearly hit the horse. I was blazing mad and jumped down from the saddle, held the reins tight in one hand and punched her on the nose, so hard that I nearly broke my hand. The driver watched, sheepishly, as I set off back home on foot, leading the horse behind me. I told Michaela, 'That thing's going back tomorrow. There's no way we're keeping it.'

She blamed my riding and called Jamie's girlfriend, Andrea, who had grown up around horses, to see if she would try to ride it. Exactly the same thing happened with her, so Cassie was on her way. The people who had sold it to us were very understanding and apologetic and gave us our money back on the spot. She was soon replaced by Sultan who, although he doesn't like men, has never posed us any problems – unlike a few later additions to the growing animal sanctuary.

The season had almost started by the time we actually moved into Tockholes. A few months earlier, I had called Raymond to check that everything was in order. 'Carl, there are a few problems at Ducati. I might not be your team manager this season,' he said. I thought he was joking at first. 'Maybe I stop at home this year and do not run the team. I cannot get the right money from Ducati.'

I was gobsmacked, but this was typical of the way that Ducati worked. I was the last to find anything out. A couple of days later I spoke to my contact at Ducati's owners Cagiva, a girl called Paola Martignoni, thinking the whole thing would have blown over.

'What's all this about with Raymond,' I asked.

'Raymond will not be running your team this year,' she replied. 'Virginio Ferrari will be running your team. You will not be affected and you can keep Slick as your mechanic.'

'Well, it's nice to be told at last,' I said.

I knew of Virginio, a former Grand Prix rider who had held the TT F1 world title the year before my first win in 1988. He had always seemed okay, but he didn't have the same charisma as Roche. Ferrari rang the next day to tell me we would be testing the new 916 bike in Jerez. Falappa was staying on as my team-mate and a factory bike was to be provided for Fabrizio Pirovano, who would be managed by Davide Tardozzi. Ducati also provided a bike for Jamie Whitham, under the management of Moto Cinelli's Hoss Elm.

It was great having Jamie on the scene again, as we had not seen much of each other since the Macau trip. But the welcome from Virginio in Jerez was decidedly lukewarm. He just about managed to shake my hand and say 'Hello'. When I suggested we should all go out for dinner to get to know each other there was no response, so I hooked up with Jamie and Hoss. The following day Virginio approached me with a little notepad and asked, 'Is there anything you want this year?' Nothing sprang to mind at the time, but I was sure something would crop up as the season progressed.

Virginio seemed perfectly nice and more professional than Raymond, but weird at the same time. 'This is what we have planned for you today. You will ride the old 888 bike and test a lot of tyres for Michelin,' he said before the first session at Jerez. So I only managed a handful of laps on the new bike, as the mechanics found it easier to understand what Falappa had to say about it.

But those few laps didn't prove anything. The bike was good – and looked beautiful – but didn't feel great. It seemed more like I was sitting on a 500cc because, without much fairing around the engine, I felt right on top of it. It also seemed twitchy, as a lot of new bikes do. I didn't even sit on the thing again until practice for the first round of the British championship at Donington, which was being treated as my first real test of the 916. I won both races, which delighted

Ducati, as their new bike was hitting the headlines straight out of the crate.

That performance increased expectations for the first world championship round, again at Donington in May. When a new 40-foot articulated lorry arrived, doubling up as sleeping quarters for Virginio and the team's hospitality area, I realised that Ducati meant business this year. A hospitality area was almost unheard of until then. But nobody was more surprised than I was when I won that first race, because I didn't like the bike one bit. Okay, it was very fast, but I couldn't carry any corner speed. Setting the bike up needed more attention, as it was still twitchy and nervous. Jamie crashed in practice, breaking his wrist, which would prove to be part of a bizarre coincidence — I suffered exactly the same fate shortly afterwards.

Honda were experiencing similar problems with their own new bike. Russell, on the other hand, was on a proven Kawasaki and appeared to be a lot quicker. This was the case in the second race, when he won with Slight second and me in third. I was somehow leading the championship after the first round riding a bike I hated.

I was sure the bike would improve but I didn't give it a chance at Hockenheim after crashing out in practice. It was a stupid crash, on the second lap of the final qualifying session. I still don't know what caused it, as I wasn't pushing that hard at Sachs Curve. Photographs show smoke coming out of the back of the bike, although I was also told that there had been oil already on the track. Whatever the reason, the rear end came round and the bike threw me over the top — a proper high side. My wrist probably broke before I landed, as my glove seemed to catch on the bar and locked my arm in an awkward position. Michaela, who was pregnant at the time with Claudia, usually never watches from anywhere but the pit wall. But, as soon as I stood up, I could see her at the exact spot where I had fallen.

It was a bad break, in two places, and the doctors decided to straighten it out there and then in the *Clinica Mobile* that follows the series around. It was one of the most painful things that I have experienced, worse than my broken legs. Two doctors grabbed hold of the top of my arm, another two were at the bottom of my arm, and all four pulled their hardest. I was swearing my heart out in agony. These Italian doctors, employed by the championship organisers Flammini, couldn't speak good English but I think they got the message. When the bone was reset, my arm was put in a pot all the way up to my shoulder. My mood got worse when Russell won both races to claim an early 39-point lead. The next race, at Misano, was three weeks away. It was crucial that I should be fit for that date.

Virginio drove our motorhome through the night straight to Milan, where his workshop was based, so I could see the best Italian doctor, Dr Claudio Costa. His X-ray showed that the bone had been set well, but the pot had to stay on for 10 more days. I flew home down in the dumps. Jamie came over to cheer me up and we must have looked a right old pair in The Rock pub at the top of the road, trying to eat our pie and chips, each with a pot on our arms. Some 10 days before Misano, I flew to Austria to meet up again with Dr Costa, as he was working at the Grand Prix in Salzburg. When he took the cast off, my arm quivered and flopped onto the bed. It had lost so much strength in such a short space of time. Surely there was no way that I would be back in action in just over a week.

I was like a bear with a sore head for the rest of the weekend. Slick had driven our motorhome to Austria from Italy and had scraped its side after trying to pass another car in a tunnel that was too narrow. Accidents happen, and that didn't bother us as much as when we found some conspicuous stains on our sheets . . . and curtains. He had obviously picked up some bird along the way. He was pulling girls without any problems in those days, when he didn't have the extra pounds to carry!

Michaela, who was heavily pregnant with Claudia, was livid and I tried to be angry but couldn't help seeing the funny side. 'Don't do that in my bed again,' I warned. 'Go and do it in the front seat or somewhere like that.'

My foul mood didn't let up, even when Michaela had made a real effort to dress up for a meal we were going to. 'Bloody hell! You're not going out like that are you? You look horrible,' I snapped. Our motorhome was parked within earshot of Neil Hodgson's, who was struggling on the 125cc Grand Prix circuit. He looked horrified and his mum, Maureen, later said she had wanted to smack me in the face because Michaela was crying her eyes out. My problem is that I struggle to switch off about racing. If I have a bad result, I know that I can be a real pain for days.

It was also around this time that I decided to call in the favour that Virginio had promised before the season had started. Slick was pretty fed up about his workload and again felt a bit isolated, working among a bunch of Italians. He wanted some help and I thought it would be good to have another Englishman around. And I knew just the guy.

My best man, Gary Dickinson, was still working in a factory in Blackburn but I knew that he could do better for himself, as he was fairly handy around bikes. Virginio agreed and Gary jumped at the chance to start at Misano. It was all fairly new to him, and we had thrown him in at the deep end. Slick wasn't too sure about him at first, until I reminded him that Gary would need a bit of time to learn the ropes. Gary knew that he'd landed on his feet. It was an easy life in a lot of ways. His accommodation in Italy was paid for, he did a couple of days' work on the bike each week and spent the rest of the time drinking with Slick. He never looked back and is still on the racing circuit, working for Kawasaki in the British Superbike championship, having also worked for Suzuki for two years in World Superbikes.

With time running out before Misano, Dr Costa had replaced the big pot with a smaller carbon-fibre cast. At last I could scratch my arse or comb my hair. But he wanted to see me again at his Bologna clinic on the Thursday before the meeting to continue with a laser treatment that was supposed to speed the healing. The cast didn't make riding too easy during qualifying, as my hand was pushed into a strange position whenever I braked. A new cast was made, which was much more comfortable, and I qualified in 11th. That wasn't bad considering there were riders behind me who had nothing wrong with them.

But the race posed new problems. Although I was running well in fifth, I couldn't use the clutch properly and had to stamp through the gears to downshift. It must have placed too much of a strain on the gearbox, because it packed in when I had fifth place in the bag. Needless to say, Russell went on to win and I was devastated again. At such an early stage of the season, I was already a massive 56 points behind. I rode the spare bike for the second race and this time managed to finish in fifth while Russell was second.

It didn't take long for Gary to prove his loyalty. He was as annoyed as I was that Russell was pulling away in the championship simply because I was injured. So, when the American walked past us in the paddock, Gary muttered under his breath, 'Do you want me to break his legs to even things up?' Russell heard him, turned round and growled 'I'd still win, man!' I had a quiet word with Gary that he shouldn't really be saying things like that. That was my job!

Falappa had won that second race at Misano – his last ever ride. Ducati had booked a three-day testing session at Albacete, after the Misano races and before the Spanish round two weeks later at the same track. My cast was off and we were able to try a few minor adjustments like different head angles or lengthening the swinging arm, the section at the back of the bike that the wheel is bolted on to. I was more than one and a half seconds faster than Falappa and he was trying desperately hard to approach my times on the third and final day of testing. Virginio told me, 'I think Giancarlo is very confused. He cannot understand why your times are so much faster.'

I was packing up for the day when the noise of Falappa's bike, roaring round the other side of the track, which has slow corners and is usually very safe, suddenly merged into a dull thud. 'Giancarlo's crashed again,' I told his girlfriend Paola, who was walking across the paddock with a tray of coffees. She seemed to shrug it off and sauntered off to see how he was.

He had high sided at a slow corner in first gear and landed straight on his head – the worst kind of fall. He was taken straight to hospital and I was told he had just suffered concussion. So we continued with plans to sneak in a few days in Benidorm with Jamie and Andrea. We bumped into Aaron Slight and Doug Polen, who were also relaxing in the resort, and they told us that Falappa was in a critical condition with a blood clot on the brain and needed artificial help with his breathing.

When we returned to Albacete, on the Wednesday before the race, the mood of the team was low and everyone was walking round with long faces. The mechanics told me that Falappa was not expected to survive the week. I couldn't believe it.

The least I could do to improve the mood was to win both races in Spain. On the Saturday night Michaela actually said, 'You never know, Russell might crash out of both races and you'll be back in with a shout of the title.' Her prediction came true, I did win both and the points difference was back to 24. And there was even more good news as Aaron Slight had been docked his Donington points for using an illegal fuel, pending appeal.

After Albacete, I had time to include a testing session at Mugello, to help me get to know the new fuel-injected Cagiva bike that I would ride in the British Grand Prix. We also carried out tests on the new 916 there and Doug Chandler, who was also at Mugello, was recording faster times, which I found embarrassing as he was a 500cc rider testing a superbike. But the next day they let me ride his bike. It was almost perfect and I knocked a second off his time immediately, to lap in 1 minute 55.6 seconds. I don't think that time has been bettered on a superbike around Mugello to this day. The geometry of the bike had been totally altered and I could now carry much more corner speed.

'I want this bike. I've got to have this bike,' I pleaded with Virginio.

'You will, you will. We just wanted to know what you thought of it after riding your own bike,' he grinned.

All this time, Giancarlo had been in a coma so you can imagine the relief when he came round during the next round at the Oster- reichring in Austria. Our mechanics unfurled a huge banner containing a warning to the other riders, 'Enjoy it while you can. The lion has awoken.' He was off the critical list the following week but he doesn't seem to have fully recovered from those injuries even now. Giancarlo still spends a lot of time around the Ducati team, wearing the same kind of clothes that he wore at the time of his crash. He is very forgetful and can congratulate me after a race before doing exactly the same thing five minutes later without realising. It's a real shame.

The impact of the bike's new set-up was immediate as I clinched pole position at Osterreichring. Somebody then told me that I had to attend an official function on the Saturday night because I was on pole. I wasn't keen and felt, as usual, that I was being pulled from pillar to post. I changed my mind when I was told that I had won my weight in wine. A pair of giant scales was set up on a stage and I sat on one side, while the wine was added to the other until the scales were tipped. They didn't realise that I had jammed my foot under the carpet, stopping my side of the scales from rising. More and more wine was piled on until my foot was forced clear. I think I took eight crates back to the motorhome.

Race day coincided with the football World Cup final in the States between Brazil and Italy. The Ducati team were not impressed when I turned up wearing a Brazil shirt, which had been given to me the previous year by a Brazilian Ducati mechanic. I carried on winding them up as I crossed the finishing line following my second win of the day. Instead of pulling the usual wheelie, I stood up in the saddle and imitated Brazilian striker Bebeto, who had celebrated his goals in the World Cup by making a cradle out of his arms because he'd just become a father. Russell's confidence had been shattered at Albacete and he was nowhere again in Austria. His 12th and 14th positions meant that, from nowhere, I was leading the championship.

The Austrian races were finished in time to watch the World Cup final at a special marquee set up at the track. I was one of a handful of people supporting Brazil, among around 300 Italians. One of the mechanics was nicknamed Arnie, a massive Croatian bloke who looked and talked like Arnold Schwarzenegger, and was on crutches for some reason. He would never dream of causing trouble as he was a nice guy but, if it all kicked off, you would want him on your side – he had been known to throw Slick over his shoulder with one arm.

The game was boring so people started chucking plastic glasses across the marquee, and quite a few hit Arnie. He managed to keep his cool until a full cup of beer landed on his back. That was the final straw and he lost his rag. He picked up a chair and, still on his crutches, heaved it to the other side of the room. Suddenly the whole thing was out of hand. I was one of the few sober ones and tried to calm it down, as it had been a great night until then.

The match itself went to penalties of course, and when they were over, and Italy had lost, I looked for Gary and Slick. I had specifically asked them not to get drunk, as I wanted to set off back to England straight after the game in the motorhome, not least to see Michaela who, being by now eight months pregnant, had made the right decision to stay at home. Surprise, surprise, when I found them they were both pissed out of their heads and Slick was round the back of the marquee with some bird. So I had to do the first stint behind the wheel, although they promised to help out with the maps.

Within five miles, they were both unconscious in the back, snoring away. I was furious, especially when I got lost a couple of times. It was a good bet that Mick Doohan, who was leading the Grand Prix championship, didn't have to drive through the night for eight hours after just winning two races.

By 7am, there were signs of life in the back. I pulled in and shouted, 'Right, one of you two will have to drive now, I'm fucking sick of this. I need some sleep.' I might as well not have bothered because, after a couple of hours, I was wide awake and listening to those two idiots arguing because we were lost in the middle of Germany.

The fuel-injected Cagiva bike that I was to ride in the British Grand Prix at Donington was totally under-developed. I hated the thing. It broke down twice before I reached the end of the pit-lane during practice on Friday. It would come out of one corner sounding like a long slow fart then, at the next, there would be a short, sharp, parp when there was no power at all. Obviously the computer-run fuel injection system was just not working properly. Every lap the bike seemed to adjust its power band, the point at which the revs kick in. And, at a meeting where I was riding a new bike and needed more practice than anyone else, I was actually getting less. Virginio had decided not to turn up, as he didn't get on with Giacomo Agostini, who ran the Cagiva team. And Slick was not invited to join the Cagiva mechanics, so I was pretty miserable. To make matters worse, the press had built my chances up all week and everyone was expecting me to win the race.

On the Saturday morning, the bike threw me off after almost cutting out coming out of the hairpin and I banged my hand. In the afternoon, it cut out twice going round Redgate. 'That's it,' I thought, 'I've had enough.' There was no point even trying to ride the thing. Ducati didn't want me to risk injury because I was leading the World Superbike championship. But Cagiva wouldn't let me ride the same bike as Chandler and John Kocinski, their other GP rider.

I was obviously just a guinea pig for their fuel-injection experiment. But it would have looked bad on the Cagiva group, and Ducati, if I had just pulled out there and then. So, Claudio Castiglioni's secretary, Paola, took me to the *Clinica Mobile*. She convinced the doctors to strap my hand up and I emerged to talk to the waiting press wearing an ice pack. 'Can't ride,' I lied through my teeth. 'Nothing I can do about it. I hurt my hand in this morning's fall.'

So I hopped on a scooter and rode away, which was perhaps not too smart as I forgot that I was supposed to be unable to ride. As soon as I left the paddock, I threw the bandage away and within an hour I was in my motorhome and driving back to Blackburn.

Whether my mind was still at the meeting, I don't know. But on the way home I nearly killed a family that were setting off for their dream holiday. It was dark and, as the motorhome was a left-hand drive vehicle, I checked in the right-hand wing mirror before over-taking a car in front. I even double-checked and the lights behind were the same distance away. But those particular lights were obviously those of another car as, unknown to me, the first was already alongside me. So, when I pulled out, I clipped the back end of the first car, spinning it in front of the motorhome, down the hard shoulder and banging around from barrier to barrier across the M62. 'Oh fuck! I've killed them,' I thought, and stopped to check if everyone was okay.

Some road workers had seen the whole thing.

'Did I do that?' I asked in all innocence.

'Well, yeah mate, of course you did,' was the blunt reply.

A policeman soon arrived and asked, 'What are you doing here? Shouldn't you be racing in the British Grand Prix tomorrow?'

'I've come home,' I said. 'My bike was a pile of shit and I didn't want to ride it!'

The family had suffered nothing more than whiplash, but their car was a right-off. I was fined and docked three points for driving without due care and attention. Some would say that I'm safer on two wheels than four. Having spent so much time around Italians during my time with Ducati, I now drive like an Italian. In fact I get flashed at for going too slowly over there.

To put the lid on a terrible weekend, *Motor Cycle News* reporter Chris Herring rang me two days later to tell me that Honda's appeal had been successful and Slight's points from Donington had been restored. Ducati announced that they would launch their own appeal and there was now genuine bad feeling between the two camps. It was around this time that I also started falling out with Slight. I think he took exception to me criticising the Castrol Honda team.

I didn't actually believe that anyone at Honda knew they were doing anything wrong, but I wasn't surprised they won the appeal because they were a huge corporation. Still, it helped me to have two rivals that I hated, instead of just Russell. So, when we christened our two new Vietnamese pot-bellied pigs Scott and Aaron, I had to make sure that I won the title!

There was another name to think about, too. Our second daughter, Claudia, was conveniently born before I had to jet off to the Far East for the next two world championship rounds. Though we both liked the name, my fixation with supermodel Claudia Schiffer was the deciding factor. If Claudia had been born five years later, her name might have been Jordan!

This time I was on hand for the whole thing and, as every dad will tell you, it's a fantastic feeling. What wasn't so good, as Michaela started her contractions, was that I could see a Kentucky Fried Chicken restaurant out of the hospital window.

'I'm absolutely starving, Michaela, I'm going to have to nip out for two pieces of chicken and some corn on the cob.'

'You can't do that,' she pleaded, 'I'm just about to give birth any minute now.' 'I can't wait. Anyway, I'll be back in a minute.'

When I returned, Michaela was in agony and didn't see the funny side when I offered her a bite of one of the pieces of chicken. 'Get that thing away from me,' is a rough translation of what she said. All the photographs of Claudia straight after the birth have an empty box of Kentucky in the background next to the bed.

My job during labour was to monitor the machine that tells you when a contraction is due. As the graph rose, I sussed it when Michaela was about to feel the pain and gave her some gas to try and relieve it. Even if I say so myself, I was getting pretty good at this. So much so, that it was becoming a bit boring. I decided to spice things up a bit. Just when Michaela was confident that her reliable husband was going to warn her when a contraction was due, I deliberately missed my cue and forgot to give her the gas. The scream was heard in Yorkshire and she made it quite clear that I wouldn't be able to father any more children if I played a trick like that again.

Claudia's birth was a real boost before my WSB campaign resumed in Indonesia at Sentul. I did everything that had been asked of me to lead the first race by eight seconds with about seven laps remaining. But the machine let me down when the engine broke. Apparently Ducati were having trouble getting their hands on some new crank casings that were needed. On the back of the Grand Prix disaster, this was the last thing that I needed.

It might seem trivial to some people – to lose one race. But it's hard to grasp just how seriously I took every little thing about my racing in those days. I had made bold public predictions about the championship after Honda's reprieve, claiming that it wouldn't be long before I was back in the lead, but I was being made to look stupid when the bike didn't perform. And there was nothing I could do about that. It's no exaggeration to say that I felt like quitting. I just didn't need this kind of shit. Even the fact that Jamie had secured his one and only race win, beating Slight on the last lap, was small comfort.

My mood quickly changed when I won the second race to whittle Slight's lead down a bit. And I was in a mischievous mood by the time of the presentation ceremony. The race organisers invited the two winners, me and Jamie, up onto the stage for a special cake-cutting ceremony. The master of ceremonies was a big stupid Indonesian idiot, who kept turning his back on us to crack jokes to the audience. But, whenever he turned round, I fired huge dollops of cream cake onto his back with a spatula.

Jamie was literally crying with laughter and the audience was in stitches. The compere thought they were laughing at his jokes and had no idea what was happening until his brand new suit, that he'd probably saved up for all his life, was being sponged down by three little men.

Problems with the throttle in Japan meant a fourth in the first race followed by second place, while Russell returned to form to take both wins. Now I trailed him by eight points in what had developed into a three-way fight for the title. Slight's points were still up in the air, as the Ducati appeal into the fuel wrangle had still to be heard. That was not my concern. All I could do was take my customary double win from Assen, where Russell had another disastrous day. And, by the next round in San Marino, the French based International Motorcycling Federation (FIM) had made their decision to dock Slight's 17 points from the Donington races. In the end it was decided just to dock the points from the race in which the fuel was tested. But, without moving a muscle, I found myself back in the championship lead.

Russell was quicker than I was in San Marino and there was nothing much I could do to stop him winning the first race. He was also pulling away in the second race when it was his turn for some bad luck, just as I had experienced at Sentul in Indonesia. His bike broke down and I was guaranteed another victory. With two rounds remaining, I was 18 points ahead of Slight. Russell was virtually out of it.

Next up was Donington, where the crowd was keen to rub my rivals' noses in it. There were plenty of banners out like, 'Fast furious Foggy flattens fuel fraudsters' and 'Russell, Russell, kiss Carl's ass, there's no pace car and Foggy's too fast.' Everyone expected two more wins, but this season had taught me to expect the unexpected.

The weather wasn't good but had cleared slightly before the race. I was advised to try a new hard wet tyre, which was supposed to suit a drying track. I had never used one before and the gamble proved to be a disaster. From pole position, I was challenging at the front when the rain became heavier. For a supposed wet weather tyre, the grip proved completely useless and I slipped right down the field to finish in 14th, almost crashing three times on the last lap.

I was in a tricky position for the second race. Russell rode a brilliant first race to win and claw himself right back into the championship frame. But I couldn't afford to push too hard in another wet race, crash out and concede even more ground. Virginio told me that fellow Ducati riders Troy Corser, who had just won the American Superbike championship and wanted to establish himself on the world stage, and Mauro Lucchiari, who had taken over from Falappa, would help me out.

Sure enough, they both came past me early on as I settled for fifth place, knowing they would let me through at the end. Or so I thought! Corser finished second and Lucchiari was third, behind none other than Russell. I was blazing mad and stormed in to see Virginio for an explanation.

'Carl, it is better this way. Team orders are not the correct way to win things,' he said.

'That's fine,' I replied, 'But tell me first, you dickhead. If I had known they were not going to let me through, I might have pushed harder to try and beat Lucchiari.'

And I didn't keep my feelings to myself. Under the headline 'Fogarty slams team orders', I told *Motor Cycle News* that it had been 'the worst decision that I had experienced in all my career'. The paper conducted a public poll and the majority voted that it would have been unsporting to let me through. But that is typical of the British sporting public, more concerned with fair play than actually winning. I had no problem with the reasons; it would just have been nice to know what was happening at the start of the race.

As a result, my championship lead over Russell had been cut to five points overnight, but Slight wasn't really a threat a further 12 points behind Russell.

The pressure was on for the final round at Phillip Island in Australia. And I had nearly four weeks to sweat on it. In many ways, Russell was now the favourite to go on and clinch the title. He rode superbly at Donington and I felt that his bike was quicker. But Ducati promised me that they would use the four-week gap to make sure my engine was in perfect working order. Russell was shouting his mouth off, saying that he didn't have to worry about me, as he would be way out in front. I was quietly confident, and decided for once to keep my mouth shut.

We travelled out early, as Honda had booked the circuit for a few days' testing. Ducati muscled in for a day, as did Kawasaki, sharing the cost with their Honda rivals, which is common practice. Russell was quicker on that day but it gave me the chance to work out some minor improvements. Phillip Island is a specialist's track, all about keeping corner speed flowing. On the second day's testing, Russell fell off, which led me to believe that he was riding at his limits. I knew that I wasn't.

We had a week to kill before the race, which left time for a spot of sight-seeing or anything to take my mind off the impending races. We visited Melbourne and also took in a bit of deep sea fishing with Australian rider Anthony Gobert's dad. The first thing loaded onto the hired boat were the crates of beer and these tinnies were cracked open almost before the boat left the dock. However, me, Gary and Slick were so seasick that we couldn't even stand the sight of beer.

The ship's captain was a typical bollock-scratching, hairy-arsed Aussie. 'What's up with ya, ya soft pommie bastards,' he laughed. His opinion of us didn't improve when none of us wanted to touch the parrotfish that we had caught. 'Here, let me do it. Don't touch that bit, though, it's poisonous and will kill you,' he said, after whipping the hook out without blinking. I caught eight out of the boat's total of 11, mainly because everyone else was pissed by the time we dropped anchor out at sea.

The break helped me relax before the race, although I wasn't that nervous. My attitude was, 'Whatever will be, will be.' I was confident that if I did what I had been doing all year, the races would look after themselves. My times improved throughout qualifying and I was second on the grid behind Gobert. But two guys had slowed me up on my fastest lap, so I knew there was something in reserve. Again, I kept that quiet.

Come race day, it started to rain, which was just about the worst thing that could have happened for me. It was obvious, though, from the clearing skies that it was just a passing cloud. Barry Sheene was doing some TV work and I pleaded with him to take his time and try to delay the start until the track was properly dried out. He did what he could and we all started on slick tyres, although a few damp patches still existed around the track.

I went straight into the lead but the nerves had caught up with me. My chest felt tight and I was struggling for breath. Russell came past and I stole a quick glance over my shoulder to see who else was up with us. Gobert was behind me on a Muzzy Kawasaki but, as I looked back, I almost crashed. I hit neutral, which is like hitting an eject button on a Ducati as it shoots you forward.

As a result I ran wide going round Siberia and the bike was about to roll at the front when I just managed to find second gear and pull it round. 'For fuck's sake, pull yourself together,' I shouted, trying to pump myself up. I caught up with Russell around the back section of the circuit, where I was quicker, and pulled out of his slipstream on the start-finish straight. I knew then that my bike was quicker than his. Then I put in some really fast times and broke the lap record, which stood for a few years. The board showed +1, +2, +3 as my lead in seconds increased. Go, go go! I won the race and had one hand on the trophy. Although Gobert slowed down after passing Russell to allow him to finish second, I now had an eight points lead.

I lifted my hand to acknowledge the crowd but that was it as far as celebrations were concerned. This wasn't about winning one race – it was about winning a world championship. My task was clear. All I had to do was follow Russell round to become the world champion.

The next two hours were the longest in my life. The skies cleared and conditions were perfect for the second race. But I had a bad start and had to work my way through the field from fourth. Corser was one of those in front of me. But, again, there were no team orders and I had to out-brake him at a corner to move into third. I soon caught up with Russell and Gobert and thought, 'The best way to win this is to ride the only way I know how.' So I started to mix it with them and passed Gobert. But then I had second thoughts. 'What am I doing? Gobert has nothing to lose here and he's a bit wild at the best of times. He might try and ride even closer to the edge and become Kawasaki's hero. Let him go, keep out of his way. He can win by four days for all I care.'

So I sat in behind Russell and decided to follow him round. It really bugged him, as there was nothing he could do about it. With three laps remaining, he slowed right down. 'I don't like this. He's up to something. If I try to go past, he might try and knock me off,' I warned myself.

Coming down to Honda Corner, he took his hand off the bar and made a throwaway gesture, as if he was conceding defeat. Keith Huewen, on the Sky Sports commentary, said, 'If he'd had a towel, he would have thrown it in there and then.' I passed him straight away but he stayed right behind me and I still couldn't work out what he was up to. With two laps to go, Russell pulled into the pits. I knew that all I had to do was keep my head and finish the race.

At the start of the last lap my board said 'P2, Russell out'. This was it. All I had to do was slow down and stay upright. It was the best feeling I had ever had in racing. After such a troubled year, I was about to win the World Superbike championship in the final race of the season and on the other side of the world. It was too much for me. I cried all the way round and didn't stop when I got back to the pits, completely drained. The whole Ducati team dived on me, and plenty more besides, including Sheene, who was trying to stick a microphone in my face. I pushed him out the way and shouted, 'Where's Michaela?' There was only one person who had shared all the ups and downs of the year and knew exactly how much the title meant to me. Our embrace was shown around the world and captured the unbelievable emotion of the occasion.

Russell came over and said, 'Well done. You've deserved it.' That went some way to healing old wounds and, from that day on, I think we had a bit more respect for each other. But I still believe that he was finished as a rider the second that he made that gesture of defeat. He even joined in the celebrations in a place called Banfields, where we stay every year. If I had been in his shoes, I would have locked myself in my room. Jamie and Andrea were there, as was Terry Rymer. Surprise, surprise, I was the first to be thrown into the swimming pool after a lot of drink. Jamie and Terry decided to follow but chose to jump into the shallow end. When they surfaced, Jamie had bust his lip and Rymer had cut his head.

The idiots who arranged the travel for World Superbikes booked me on a Garuda Airlines flight which stopped at every city in the world on the way home. So I didn't arrive back until Wednesday morning, absolutely knackered. But the reception was amazing. Sky Sports, the local press and local television stations were waiting for interviews at Manchester Airport. There wasn't a great deal of coverage in the national newspapers as, by this time, we were well into the football season.

But the invites for personal appearances flooded in. I was asked to light the big bonfire in Blackburn at Witton Park. Blackburn Rovers also wanted me to parade in front of their supporters at the next home game against Tottenham, in the year they won the Premiership title.

I'm not sure how many of their supporters knew that I had supported Manchester United since being nine years old. I do actually go to watch a lot of Blackburn's home games now. Maybe my loyalty would be tested if there were to be another battle for the title, as I have fallen out with Old Trafford over ticket arrangements. It's no fun for me to sit among the crowd and miss half the game signing autographs.

If you were to analyse my season it was probably the points from the Misano races, where I rode with a broken wrist, which secured my first world championship. If I had missed that race, I would have been left with a mountain to climb. And, without my aggressive, obnoxious approach to anything and anyone who stood in my way, I would probably have sat the race out. The fuel controversy and personal rivalries also helped to fire my motivation.

Cash bonuses never really entered the equation because, when I negotiated the contract I was given two options. I was greedy and took the first – a bigger lump sum without bonuses. The second had bigger bonuses built in but with a smaller sum up front, and I probably lost around £50,000 as a result.

But money was the least of my concerns. Success in the world championship had lifted a huge weight off my shoulders. I felt that I had proved a point and I was now in a position to relax more and enjoy the following season. For sure, there was a responsibility that went with carrying the number one plate, but now there was no question over who was the best. It was all set up for 1995, when I reached my peak as a rider . . .

CHAPTER ELEVEN

Reaching my Peak

Being world champion had increased my bargaining powers. Neil Tux-worth was still desperate for me to be back on a Honda and approached me again at the end of 1994. Doug Polen had under-performed that year but was on a two-year deal, so Honda were looking for a way out for the following season. This time it was very easy for me to say no. I had already negotiated a very good deal with Ducati with good bonuses. My new leathers and helmet contracts were also in the bag at decent money.

All this meant that I had been able to buy a few new toys, including a brand new red BMW M3. I soon found out that there was more than just the cash price to pay for owning a few luxuries. I always parked the car on the drive next to the house at night but one morning it had disappeared. After ringing the police, I contacted my insurance people, who asked if it had a tracker system. At first I told them that it hadn't, but later remembered the salesman telling me that the tracker could be activated any time I wanted and had a 98 per cent success rate in finding stolen cars.

Within a couple of hours the garage told me that it would cost £60 to have the tracker reconnected. 'I'll pay it,' I said, although I thought that the car would be on some ship to Holland by then. Five hours later the police located it, being stripped down in a barn in nearby Bolton. The bastards claimed that they were just doing some work on it for another guy who had dropped it off. And, as usual with the British legal system, they got away with it and are probably out there nicking more cars today.

Meanwhile the animal sanctuary was still in full swing. The first of the pigs had arrived the previous year. Unusually for a Vietnamese pot-bellied pig, it was pink. Most of them are black so we soon decided to buy a normal coloured companion, as the first one was really clean and didn't need much looking after. It never once shit in its hut and, during the day, was happy to roam around the half an acre in which it was penned.

We needn't have bothered about it being lonely because, unknown to us, the neighbour's pig had escaped and shafted ours before being caught. We weren't even sure whether it was pregnant because it was so fat – until all hell broke loose when Michaela was out with some friends one night. Piglets were coming out at all angles. I needed help.

One of Michaela's mates, Mandy Wrigley, who later took Bridget the Great Dane off our hands, had just bought a pub in a dodgy area of town. I rang the Elma Yerburgh pub and asked them to stop the live music to get an urgent message to Michaela. 'You've got to get home quick,' I shouted. 'She's giving birth.'

We sat up all night as, one by one, Michaela's friend Tracey delivered the pigs while we supervised from a safe distance. In all she gave birth to 11 healthy piglets and one runt.

When we returned in the morning there were only eight still alive, as the mother had rolled over and crushed four of them. And we weren't prepared for the chaos they would bring. If they ever broke out of the pen, it was like having eight big rats running and squealing through the fields. It was once down to me, with some help from Slick, to round up all eight of them and I've never been so exhausted in my life. We both had to rugby tackle the last and most stubborn one and even then it nearly wriggled free. Passers-by must have thought we were murdering it, as the noise the thing made was unbelievable until it ran out of breath.

Another time, it was down to my dad. He had trapped one, the size of a small dog, between the stable and a barbed-wire fence, which separated our land from a stream. It was a classic case of a 'pig in a ginnel'. The rest of us couldn't see what was happening. But we could hear all right! First the squealing got louder as dad slowly approached the pig. Then everything went quiet before there was a dull thud. And, as the pig came hurtling round the corner of the stable, we could hear dad moaning 'Help, help'. The pig had charged him and knocked him over the barbed-wire fence and down the stream's embankment. His face was cut and he stank of TCP for three days.

It was obvious they would have to go. Again it was up to dad to take them to an animal sanctuary place called Only Foals and Horses, which had agreed to take them off our hands for a fee. He counted eight piglets into the Jeep but, when he counted them back out, he could only find seven. The last one had jammed itself under the driver's seat.

It was even harder to get rid of the adults, who, as I mentioned earlier, had been named after Scott Russell and Aaron Slight. Aaronetta, as she came to be known, just didn't want to enter the box trailer. Perhaps they knew that we didn't have the necessary licence for transporting them! Dad decided to lasso her round the neck and drag her up the ramp. But this pig just would not budge. I was crying with laughter as dad kept slipping on his arse, trying to heave a quarter of a ton of pork into the box. Even when I whacked it on the backside with a wooden plank, it only budged an inch at a time!

Before the pigs were finally out of the way, another problem cropped up. I had asked my mate Howard Rigby to fetch a couple of ducks from his uncle's farm, which was just across the neighbouring fields. He turned up with sacks containing hens, cocks, geese and ducks and emptied them all into the shed. The next morning, when I opened the doors to let the ducks out, a huge riot spilled out into the fields.

The four cocks were at each other's throats, a goose was spitting feathers and out waddled a half-dead duck, which we had sprayed with the word 'Duck-ati' on its back in red paint. God knows what it must have been like in there during the night. I had to kill two cocks by hitting them over the head with a shovel because they would not stop fighting. Then I had to sack the rest of them up and take them back to Howard, who was pissing himself laughing. Nothing seemed to last long at that house. At times, there was lots of nice wildlife in the fields. The next day almost everything was dead because a fox or one of the dogs had got at them, so we had to stock up all over again.

It may seem that our animals have brought nothing but hassle. But I really like animals – except horses and cats. Maybe I should have taken more time to train them, the dogs especially. But I'm not one to sit down with a bag of goodies and go, 'Shake a paw!' I think they should train themselves – I had to! So, if there's a problem with one of the pets, you have got to do something about it, especially if someone says they will take it off your hands. For instance, we had a Boxer which only lasted a few weeks because it was just completely stupid and wriggled around like a trout out of water. We had to give that away and, when someone brought it to a Christmas party we went to in 1999, I'm surprised it didn't bite me!

While all this mayhem was happening at home, at least the Ducati set-up provided some stability. Mauro Lucchiari, who had taken over when Falappa was injured, was staying on as my team-mate for 1995 and I expected him to have a good season. That was fine by me, although his close relationship with Virginio worried me a little bit, as I didn't want him to have preferential treatment. Mauro was obviously his favourite and the two of them used to train together, as Virginio was a very fit guy. But he was a nice lad who kept himself to himself and, because he did not speak much English, we didn't bother each other too much.

Slick was also still on the team, but only just. It was clear that Virginio no longer wanted Slick around and the row that I had with Virginio over this had been only my second big bust-up with him, the other being the team orders cock-up at Donington. He told me that Slick's work hadn't been up to scratch and that the other mechanics were fed up with his shouting and bawling. I don't think they were too impressed with his drinking and his scruffy appearance on race days, and felt that he should socialise more with the rest of the team. But that was difficult for Slick. All the others were Italians, who had grown up in the same area around Bologna.

I realised there was no point trying to keep hold of Gary, and he wasn't too bothered. He had seen a bit of the world but I think he was more comfortable at home in England. The previous season had opened a lot of doors for him and, when he told people that he'd worked with Carl Fogarty, he had no problem finding a new job in racing with a privateer Ducati team which had Steve Hislop riding for them. But I dug my heels in over Slick.

Virginio argued, 'Carl, he did not win you the world championship, you won the world championship on your own.'

I was insistent. 'Look, I want Slick, and that's that.'

At that time, he was a very good hands-on mechanic. Nowadays the word mechanic doesn't really exist. The team is full of engineers and specialists in different areas such as tyres and suspension. He was also English and a friend, and I needed someone close around me. This dragged on for a full day and everyone started falling out. 'Believe me, Slick will be better in 1995, no worries,' I promised. 'It's been hard for him this year because he was looking after Gary, who was new to the team.'

Eventually I got my own way, but not without Virginio warning me that Slick would be out of the door at the first sign of trouble. He also moved two of his mechanics across from Lucchiari's team and gave them the responsibility of making the final decisions. Slick might no longer have been the official chief mechanic, but he still was in my eyes.

We decided to start the season by returning to Daytona. As a world champion and a member of a big factory team, I mistakenly thought that I would get fair treatment from the Americans. But it didn't help matters when I was quoted in MCN as saying that I hated Daytona, the track and all Americans. What I actually said was, I didn't like Daytona and didn't particularly like the track.

It was only when I arrived in the States that I realised just how much the Americans hated me for it. Dunlop America had even posted copies of the newspaper cuttings all around the track. Yanks just don't like criticism of their country and the build-up to the race was like the hype surrounding a big fight. At the time it was a bit worrying but, looking back, it generated a lot of interest.

Troy Corser, who was riding for the rival Ducati team run by Davide Tardozzi, was handed the number one plate because he was the reigning American champion. I needed a number that was a bit stupid and different, so I chose 99. (Jamie Whitham always used to choose 69 because it read the same way when his bike was upside down in the gravel!) Having qualified in third, I was up with the leaders before Scott Russell crashed on the second or third lap. I couldn't believe my luck, even though I had to run wide to miss him and lost a couple of places. But Russell received help from the marshals in getting back on his bike, which was illegal. Then there was another small crash. Nobody was injured and there was certainly no debris on the track.

Still, the Americans decided to bring out the pace car while I was in fourth. No rider was allowed to pass another while we followed the car round for a couple of laps. Yet, when I looked around, I could see Russell weaving through the pack without a care in the world. If the rules were there to be followed, he should have been disqualified. But he was American, so he could do what he wanted.

After that, though, he rode really well and was the quickest man out there. While his pit stops were ultra-fast and professional, I had to pull in once because I couldn't even see my board. When I got into the pits, Slick and the rest of the team were sat on the wall having a natter and I lost 30 seconds on Russell. But I still managed to finish second despite a splitting headache. I was pleased to leave the place alive and I will never go back there again as the track is dangerous and the rules are bent.

After tests at Laguna Seca in California and Misano, where I was presented with a gold engraved Rolex Daytona watch from Michelin for winning the world title, it was obvious that the improvements that had been made to the 916 had worked wonders. The suspension had been altered at the front and back, and the engine was smoother and more powerful. To this day, that 1995 model was the best bike I've ever ridden.

The first race was at Hockenheim in Germany, where I had never won before. But I won both races and, to be honest, the season was pretty boring from then on! The team was working well, Slick seemed to be fitting in better, my confidence was sky-high and I was much more relaxed. And people had tried to tell me that it would be harder to retain my title!

At Misano, I'll hold my hand up and say that I was riding on the limit to stay with Lucchiari, who won both races by close margins. But Corser and Slight were clearly going to be my main challengers, if you could call them that because I was already 31 points in the lead. Then I had a bit of a dice with Russell at Donington but, after I out-braked him at the hairpin, it was the last I was to see of him in superbikes for a few years. He walked out on Kawasaki, using a loophole in his contract and blaming his bike, to take Kevin Schwantz's place with Lucky Strike Suzuki in GPs. But Slight was still around for me to wind up. I actually think that I made Slight a better rider because he hated me so much for saying things like, 'The new Honda is too good for him.'

By the next round at Monza, the other teams were moaning that the Ducatis had too much of an advantage. They claimed that the twin-cylinder Ducatis had 1000cc engines and were much lighter than the four-cylinder bikes. And their whines found some sympathy with the FIM. So the rules were changed halfway through the season in time for the Monza races and weight was added to our bikes. It didn't make much difference to the results.

I won the first race and was leading the second with a lap to go when I had to slow down because of engine problems. Pier-Francesco Chili came past me . . . on a Ducati, of course. I told the press conference, 'Yeah, I think the new rules have made a difference. They have made the Ducatis better as, before, they were a bit too light and jumped around.' That comment annoyed Ducati more than the people it was intended to wind up, because they didn't want things stirred up any more than they already had been.

Elsewhere in Italy, I could do no wrong. The profile of the sport over there is huge, as motor sport is second only to football in popularity. You only have to walk along the streets to see why, as the number of scooters on the road is huge. My world championship had received a lot of publicity because the fans aren't bothered about the nationality of a rider if the manufacturer is Italian. So victory on a Ducati had made me something of a national celebrity. Later in the season, the Italian press started referring to me as the Lionheart.

Nowadays I can't really walk down the street in Italy without having to sign autographs or having scooter riders shout, 'Ciao, Foggy!' My profile is also quite high in Spain, which is another big biking country, and perhaps in America as well – for the wrong reasons after Daytona! I am quite well known in superbike-mad countries like Germany and I've raced enough in Australia to have a pretty high profile there. The Far East is a different matter, and I would almost definitely not be recognised in Japan – most riders wouldn't. In Italy, though, support for me is phenomenal and is still growing year by year. Only recently I was the fifth most photographed sportsman in a poll run by *Gazzetta dello Sport*. Not bad for a working-class lad from Blackburn.

Slight managed his first win on a Honda in the first race at Albacete by holding me up in the corners. He made the most of it afterwards, saying, 'This is what you get when you work hard on something for 12 months.' I couldn't wait to put the record straight and, sure enough, I stormed to victory in the second race. I walked into the press conference and said five words, 'Normal service has been resumed.'

But the Honda was starting to worry me a bit because it was seriously quick. If Polen hadn't been axed at the start of the year after some slow testing sessions, robbing Slight of a proper team-mate, the two Hondas could have posed me a problem. As it was, Slight only had Simon Crafar on a non-factory Honda as back-up. And my little digs were really getting to him. When I said that his Honda would be faster than my bike in Austria at the next round, he grabbed the mike off me and sarcastically said, 'Yep, that's it. I'll just wobble round the corners and blast away from everyone down the straights.' It was his sarcastic way of saying that he didn't think he had any advantage.

That race at the Salzburgring was a real battle, literally, but not between me and Slight. Some oil had been spilled near the start-finish line and Falappa, who had made the trip to support the Ducati team, tried to alert the marshals. They didn't take him seriously, so he started shouting at them to put their flags out. Finally, one of the marshals pushed Falappa away and he fell over. The Ducati team saw this from their garage and all hell broke loose.

Virginio fancied himself as a bit of a karate expert and struck up the classic Bruce Lee pose. The only problem was that most of the marshals were also black belt kung fu experts. The Ducati team got a right pasting. Virginio's nose was broken and Lucchiari's dad's collarbone was dislocated when one of the marshals put him in an arm-lock.

While all this was going on, I was on my way to second place after tangling with a slow rider, having won the first race. When I got back to the pits, there was hardly anyone to be seen.

'Where is everyone?' I asked Slick.

'You've missed all the fun,' he replied. 'Most of them are at the clinic. There's been a huge punch-up!'

Amazingly, our team was fined for misconduct as, by all accounts, it was the marshals who were looking for a fight.

By coincidence, the Salzburgring also saw the start of another fight – for my signature for 1996. Davide Tardozzi was running the other Ducati team as Team Promotor for Ducati with Troy Corser and Andy Meklau as riders. The team had financial backing from an Austrian businessman called Alfred Inzinger, who made his money from the Power Horse energy drink. Tardozzi approached me in Austria, offering a two- or three-year deal. But I was still wary of signing for anyone except a full factory team after what had happened in previous years, and Tardozzi's plans were only built on Inzinger's promises. It was a good decision. To this day Troy is fighting a legal battle to try and recover money that he was not paid from 1997, when the Promotor team left superbikes and tried to set up a Yamaha team in Grand Prix racing.

Back in America for the Laguna Seca round, the reception was just what I wanted. The Yanks hadn't forgotten my Daytona comments and they made sure I was aware of it. There were banners out saying, 'Fuck off home Foggy' and the rest of the crowd were either flicking 'V's at me or giving me the finger. I just love all that stuff as it really pumps me up and makes me determined to prove a point. I was also in the right form too, having not finished lower than second all season.

The only problem was that Laguna Seca just doesn't suit the way I ride a motorcycle. It's almost impossible to carry any corner speed because the corners are flat and don't have any camber to help you lean the bike over. Instead, if you try to carry speed, you end up running wide. I crashed in practice and only qualified in 12th. 'Not here, in front of these bastards,' I thought, especially when they didn't appreciate the problems. Instead, I tried to change something on the bike after almost every session, which probably did more harm than good. As it turned out, fifth and seventh places were enough to extend my lead in the championship, although Corser had moved into second, ahead of Slight.

This was not the time to be entering the unknown of Brands, another undulating circuit and somewhere I had never won. Nobody was more surprised than me when I was quickest after the first timed session. And my times continued to improve throughout the weekend until I qualified in pole.

On Sunday morning I looked out of the motorhome window to find the biggest crowd I had ever seen. The official attendance was 50,000, but I think it was more like 60,000 when you took into account the number that had climbed over the fencing. It turned out to be one of the best days I had ever had in racing. I was at the absolute peak of my racing career. I was even enjoying the travelling, qualifying and practice, which is unusual. The bike was doing exactly what I wanted it to and I could control races almost at will. If I felt that someone was catching me up, I could just put in a couple of faster laps.

Maybe my previous results at Brands had just been down to a spate of bad luck because, on that day, there was no contest. I won both races and set a new lap record. I had a 136-point lead in the championship and already had one hand on the title. It was time to party with my Blackburn mates at the nearby home of Barry Sheene's sister, Maggie Smart, and then back at the motorhome in the paddock. The drive back to Blackburn with the hangover from hell on a red-hot Monday morning was not a pleasant experience!

In the few weeks' gap before travelling to Japan for the next round, we put up a marquee in the back garden and held a big summer barbecue to celebrate Claudia's christening. During a game of rounders, I noticed that Jamie was really out of breath. It wasn't like him because he was normally pretty fit. Then he went to bed early, which was certainly not like him. I even noticed that he was looking thin and gaunt at the christening.

A week later he was diagnosed with Hodgkin's Disease, a cancer of the lymphatic system. The word 'cancer' is enough to make anyone fear the worst. But he coped very well and refused to let it get him down. His attitude was, 'Well, I've got the thing, now let's get rid of it.' And that made it a lot easier for his friends and family to cope. He's a tough character and underwent a course of chemotherapy, sometimes asking for double the dose, even though he knew it would knock him for six. Amazingly, having missed the end of that season, he was back in the saddle for the start of the next.

Japan provided a blip in my own fortunes, but on nothing like the same scale. It was actually possible for me to clinch the title at Sugo, if I had won both races. But I didn't really want to win in Japan! It was a long way from home and there wasn't much of an atmosphere about the place. It would be much better if I could seal it at Assen in front of tens of thousands of British fans.

It turned out that I didn't have a choice. Having qualified in pole, I had just passed Slight, Corser and a Japanese rider called Yasutomo Nagai. Coming out of turn two, I had the biggest high side of my life. The back wheel had almost slid round enough to just carry on the slide. But then it fired me off with so much force that the petrol tank flew off the bike. I went so far up that I had time to run in mid-air to regain my balance. And, for the first time ever, I was able to try and limit the damage from the fall. I remember thinking, 'This is going to hurt. Come down on your side and cushion it because, if you come down straight, you're going to snap your legs.' When I hit the deck I was tossed and thrown but was able to stand up and limp away with what seemed like nothing more than cuts and bruises down my right side.

The fall had been captured on the TV monitors and Slick rode straight over on his scooter to pick me up and take me to the clinic, where I tried to lie still for a couple of hours. My hand was swelling up as I had cracked a bone and I was given a couple of injections to stop the pain. Michaela was back in England at the Sky Sports studios. I rang her and said, 'I don't think I'm going to be able to ride in the second race, the pain's too bad.'

But just before the second race it started to rain, which meant there had to be a 15-minute practice in the wet. I decided to give it a tentative go, but people were coming past me easily and I pulled in and told the doctor that I couldn't ride. Sat in the garage, as the sun came out, I changed my mind and decided to try and get a few points at least. The doctor gave me a couple more injections that he called 'mesatherapy' to numb the pain in my hand and foot, where I had chipped bones, and my knee, where I had stretched some ligaments. And out I went. On the start line I pumped myself up, 'Come on, come on, you can do this.'

And I did it. I won the race. In fact, I absolutely blitzed it. If I was to chose one moment in my whole career, that was the point when I was at my ultimate best as a rider. I don't think I could ever do that again. Right from the first corner I was bashing fairings with Nagai. Then he cut me up at the next corner. 'Right, you little bastard, if that's what you want.' I passed him back and he cut me up again and almost knocked me off. I was fuming. At the chicane at the end of the first lap I passed him for a second time and turned round to give him the finger.

Then I got my head down and was off. The gap stayed at around three seconds, with one lap remaining. I eased off a bit – but so did the adrenaline. The nausea set in almost immediately. As soon as I finished, I felt sick to the core. I almost threw up in my helmet on the slowing down lap and didn't even want to climb onto the rostrum. I was white as a sheet and had to lie down before I fainted. I had just enough strength left to hug the doctor who had got me through the race. Then the series organisers, Flammini, had the nerve to bollock me for not attending the press conference!

Like an idiot, I went for a few beers in the hotel bar on my crutches. I had almost made it back to my room when I bumped into Gobert and Colin Edwards. The Texan was another rider who I didn't like that year. He had come over here over for the first time and was one of the loudest to shout his mouth off about me and Ducati. I told him, 'If I was as slow as you are, I'd wait until I could beat my own team-mate before I started gobbing off.' Earlier, in my room, I had trapped a cockroach in a plastic cup, pricked a hole in the top and named it Colin the Cockroach after Edwards. And, while Colin the Cockroach was still a prisoner upstairs, Edwards said, 'I know we don't get on, but what you did today was incredible. Let me get you a drink.'

The pair of them got me drinking Jack Daniels and coke, which I hated. When I made it to my room, I spewed up everywhere but couldn't make it to the toilet so there was a big pile of puke next to my bed. My room-mate Lucchiari had been drinking the same stuff and he was spewing at the other side of his bed.

It was not until the next day that I found out that I had suffered two broken bones in my hand, the chipped bone in my ankle, a hairline crack in a toe as well as knee ligament damage. But all that was nothing compared to travelling home for 24 hours with the worst hangover ever.

Nagai had been annoying me all year, by latching onto me in qualifying for slipstream tows. He was a bit out of control at the best of times. At Assen, in the next round of the championship, he was dead. It was obvious that he wasn't going to get away with that style of riding forever, but this time it wasn't even his fault. Another rider's bike had blown up in front of him and dumped oil all over the track. When Nagai's bike hit the oil he slid off and was about to get to his feet when the bike dug into the grass, flipped up and landed on his head and chest. He was kept alive until his parents and girlfriend reached Holland, when they decided to switch off the life support machine. Yamaha pulled their team out of the rest of the series as a mark of respect.

His death obviously took the edge off my celebrations. I had struggled in practice as my hand was still sore from Sugo, and Assen is the type of track where the rider needs to pull hard on the bike through the corners. But a couple of painkilling injections dulled the pain and I clinched the world championship with a comfortable win in the first race, although Simon Crafar rode well to push me in the early stages.

What little pressure there had been was off and I was miles ahead in the second race when Nagai crashed and it was stopped a couple of laps early. I hadn't really known him too well but this was not the time for wild champagne celebrations, just a few quiet beers. Later that week, *Motor Cycle News* annoyed me when they quoted me as saying that I had dedicated the win to Jamie, who was still fighting his cancer. It was embarrassing and a stupid thing to write, as it sounded as though he was dead. I made sure Jamie knew that I had been misquoted.

It was at this exact point in my career when I changed as a person and a rider. I was bored. There was nothing left to prove in World Superbikes, as I was head and shoulders above the rest on a Ducati. I was also fed up with Virginio's lack of organisation, as was Slick. So, what was I going to do next? The answer seemed fairly obvious . . .

CHAPTER TWELVE

Wasted Year

The fact that Grand Prix promoters Dorna wanted me in their championship was no secret. The TV company had seen my popularity in World Superbikes and wanted to cash in. They were even offering packages of free advertising worth hundreds of thousands of pounds, even millions, to any team that secured my signature. As far as I was concerned, the Grand Prix circuit would have provided a new challenge, for sure. But there was no point in me switching from superbikes unless I was going to be riding a bike on which I could challenge for the title.

Garry Taylor at Suzuki was again the first to make a move. But he wanted me to ride in the World Superbike championship, as Suzuki were intending to make a comeback in that competition.

'Is there nothing available in GPs?' I asked.

'I don't think so,' Garry replied. 'We've got our riders sorted out and I don't think our bosses will expand the team to three riders. But . . . wait a minute,' he continued, 'Kenny Roberts might be looking for a rider. I'll see what I can find out.'

He was true to his word because I then received a call from Roberts' co-ordinator, Chuck Aksland, who wanted to set up a meeting.

By now the other superbike teams had realised that my services were up for grabs for 1996. Neil Tuxworth was again seriously asking me to join Castrol Honda and I also had offers from Yamaha and Kawasaki, although I didn't take them too seriously because their bikes would not have been capable of winning the title. But the lure of GPs was still strong.

Scott Russell had moved over earlier that year and was doing quite well. I knew that I was better than him and, having already raced

177

against the likes of Mick Doohan, I knew that I could win Grand Prix races. But a ride was not just going to land in my lap. So a friend called Alan Pendry, who imported the No Fear brand of clothing which supplied some of the GP teams and had done a couple of deals with me in 1995, suggested that I travelled to the Spanish Grand Prix in Barcelona. The aim was to show my face and quietly make contact with Roberts and Dorna. But there was no chance of doing it quietly because the media attention was amazing. I had to do more interviews than I would have done at a normal WSB round. And I seemed to be attracting more publicity than the top stars like Doohan and Darryl Beattie.

The meeting with Roberts was arranged in the Marlboro Yamaha team bus. It was a bit weird because, despite the fact that he was my childhood hero, there had been a bit of history between us. He, like me, is not the kind of bloke who is going to keep his mouth shut if something is upsetting him. I had said my piece about Grand Prix riders in 1990 and Roberts was one of the GP men who liked to put superbikes down, until Scott Russell switched over and made a good impression. So, by the time we met in Spain, we both had a lot more respect for each other. He said, 'Look, I don't know what's happening with Marlboro or with Yamaha for next year. For sure, I'd like you as a rider in the team but it all depends on sponsorship. I'll keep you informed.'

Whether that was true or not, I'll never know. We also met up with the boss of Dorna. They were desperate to steal the best superbike rider, in an attempt to stop our growing championship from threatening the status of Grand Prix as the sport's top prize.

Today, there is not a lot to choose between the two championships although, worldwide, the history and nostalgia of GPs probably still give them the edge. Obviously superbikes is bigger in Britain because of my success and its relative popularity in other countries also depends on the success or failure of their own riders. For instance, superbikes has recently been bigger than GPs in the States but, now that Kenny Roberts Jnr is starting to have success, GPs are starting to pick up again over there. Strangely, even throughout Doohan's period at the top, superbikes has remained very popular in Australia.

We left Spain none the wiser. And all this time the superbikes world was on hold. There was only a couple of irrelevant races of the 1995 season remaining, but no team wanted to name their riders for 1996 until I had made my decision. I hadn't talked figures with the likes of Yamaha, Suzuki, Kawasaki or even Honda, as creating an auction is not my way of going about these things. And, of course, Ducati desperately wanted to know what was going on.

They had made me an offer, but it was pretty disappointing considering my success, which continued in the next to last round of 1995 at Sentul, Indonesia. But the first race win meant nothing to me and, when the breather pipe developed a problem in the second race, I pulled in without any second thoughts. 'There's a bit of a problem, I can't ride it,' I told Virginio, after my first breakdown of the whole year. He wanted me to fly straight from Indonesia for some testing in Phillip Island before the final round in Australia. 'I'm not testing,' I told him. 'I've just won the world championship. What do I want to test for?'

Instead, I went to Bali for a week's holiday and was joined by Michaela, Slick, a few mechanics and a couple of Italian riders, Fabrizio Pirovano and Piergiorgio Bontempi. By now Honda, Suzuki and Ducati were frantic for a decision. I wasn't sure that Suzuki would be competitive enough.

And I had pretty well made my mind up over Ducati. I hadn't told them, but I really didn't want to stay there for another year. It wasn't because I felt that I had nothing more to prove. The reason was the lack of overall organisation. There was also a lot of politics within the company and their offer was not as good as some of the other figures that had been mentioned, probably as a result of those internal arguments.

Deep down, I really fancied a shot at the GPs. But that was the least concrete of the offers. I needed to force the issue. Before Michaela arrived in Bali, faxes were flying to and fro between Blackburn, Kenny Roberts Snr in the States and Aksland in Europe. Eventually, I managed to speak to Roberts.

'What's happening, Kenny? Is there a ride or isn't there?' I asked.

'Carl, I just don't know and I don't think anything will be sorted out before Christmas. One thing is for sure, I can't guarantee anything. If you get a good offer from another team, I would take it if I were you,' said Roberts.

I don't know how much truth there was in what he said, but it was clear that I would be stupid to go down that road. I came off the phone and said to Michaela, 'I'm going to go with Honda.'

179

There were a number of reasons. I had always been impressed by the team's set-up. It appeared well organised and somehow more professional than Ducati. Their riders travelled business class all the time, and that wasn't always the case with Ducati. Little things like that all added up. I had always worked well with Neil Tuxworth, despite taking the piss about his tightness and sulking. Their bike had looked fast in 1995 and there was no reason why it couldn't go even quicker. And the money was good, nearly double Ducati's previous deal. I've no idea whether I was paid any more or less than other riders. I don't even know whether I would have earned more in GPs. These things have never bothered me. As long as I have been happy with my deals I've let other people get on with their own negotiations. If someone sorts out a better deal than mine, good luck to them – you won't find me bitching.

The questions about my future were almost constant as soon as I set foot in Australia. But Virginio needed to be told first. 'Okay,' he conceded, 'If that's your final decision. I just wish you could have told me sooner as I need to sign up other riders.' Then I found Neil. 'You've got me,' I told him.

Nothing more needed to be said. He didn't do cartwheels, but his relief was evident, as this was the third year in succession in which he had tried to sign me. Slick was included as part of the package, as well as Nick Goodison, who had worked with him in 1989 for Honda. The actual races at Phillip Island were something of an anti-climax although Gobert gave me a good second race, beating me by half a machine after I had finished fourth in the first race. Then I announced my decision to leave Ducati publicly at the post-race press conference.

Neil's first act was to bring Aaron Slight, his other rider for 1996, round to my room the following morning. Neil said, 'Look, I know you two have said stuff about each other in the past, but I want to clear the air right from the word go. I can tell you now that you'll both be treated the same.' I didn't like Aaron and he didn't like me. There was no getting away from that fact. But neither of us had a problem with being team-mates. And it was good for me to know that I had a team-mate who I knew I could beat!

It wasn't until later that week that the deal with Honda was announced in the press. I think a lot of people were pleased, as it got me off a Ducati and opened up the championship. But, on the way home, the split with Ducati proved very upsetting. We flew with the team to Singapore, where I changed flights for England and they switched for Italy. Virginio gathered us all round at the airport and gave a little goodbye speech. 'It has been fantastic over the last two years and everyone is going to miss you. But we wish you well and hope that you might be back with us some day,' he said. His voice started to crack with emotion, which made me and some of the mechanics fill up with tears. It was a touching moment.

The discussions with Kenny Roberts proved to be the closest I ever came to a regular Grand Prix ride. But that's not something that I regret in the slightest. I have absolutely no doubt in my mind that I would have won Grand Prix races, given the right package and the right bike. Whether I would have won a world championship is a different matter. To win a world title there also has to be an element of luck involved. It is always difficult to stay out of trouble for a whole year. Mind you, at that time, there was only really Mick Doohan to worry about, as Kevin Schwantz had just retired.

Some riders who left superbikes have adapted to the Grand Prix scene, some haven't. It all boils down to an individual rider's personality. For instance, Simon Crafar never won a World Superbike race but won the British Grand Prix in his first year on a 500cc. At that time, the package was working for him. The following year he changed his tyres, didn't win anything and lost his job. Max Biaggi left 250ccs, jumped on a 500cc bike, smashed a lap record and won his first ever Grand Prix race. Yet people say that 500cc bikes are hard to get used to. Yet even Mick Doohan says that they are easier to ride now. I've raced Alex Criville twice in GPs and beaten him twice – and he is now the reigning world champion.

But I've also seen it work the other way. Troy Corser joined the factory Yamaha Grand Prix team as World Superbike champion but didn't do a thing for them and was sacked halfway through the year. Anthony Gobert, who is always difficult to judge at the best of times, has ridden fast laps on a 500cc, just as he has done in superbikes. But he has never been fit enough or motivated enough to do it consistently for the 25 laps of a race. He has a lot of talent, but was too young and stupid to be handed the chance to ride in GPs. John Kocinski won 500 Grand Prix races on the Cagiva, which nobody thought would ever happen, and on a Yamaha. When he returned to GPs from superbikes, he was as fast as anyone on a couple of tracks but crap at the others. Again, his style is more suited to some bikes and tracks than others. I know that I've always been able to adapt to riding different bikes. And, if I had been given a good bike with a good team, I'm sure I would have been a GP world champion.

It was no time at all before I started to have serious doubts about my decision to join Honda. After briefly meeting the team in Louth, I flew out to the first test in Malaysia with Chris Herring, who had been a reporter on MCN but had also just joined Castrol Honda as their public relations guy. He was a good bloke and I had always respected his work so it was good to have him on board.

As on any long distance flight, I had plenty of time to think things through. And it just hit me. What the fuck have I done? Why have I changed teams at this stage of my career? Why leave something behind that I've built up over three years, and that worked so well? I drifted off to sleep and put it down to an attack of nerves on landing in Malaysia. And Honda's smooth organisation helped ease those fears. Someone was waiting at the airport with my car for the stay, exactly the kind of thing that hadn't happened with Ducati. They had also given me a Honda NSX Supercar for use in England, which was fantastic to drive.

Slick and Nick had travelled in advance and were already working on the bike at the Shah Alam circuit. My first impression of the machine was quite good, especially when I pulled a wheelie on my way out of the pits to announce my arrival. After two days of testing, I was only half a second slower than the best lap time of the three days.

It was a wonder anyone could set decent times, though. One session was stopped for 10 minutes while the marshals chased a family of baboons off the track with sticks. I saw a whole family wander casually across a fast part of the circuit. I hit the brakes and just missed one of them, who looked at me as if to say, 'Piss off, you don't scare me, mate.' And they weren't the only wildlife hazard. It's not so bad on race day, as the place has usually been cleared by then. But in practice sessions, especially when the circuit hasn't been used for a while, I regularly ran over little long black snakes which had slithered onto the track. I once saw one rear up at a 125cc rider and nearly knock him off as he sent it spinning across the track. You certainly don't lean your bike over if you see them at a corner!

And, if you ever fall off in those places, the first thing you do is get out of the grass, however badly hurt you are. Big iguanas have even been known at Shah Alam. So, all things considered, the results from that test seemed fine for my first time out. What wasn't so good was the number of meetings that I was expected to attend to be quizzed by little Japanese men. Honda seemed to call a meeting every time I farted.

My testing time had to be cut short so that I could attend the Sky TV Sportsman of the Year awards in London, a three-hour spectacular live on television. This was a real star-studded occasion and the audience contained the likes of Sylvester Stallone, Noel Gallagher out of Oasis and lots of soap stars from *EastEnders* and *Coronation Street*. They all went mad when I rode the new Honda onto the stage. I was pipped into second place by boxer Prince Naseem Hamed, while Frank Bruno was third. But Sky Sports did present me with a special Get Up And Go award for my performances during 1995, especially at Sugo. At the BBC Sports Personality of the Year awards before Christmas, I was interviewed about my world title but didn't make it into the final three. I was sat next to Colin McRae, who was third in the poll after winning the World Rallying championship, while Frank Bruno was second and triple jumper Jonathan Edwards first. When Edwards' name was read out, McRae and I just looked at each other and said, 'Who?' We had never heard of him!

I have been invited down to that BBC ceremony ever since I claimed my first F1 TT title, but didn't always accept the invitation as I knew that I wouldn't feature in the programme. As my popularity grew over the years, though, and the voting system supposedly changed to a 'live' phone vote on the night, people started thinking that I had a chance of winning, especially after the 1999 season.

In my opinion there's no question that it is biased towards sports that the BBC has coverage of, so World Superbikes was never going to get a look in while it was on Sky. The winners in 1999 all seemed to know when it was going to be their turn to stand up and collect their awards. At that same ceremony, when I told the nation that it was great to have more fans than Manchester United, the interviewer, John Inverdale, said, 'If you win it for a fifth time in 2000, you may have a chance.' In an Olympic year? I don't think so! But, with the BBC having won the rights to screen the World Superbike championship in 2000, there might be less bias against me.

After the Sky awards, the next testing session was in Australia, where the team staged all their publicity shots. Honda's discipline was already beginning to get on my nerves. I had to wear certain shirts to certain events, which is not my style. The only time I got a real bollocking from Neil all year was at Laguna, when I wasn't wearing the correct shirt at the right time. So I lied and told him that someone had nicked it from my cupboard.

To make matters worse, the testing didn't go well. It was cold, wet and windy and I seemed to be going round in circles – literally. I was doing a few laps, putting new tyres on and doing a few more. There was not much effort, or thought, going into it on my part, so I wasn't learning anything about the bike. This was yet another sign of the change in my attitude to racing. I had lost some of the motivation to analyse the bike in winter testing. And when the next two testing sessions, at Mugello and Misano, were ruined by the weather, I was entering the season under-prepared.

What's more, Honda just didn't feel like my team. It seemed to be geared up more for Slight's success. At the first round in Misano, I noticed that he had a different set of forks on the bike. 'What are they?' I asked his mechanic, Adrian Gorst, who I didn't like one bit. He was a real teacher's pet type who kissed the arses of the Honda top brass whenever they were around. He also had it in for Slick from day one.

'It's just a different set, no big deal. There was only one set left,' Gorst replied.

I pulled Neil up immediately. 'Look Neil, we either test the same things, or we don't test at all,' I insisted.

Neil saw my point and it didn't happen again.

I missed most of final qualifying as I was laid out in my motorhome with concussion after my first big crash on the new bike. Having spent two or three weeks on the road travelling between tests, with Danielle and Claudia to look after, I wanted to race, pack up and get home as quickly as possible. I was still beaten up come race day and was fairly happy with a sixth and seventh place, just behind Slight in each race. I felt there was something to build on. But yet again, when another test was set up at Snetterton so that I could spend more time on the bike, it was cut short by rain. But at least I was now quicker than Slight and had Donington to look forward to. Or so I thought.

The bike was not at all bad to ride. The braking was good, the gear changing was positive and the acceleration was smooth and powerful. But it just didn't suit my style of riding. Whenever I leaned over in mid-corner, to try and carry as much corner speed as possible, the rear end tended to come round. Slight didn't have the same problem, as his style was different. He braked late, was slower through the bends, but would squirt the bike out of the corner. And at some tracks the effect on me was worse than at others. That was to be the story of the year. And Donington just happened to be one of the tracks where the bike wouldn't perform. I was ninth and seventh, which was an absolute disaster for the reigning world champion on his home track. Slight's second place in the final race just rubbed salt into my wounds. It was the perfect chance for my rivals like Colin Edwards to open fire with comments like, 'We told you he was shit' . . . blah, blah, blah.

Sat in the bath, back home that Sunday, I was thinking that the season couldn't get much worse. Then Michaela walked in and said,

'They're going to sack Slick tomorrow.'

'What are you talking about?' I said.

'I've been speaking to Neil and he's going to call you later tonight. They've been having a lot of problems and the other mechanics have been complaining about him.'

Sure enough, Neil rang to break the news. 'Look Neil, I'm not happy about this. But if that's the way it has to be, then that's the way it has to be,' I said.

The real problem was that it was my own mechanics, people like Nick Goodison, who couldn't work with Slick and not the ones on Aaron's side of the team. Slick has always been outspoken and will say things that perhaps he shouldn't say. He will also do things his own way, instead of looking for a compromise. He can shout and bawl and occasionally doesn't speak to people properly. And it didn't help his cause when he turned his company car over in a ditch.

When Slick looks back on his career, I think he'll wish that he had done things a bit differently. He was always the one who would be urged to do something daft by those around him. Then, when he gave in, he invariably got into trouble with the team bosses. In a team as strict as Honda, it was probably only a matter of time before it came to the crunch. Slick told Neil, 'I don't even like it here; I only came because of Carl.' But he was very upset and came up to Blackburn for a few days.

It didn't help his mood when we went to play golf at Blackburn Golf Club and he put his first shot into the allotments next to the first fairway and smashed a greenhouse window. He had also heard that Nick Goodison had complained about him, but I couldn't believe that Nick would do that. Those few days were not a bundle of laughs, because I was still depressed about Donington.

My mood had not changed by Hockenheim. In all honesty, I didn't really want to leave my motorhome. I was just sick about everything that had happened. Surely the team should have been bending over backwards to make sure that I was okay. That's what my current boss Davide Tardozzi would have done. I was in a new team and had just lost my mechanic. Yet nobody was trying to make me feel wanted. And I was sure that Slight was loving every minute of it, smirking behind my back.

Yet another crash in practice shattered my already fragile confidence. I was convinced that I had broken my wrist but, when the ambulance took me to the clinic, there was nobody waiting for me from Honda to check how I was. Nobody even called into the motorhome to see if I was okay.

Slight won the first race, while I clawed my way up to fifth from a low start on the grid. I have always been a bad loser and couldn't stand the thought of having lunch in the hospitality compound, where Slight would be celebrating. Michaela brought me some pasta from hospitality, so that I could stay out of the way in the motorhome.

But I wasn't even safe there, as Danielle, my own daughter, had turned on me by then. She had obviously inherited my competitive streak and was disgusted that I was losing races.

'Why are you not winning any more, daddy?' she growled.

'Daddy had a problem with the bike,' I said, apologetically.

'No, not the bike. It's you,' she said with a stony face. 'When are you going to win again?'

'I'll win the second race, don't worry,' I assured her, without much conviction.

I had probably never felt as low in racing and, at that moment, I was planning to quit as soon as I got home.

As I prepared for the second race, I spotted the mechanics pushing our two bikes back to the garage from the compound in which they are held after the race to be scrutinised. For the first time I noticed that Slight's was a lot higher at the back compared to mine. It set me thinking. After studying some information on Aaron's set-up, I decided that lifting the rear end higher might stop me from running wide at corners and might help turning into corners. It could make the bike less stable down the straights, but that was a risk worth taking. The changes were made and I got a flying start.

It was a massive improvement. With five laps remaining, Slight and John Kocinski, who had taken my ride on the Ducati, were holding me up. At worst I was going to be third but I could almost feel everyone willing me on to win – the people at home, the press, half the paddock, and Danielle, of course, whose outburst was probably another big reason behind my new attitude. I was in the perfect position entering the final lap. And whoever enters the stadium section called the Motodrom first usually wins the race at Hockenheim. Slight would be good on the brakes for the final bend, I knew that. It didn't matter. Because, wherever he braked, I was going to brake later. Sure enough, I out-braked him, held on and won the race. I felt as though I could stick my finger up at the world again and say, 'Fuck you lot.'

All of a sudden, I couldn't hear the digs from Colin Edwards. In fact, I was so pumped up that I wanted to drag him out of his motorhome and say, 'What are you going to say now, you tosser?' Chris Herring told me that the pressroom went wild as I crossed the line. At the press conference I said, 'This has proved I can win on any bike and the whingers can go and crawl back under their stones.'

Aaron Slight was sat next to me in silence!

We packed up and set off for home immediately as I wanted to get as far away as possible from the paddock back-stabbers. We drove as far as Luxembourg and parked up for the night at a nice motorway service station and enjoyed a few beers outside the motorhome on a nice warm evening. It was really good to be able to relax once more. And Danielle was talking to me again!

Back home, I received faxes from Davide Tardozzi, Virginio Ferrari and Garry Taylor, saying 'Well done'. Even Scott Russell, who was struggling in GPs, rang me in the four-week gap before the next race to offer his congratulations.

Slick didn't know how to feel. He was delighted for me, but in some ways he felt that it was his fault that I hadn't won before. That wasn't the case. It was simply that my own confidence, and that in the bike, had been restored. And I was sure that I could win at the next round at Monza.

Sure enough, I won the first race and should have won the second. I was quicker than the guys in front of me in the chicanes and had it all weighed up to pass Slight at the last corner until Chili came flying past and nearly T-boned me off the track to win it on the line. Slight's bike was quicker and I made a mental note of that fact, but brushed it off as one of those things.

I had obviously convinced people that Hockenheim was no fluke, as Edwards approached me at the Monza paddock party to apologise. 'I've said some things about you, but I was wrong,' he began. 'Let's be mates. This is silly, especially as I'm good mates with Aaron and hanging round you guys all the time.' So we made up there and then and have been okay with each other ever since.

The next round at Brno was always going to be a big test, at a circuit where I expected the bike to be a problem due to the large number of off-camber bends where I would struggle to lean over against the gradient of the track. The races also confirmed my belief that Slight's bike was quicker. On a couple of the straights, especially an uphill section, I was struggling to even stay in his slipstream. Corser cleared off in both races but I managed to beat Aaron in the first before panicking in the second, when I saw some oil coming from a broken seal of Corser's bike. Slight took advantage to push me into third. I was blazing mad and started to shout my mouth off in the press conference. 'Perhaps, if I was given the same bike as my team-mate, I might have won those races,' I fumed.

Neil was told in no uncertain terms that I was not happy with the situation. 'Honestly, Carl, both engines are the same,' he insisted. And I believed him, but that didn't solve the problem. Even the fans had noticed on television and a couple of letters in MCN asked why Honda weren't prepared to give me the same bike as Slight. It might seem as though it was just another case of me moaning or complaining all the time. But the facts were there. His bike was pulling away on the straights. Did I not have a right to ask what was going on? Many people don't say a thing and just get on with it. But, when I'm mad about something, I want action and so I say what's on my mind.

At Laguna Seca, where I have never gone that well, it was not really possible to tell whose bike was the quicker. I was eighth and fourth, but Slight just beat me in both races. Then we had to travel to Japan for the Suzuka 8 hours, which I hated and was absolutely dreading. But, being in Honda's number one team with local rider, Takuma Aoki, we were favourites and expectations were high in the biggest race of the year for the Japanese.

In hideously hot conditions, we were leading because Aoki was riding really well. But Yamaha were closing in on our lead with a couple of laps left in one of my stints. I wanted to hand over to Aoki with the lead intact and was pushing extra hard. Then, more through exhaustion than anything else, I fell off at the hairpin and we dropped down to third or fourth before I could remount and hand over.

As soon as I got off the bike my leathers were ripped off by a couple of Japanese girls. It sounds kinky but, believe me, it wasn't. Then I was dragged to a deep tub filled with icy cold water at the back of the garage, where I had to sit and return my body temperature back to normal. But I had been taking so much water on board before my stint that I was dying for a piss. I couldn't be bothered getting out and going to the bogs. So I let it all out in the tub. After I had finished it was the turn of another Japanese rider, Tadayuki Okada, to sit in the tub while I was led away to have a glucose drip inserted in my arm. He had no idea what I had left in there and was quite happily washing his face in the tub's water. Nobody could understand why I was pissing myself laughing all the way through my massage in another air-conditioned unit!

All this time I was being fed energy food, as well as breathing in oxygen through a mask. By the time everyone had finished getting me ready to ride I was in a daze. It's no wonder they call it an endurance race. We finished in third, which was not a bad result, although Aoki was a bit annoyed with me for crashing. Still, the race meant absolutely nothing to me.

Back home, there were only a few days before the next world championship round at Brands and I was still knackered from Suzuka. A crowd of 70,000 had turned up – but only to witness the same problems that had dogged me all year. One picture that was taken shows me in a kind of speedway pose, fighting to stop the rear end of the bike coming right round on me. Still, I managed to come fifth in the first race although I knew that I could have won on a Ducati.

Again I was fuming with the bike and pushed even harder in the second race. Fourth place was in the bag with five laps remaining and I settled for that. Then, for some reason, I tried to take a corner in first gear instead of second. I didn't change positively enough, hit neutral and shot off the track. I put the loss of concentration down to fatigue from the Japan trip. In front of so many expectant fans it was a disaster and a crucial loss of points because Corser was now 48 points in front while I trailed Slight by 41.

Second and third places at Sentul were more promising but hid the story of a huge cock-up on my part. You could never really change gearboxes on a Ducati like you could with a Honda. Up to that meeting, we hadn't bothered but, after qualifying, I felt that the gap between second and fourth gears was too long. When we tinkered with it, though, I made third gear way too short, especially for two particular corners.

I felt a right idiot and kept it very quiet because I was catching Kocinski everywhere in the first race, except for those two corners. In the second race, I was third behind Chili when his throttle stuck open and he ran off. Exactly the same thing happened to my bike one lap later. It was probably the shit and dust on the track. I ran wide but managed to save it, although I lost my concentration and Slight sneaked into second. Even after that incident I had another massive heart-stopping moment when the throttle stuck open again, leaving the fast right-hand first corner. This time I hit the rumble strips after shooting wide and, at every corner from then on, I banged on the throttle to make sure it wasn't going to stick again.

The mishaps continued in Japan. I lost the front end during qualifying, slid into the foam banking and became tangled in some rope. The television cameras caught me kicking out at this stuff in an attempt to wriggle free as, not surprisingly, I wasn't in the best of moods. I had bruised a rib, or so I thought, but felt fit enough to race on the Sunday and finished eighth and fourth.

It was around this point of the season that I realised that I had missed Ducati all along. Being with Honda was too much like being back at school. Everything had to be punctual and run like clockwork. Who cared if I wasn't wearing the right shirt? Okay, Ducati were a bit disorganised at times, but in some ways I had missed that laid back Italian nature. I had found that the grass is not always greener on the other side.

But the memories of 1995 were still fresh. The Ducati was *my* bike. It worked to my strengths. And I think Ducati, and Virginio Ferrari in particular, were also missing me. He had fallen out with Kocinski and the two of them were not even speaking. I'm not surprised because Kocinski is a bit weird. Everything in the garage, like his food and towels, had to be laid out in perfect order. And, if anything had been touched, he would completely freak out. He had a phobia about dirtiness and was forever cleaning his leathers, helmet, boots – even his car keys. And, for some reason, he would not let people enter his motorhome. He blamed the team whenever he had a bad result and Virginio had had enough.

Ducati's other factory rider was Neil Hodgson, who lived just a few miles down the road from Blackburn in Burnley. It was amazing that two riders from such a small area of Lancashire were both riding in the World Superbike championship in the same season. He did really well to get a two-year deal, as all he'd ever really done was to qualify on the front row of a Grand Prix grid in Argentina, during his season in GPs the previous year with a private Yamaha team. He was capable of the odd fast lap but I think his manager, Roger Burnett, must have done a particularly good job in getting Ducati to take a gamble on him. I think he was a little bit out of his depth but I got on very well with him and, as the season wore on, I found that I was spending more and more time with the Ducati lads.

Virginio had already tentatively approached me halfway through the season, asking if I would think about a return for 1997. And he was desperate for an answer by the time we left Sugo. He didn't know that Neil Tuxworth had also asked to open negotiations after the round in Indonesia. But it wasn't a decision that I wanted to be rushed into. Whatever I decided for 1997, whether I stayed at Honda or returned to Ducati, it was probably going to be where I would end my career. That said, it was obvious where my heart was.

During that weekend in Japan, Virginio made his first official approach. 'I don't want a repeat of last year,' he said. 'If you don't want to ride for me, tell me now so that I can look for a new rider. You tell me how much money you want.' I gave him my demands there and then, which was a lot more than Ducati had ever paid me before.

Virginio was straight on the phone to Italy and he cornered me in the track's hotel toilet after the races. 'Carl, I need you to sign this, now,' he urged, thrusting a piece of paper in my direction. It was just a normal sheet of A4, which contained the most basic of hand written contracts:

I, Carl, Fogarty agree to ride for Ducati in 1997 for 'x' amount of pounds.

That was all it said. Virginio added, 'I have all these other riders like Slight and Gobert who want to ride for me, but they cannot ride a Ducati like you can.' He then pulled out a proposal from Aaron

Slight to Ducati. The money he was demanding was something like $800,000. That was about the same as me and I had already won two world titles on a Ducati. 'Sign for me now, Carl,' he pleaded. Although legally the document probably meant nothing, we both knew that neither of us would go back on our word.

I signed his piece of paper and Virginio ripped up Slight's proposal in front of me and threw it in the toilet bin! It had not even reached the bosses at Ducati.

It wasn't until I broke the news to Neil Tuxworth, on the way back from Japan, that I realised how badly Honda wanted me for another year. I had expected them to shrug it off because I had never felt that I was wanted. But Neil was absolutely devastated, and not just because we had worked well on a personal basis during the year. 'We have a new bike that will work better for you. The swinging arm would suit you more,' he said.

It also seemed clear that they wanted me a lot more than they wanted Slight. They even sent one of their main men, Mr Yoshishige Nomura, over to talk to me at the next round at Assen to try and persuade me to change my mind. It was too late. But, if Honda had shown that commitment to me during the season, it might have been a different story.

The Ducati agreement meant that I could concentrate on the rest of the season without the usual contract hassles. Fortunately, none of the other riders had stolen much of an advantage in Japan and, if I could manage a couple of wins at Assen, which was just about my favourite track, the title was still within reach.

First, though, Honda wanted me to put a stop to all the rumours surrounding my future. A press conference was called where I announced the Ducati deal and said, 'Now will people leave me alone and let me concentrate on winning the championship for Honda.'

The bruised rib was still causing me pain so I asked the track doctors in Holland to look at it again, as I was sure that it felt broken. Their diagnosis was the same – the rib was bruised and nothing else. During qualifying, the pain became intolerable so I insisted on an X-ray. Surprise, surprise, it was broken in two places. I went barmy. 'For the last two weeks I've tried to carry on as normal because you lot told me it wasn't broken,' I ranted. Injections took away most of the pain – in fact injections are all they seem to give you at the clinic, even for a cold.

Kocinski was faster than I was in one section, where I struggled to pull the bike over from the right and into the last left-hand corner. Having won the first race, I had a great battle with Kocinski in the second. He out-braked me entering the final chicane but ran wide. So I stuck it back up the inside of him, hooked it into first gear and beat him and Troy Corser over the line. It was the first time any Honda rider had won both races at a single round and the points difference between me and Slight, the championship leader, was now just 22 with two rounds remaining.

I have always attracted a large British following to Assen because it's only a short ferry ride over the Channel, and the Dutch town turned into one big English party. I had also decided to take the ferry home from Rotterdam to Hull on the Monday night and enjoy a few drinks with everyone else who was travelling back to England. I felt really rough anyway, because we'd had a skinful after I did the double. But the shooting pains in my chest were now unbearable. I went to lie down in the cabin that I was sharing with Neil Hodgson. After half an hour I was writhing in agony, dripping in sweat and suffering spasms. The weekend's painkillers had obviously worn off.

Luckily, Neil came back with a girl, who worked as one of the chefs for Honda. He'd obviously had a few drinks but was sober enough to notice that I wasn't feeling too bright. 'I'm in agony with this rib thing. Go and find the captain and get me some painkillers,' I pleaded. He went off with the girl and came back with some Aspirin, or something similar. I don't know whether he expected the pills to send me straight to sleep, but he went full steam ahead with his attempts to get the girl into his bunk. At least his drunken fumblings took my mind off my rib for a few minutes – until she decided she'd seen enough and left us to lick our respective wounds.

The injury had cleared by Albacete, where I needed to maintain some consistency and pull out another couple of wins to claw back a few more points. In both races I was running comfortably in second when the tyres lost grip and I dropped quickly back through the pack to finish in fifth and seventh. Corser won both races to take the championship lead. But my challenge was all but over, as I was now 45 points behind.

That round had summed up the whole year – two good wins at Assen had been followed by inconsistency at the very next round. Yet my season's results had been good enough for Honda to try one last attempt to wrestle me from Ducati's grasp. Neil pleaded with Michaela to try and get me to change my mind and offered around £750,000 for 1997, almost double what they paid me in 1996. As it happened, their bike was better the following year. And I'm convinced that I would have won the championship on a Honda if I had stayed for one more year.

It was perhaps fitting that I should finish the year off feeling terrible with a throat infection in Australia, where I missed a lot of practice. I managed to finish fourth in the first race but it wasn't enough to prevent Troy Corser from clinching the world title. I didn't even think that he was a worthy champion. He made hard work of an easy job. If I had not left Ducati, I would have walked the championship without any doubt. At three tracks where he won both races – Donington, Brno and Albacete – he was very good. He won seven races in total but was inconsistent and made a lot of mistakes.

After that first Phillip Island race there were only 10 points between me, Kocinski and Slight, in the battle for the runner-up slot. But, if I wasn't going to win, it didn't matter if I was second or fourth. I gave up in the second race and couldn't wait to get off the Honda and go round to the Ducati garage, to see if the bike still felt the same to sit on.

It was exactly the same. But a lot of things at Ducati had changed which were to affect my chances of winning back my title. And a few things were changing at Chapel's Farm in Tockholes . . .

CHAPTER THIRTEEN

Cramping my Style

It's unbelievable just how much fuss a simple tennis court can cause.

It was built shortly after we moved into Chapel's Farm. As far as I was concerned, I owned five acres of land and could do what I wanted with it. Call me naïve, but it never once occurred to me that we would need planning permission.

But I did call the council planner round when I decided to convert a corrugated iron garage back into stone and, at the same time, add around three feet to its height in order to build a loft. The garage was at the bottom of the drive, which ran by the side of the house and down into the fields. There had been a shed in its place before, so there was no need to obtain permission when the garage was actually built because it wasn't a new feature.

The planner who visited us was a bit of an idiot. It was obvious from the moment he set foot on our land that he was out to cause trouble and make a name for himself. He had a look at the garage but then pointed at the tennis court.

'Whose is that and how long has it been there?'

'It's mine and we built it a couple of years ago,' I replied. 'Nice, isn't it?'

'You can't just build a tennis court,' he said.

'What? It's my land. I can do what I want. The neighbours have never complained,' I argued.

'Mr Fogarty, this is greenbelt land. You need permission for these things,' he scoffed.

He then went to the stables and asked whether permission had been obtained to build them. It hadn't, of course. Apparently, they were outside the curtilage, the area around your house for which planning permission wasn't needed. He left, pleased to bits with his day's work.

Then the letters started arriving. First, we had to apply for permission from the Tockholes Parish Council. I couldn't understand why because it had to be referred to Blackburn Council eventually. It soon became clear that the stables wouldn't be a problem, and I didn't think the garage would be an issue. I had actually applied for permission to build a gym in the extra space, thinking they would have some sympathy with that because I was a sportsman.

But we had to find a way of making the tennis court blend in with the surroundings. We suggested planting conifers as a way of coming to a compromise. The first meeting of the Tockholes Parish Council accepted the stables, but rejected the garage alterations and the tennis court compromise. Their main objection was that, because the court was close to a cemetery, anyone in mourning might be upset by any grunts and groans from the court. I felt like telling them that we promised not to shag on it in future.

Then they said that raising the garage would affect the skyline. The bloody thing was surrounded by trees and was 30ft lower than the level of the house. How could an extra 3ft affect the skyline? What skyline? Who were these people? I had never met them and none of them had been to look at the house. If they had visited it, they would have seen that everything was nice and neat. It wasn't as though I was building a bloody great power station in the middle of a field.

Just a mile down the road a motorway extension was being built right next to the village. Yet this group of two-faced grumpy old farts were making stupid decisions that were affecting our lives. They had seemed quite happy to have me living there when they wanted me to open their village fete. There could only be one reason for their actions – jealousy.

The whole thing dragged on and developed into a bit of a shit fight. When it was eventually referred back to Blackburn Council some six months later, they laughed at Tockholes Parish Council and passed everything.

The funny thing was that, while all this was going on, we had decided that we wanted to move. Without wanting to sound big-headed, I had become a bit too big a personality for that house. It was not a private location as a couple of properties had been renovated either side of our house, and we also found that more and more passers-by were having a good nosey over the wall. But there was no way that I was going to put it up for sale until this dispute had been settled. That would have looked like I was conceding defeat. And, even if we had found the right house, we might have even stayed in Tockholes because we had become good friends with a few people. So I wasn't running away.

We made the most of our last few months at the house and, that summer, held our best ever party. The usual crowd of mates, mechanics, Jamie, Neil Hodgson and Slick all turned up on the hottest day of the year. We erected a marquee and brought in a chef to cook some chilli. The beer was flowing, the music blaring out.

Later in the evening, I nipped around the back of the tent for a piss and killed myself laughing when I saw two legs poking out from underneath a bush. It was, needless to say, Slick's arse that was going up and down on top of some girl that I didn't know, so I went to fetch Nick Goodison for a good look.

I didn't take long for the whole party to get rapidly out of control. People were being thrown in the pool and one girl's ankle was cut quite badly. There were around seven or eight people in the jacuzzi at one point – and let's just say there were no hands on view! Then, when I wandered inside, another girl was being entertained on the sofa by a couple of male guests. I couldn't believe what I was seeing – it was wild.

The following morning, Blackburn Shopping Centre staged a superbike day. I had to ride into the town centre under a police escort and I remember burping pure alcohol into my helmet, with a couple of coppers within easy smelling distance. I felt like shit.

Back at Ducati, I was interested in seeing if they had become more organised in my absence. This was, after all, Virginio's fourth year in charge and he was obviously learning all the time. Don't get me wrong, I liked the guy and he was good to work for. But there is a thin line between being laid back and disorganised. I was also kind of hoping that a year of John Kocinski's quirky habits might have rubbed off on the team.

There were some improvements. For instance, Virginio set up an extra testing session in December at Misano, where Slick was also re-united with his former colleagues. It was important for me to get back on their bike and for Ducati to get Slick back into the swing of things. But, when I rode the bike, it wasn't how I remembered a Ducati at all. It felt awful.

'This was how Kocinski had it set up,' I was told.

'Well, is there none of my old stuff left?' I asked.

Slick changed a few parts back, but it still felt difficult to ride. And it didn't help that I felt awful. The doctors put it down to eating too much hot pasta before riding round in the freezing cold.

On top of all this, there were a lot of changes happening at the highest level of the company, as the Castiglioni brothers were preparing to sell the Cagiva Group to current Ducati owners, the Texas Pacific Group. As a result, people like my old engine man, Ivo Bertonni, were no longer there. Still, this was an early stage in the preparations for the following year and those tests were on the old 1996 bikes and not the new 1997 model. So I thought nothing more of the bike until the next tests in Australia and America.

Neil Hodgson had remained as a factory rider and was my new team-mate. Over the previous couple of years we had become quite good friends, riding motocross near our homes and travelling to and from races together. But that is so different from working together on the same team, when you are with each other nearly every day, week in week out. There is also the professional rivalry to consider. These things put relationships under different strains and, although we didn't fall out, we didn't get on that well either.

We are two very different people. Neil is quite vain and just wants to look pretty, train and eat the right food. I'm completely the opposite. The long testing trips meant that we were in each other's pockets for long periods, and I couldn't wait to get away from him at the end. There was no hatred, I would just rather have my own space and do my own thing. And Neil was forever gassing. We shared one flight from Manchester to Heathrow with the Spice Girls. He claimed that one of them – the ugly one, Sporty Spice – smiled at him. But I didn't notice anything. I remember one of them acknowledging me, but they had no idea who Neil was.

Corser's championship-winning bike from 1996 seemed fine in Australia where I was the fastest rider, despite a massive crash on the first day when the throttle stuck open. At the next test at Laguna Seca, where I had struggled in the last two years, the bike also performed very well and felt much more like the 1995 bike. It didn't stop me having another two big crashes, though. For the first, something worked loose from the engine and locked the back wheel going up one of the hills. It threw me over the bars and I landed on my head.

This was the one and only time a bike has locked up on me. Later that afternoon I had a massive slide. The bike flipped over and threw me over the high side to land on my head once more. If it wasn't bad enough having to fly home from California, dazed, with mild concussion and a stiff neck, Neil was sat there talking me to death!

When the *new* bike was finally put through its paces at Monza, all three factory riders – me, Neil and Chili, who was in his own team – struggled to post good times. I even resorted to cutting through the chicanes, which were not coned off, to try to convince myself that I had done a couple of fast laps. The struggle continued at Phillip Island for the first round of the championship. I was running wide and the throttle was aggressive. But swapping and changing the bike made no difference. I couldn't work out how I had been fastest during the winter testing on the 1996 bike, but was now finding the 1997 one so difficult to ride at the same track. Everyone else who had been at the Australia test was matching their times, but I was around half a second slower. What was going on?

It threw down on race day and the circuit was as slippery as I've ever known. I thought, 'Steady away, here. There's going to be a lot of crashing. Just make sure you pick up some points.' As expected, the other riders dropped like flies. But Kocinski, who had swapped with me and moved to Honda, was a very fast rider in the wet. He won the race and I was second. In some ways that first round summed up the whole season. If the first few races had been held in the dry, Kocinski might not have finished halfway in the final standings. He could have lost his rag and he could have fallen out with his team.

Instead, because he was winning, everything was right with his world. In the dry of the second race, he was back down in seventh while I was second, until my tyre blew out and I had to settle for fourth. Kocinski has always seemed to rely on having the bike set up perfectly, whereas I can ride round any problems. Having said that, when he was riding in GPs for Cagiva in 1994, I thought he was the best rider in the world along with Doohan. Kocinski and the temperamental Scott Russell are probably the only two riders who have ever given me a run for my money in superbikes.

The fact that I trailed Kocinski by just one point after two rounds disguised the problems with my bike. For sure, it was more powerful but I couldn't put that power down on the track effectively enough. Rain also ruined the Misano round, where I picked up a couple of third places while Kocinski won one race and was second in the other. Donington was dry, and proved to be one track where the bike performed well. Slight overtook me with two laps remaining of the first race to steal victory, but I rode well in the second for my first win back on a Ducati. Again, Kocinski couldn't cope in the dry and was tenth and fifth – so I was leading the championship. The next round in Germany provided proof that the year was going to be tough.

When I was at Honda, Corser and Chili's Ducatis always appeared to have the legs on the others. But this year, in the first race at Hockenheim, the two Hondas were in a class of their own. A clutch problem early on meant that I lost their tow and there was no way back. But I managed to hang on in the second race. For some reason, Neil Hodgson was also up in the leading group. On this particular day and in this particular race, his bike was the fastest thing out there.

I clashed with Kocinski early in the race and knocked his fairing bracket off, which prompted him to cry and moan after the race that I should have been disqualified. Slight crashed out at a chicane and, when I had to run wide to avoid him, I lost the tow from Neil for a while. Coming out of the last chicane, though, I had managed to claw my way back into his slipstream and was in the perfect position to pull out alongside. I didn't have enough speed to go past Neil, but I beat him on the brakes at the next corner without any problem. I dived inside, edged him out and won the race. Unknown to me, he'd panicked, lost the plot and ran wide into the loose stuff and finished eighth.

Although I had stretched my championship lead to 24 points, I was in no mood for celebrations. Quite the opposite, in fact. The bike hadn't been good enough to win that race. I had stolen a victory. And, of course, I wasn't afraid to say so. 'I can tell you all now that I'm not going to win the world championship on this bike this year,' I said at the press conference.

So what if it earned me a bollocking from Ducati's top bosses? I wanted some action. I was riding on the edge, yet Neil Hodgson's bike was 10kmph faster. Typically, Virginio did nothing to sort out the problems.

The same issues cropped up again at Monza, Ducati's home track, where the Hondas blew me away. At the last corner, I out-braked them both but still finished third as they flew past me on the finishing straight. This was now really pissing me off. And Kocinski, who wasn't riding all that well at this point of the season, made even more ground in the second race when it rained yet again. I was my usual cautious self, finishing fourth after a good dice with Jamie Whitham on the Suzuki.

At Laguna Seca, Kocinski's home track, I was as sick as a dog after catching food poisoning from some seafood. On the morning of the race, I had a glucose drip in each arm for energy and popped loads of pills to try and stop the nausea. Considering I also hated the circuit, I rode really well to pull through from the third row of the grid and even overtake Kocinski. And, if I had just ridden a bit more aggressively, I wouldn't have let him slip back into the lead and clinch the win. It was a similar story in the second race, but this time Kocinski had cleared off by the time I made it up into second.

With two laps to go, the effect of the pills wore off and I spewed up in my helmet. Believe me, it's not a pleasant experience as there's not much room in a helmet to throw up. Back in the pit lane, the TV cameras zoomed in on the vomit dripping off my chinstrap. But I had done enough to keep my nose in front of Kocinski by four points, in what had already become a two-horse championship race.

It was at this point that Kocinski started to ride the Honda well. In contrast, my own bike seemed more and more like my Honda from 1996 and we were struggling to find the right tyres. Maybe all bikes were like this now. But there was one difference that I couldn't understand. I was unable to hang as far off the bike as usual to keep it tight into corners. It wasn't until later on in the season that I found out the bike had a new and bigger fuel tank, which was literally cramping my style. Amazingly, nobody had bothered to tell me about the change.

There was also added tension in the air in the usual intense build-up to the races at Brands. Kocinski had labelled the Ducati team 'the Mafia' and I was quoted as calling him a 'freak of nature'. I didn't like the way the guy treated and spoke to people, especially those who were looking after him. The stakes were raised after a couple of run-ins during practice, when he got in my way and was told exactly where to go.

So this was not the place to mess up and we concentrated really hard on setting the bike up properly. It ran well, although I was still struggling for grip, and I was leading the first race when Graeme Ritchie crashed out and was killed. The race had to be re-run and I made a poor start. I had made it back up to third but was really frustrated because Kocinski was holding everyone up. Maybe he still wasn't too confident in the dry. I needed really good drive down the hill to try and threaten him at the next corner.

So I leaned the bike right over – too far over – as I came out of the corner before the slope. The back end came right round and I had almost controlled the slide until the bike 'low sided' me. This is when, instead of flipping the rider off as happens in a high side, the front wheel is lost and the bike dumps you onto the track. I took Simon Crafar with me and Chili missed my hand by a millimetre. My world championship lead had been lost through impatience – and all in front of a crowd of around 80,000.

The situation reminded me of Donington in 1992, where I was desperate to repair the damage of my first race fall. It was threatening to rain, which also threatened my chances, but thankfully the race was started in the dry. I claimed the lead by passing Chili on the inside. He didn't lift his bike far enough up as I came underneath him and he crashed out when his bar touched the back of my bike. But, of course, while I was in the lead, it started to rain. The race was stopped and, after a short practice in the wet, was re-run over aggregate times with Kocinski four seconds behind me.

He was sure to beat me in the restarted wet race, but he needed to win by more than five seconds. A local wild card, Michael Rutter, cleared off into the lead and, sure enough, Kocinski caught me up and came past me. 'Right, I'm either going to crash out or stay with him,' I said to myself.

It was probably the best race I have run in the wet and I matched him wheel for wheel. The crowd were on their toes, as I lost the front and back wheels in some big slides. Unusually, I even managed to put my knee on the floor, which I very rarely do in the wet as I don't have enough speed or confidence in the corners to lean over that far. Other riders, with longer legs or different styles, do it far more often and tend to get better results in wet conditions. I hung on to Kocinski and crossed the line right behind him, and within four seconds of Rutter, to win the race overall. There were no handshakes on the rostrum!

Even though I had clawed the points' difference back to seven, I had missed out on the chance of two wins. The wet weather had partly been to blame and I could see that things were starting to go Kocinski's way. Riders sense these things. You somehow know when you are going to win a championship, and when you're not. He was improving all the time on the bike and already, I had big doubts about whether this was going to be my year. And that was despite another hard-earned win in Austria. I almost felt as though it was another stolen win, because I was riding on the edge to beat better bikes like the Hondas and Kawasakis – and getting away with it.

But the effort involved made victory taste even sweeter. Another win was on the cards when I led the second race until, you guessed it, spots of rain started to fall. I was caught in two minds: whether to push hard or exercise some caution. But, when Kocinski came past me, the red mist descended.

It was the only time in my racing career when I considered knocking another rider off his bike.

I knew that I could brake harder than he could at the next slow, hairpin corner. He also knew that and, at the next corner, he braked very late. I was later. I should have let go of the brakes and allowed my bike to run through and clip him as he was tipping it over and I was coming underneath. He would have gone down, and I probably wouldn't have fallen. But I hesitated for a fraction of a second and my hand went back on the brake. I ran into the back of him and took myself out while he wobbled, ran through the gravel and stayed on his bike.

It was my fault – I'll admit that. If I had just managed to clip into him, I don't think he would have tried to come back past because he didn't enjoy riding with me like that.

Danielle didn't agree that it was my fault. She had grown to dislike Kocinski as much as I did – and was furious. 'I hate that John Kocinski, he's a horrible man. I want him to crash,' she said. Mind you, she didn't like anyone who beat her daddy.

There was another collision in the next round at Assen – between me and a fly. With just four rounds remaining, and the points still tight, I needed a double win in Holland. I led the first race until the last lap, when Kocinski passed me. But I was confident that I was quicker than he was going into the chicane. 'No problem, just stay behind him,' I thought, just as a massive bluebottle splattered all over my black visor. These things can make a mess, trust me. I couldn't see a thing and there was no way that I would have been able to see the kerbs well enough to re-take him. Having complained all year about the bike, I knew that I would have been laughed out of Holland if I had told anyone – only Slick knew the truth. I couldn't believe it. My run of eight consecutive race wins at Assen was ended by a bloody fly!

In front of a huge British contingent, I was really down. But Frankie Chili, who was one of the many riders who didn't like Kocinski, came up to me and said, 'Come on! Pull yourself together and beat him in the next race.' I did just that. Slick was told to forget the other riders; I just wanted my board to show the gap between me and Kocinski. He had a bad start, but then the gap starting to come down: +6, +5, +4, +3, +3, +3. It stayed at that margin and Chili hung onto second place. Then it was Kocinski's turn to sulk as he refused to jump on the car that takes the top three around the circuit for a lap of honour. I was really pumped up because I now trailed him by just five points.

The next round was crucial and I told Virginio as much. 'If I don't win both races at Albacete, you can forget the championship,' I said. He seemed more concerned about whether the hospitality truck looked good and clean. I was pushing for changes, and pushing the bike to the limit. But I didn't seem to be getting much response from the team boss.

In Spain I pushed too hard. Yet again I led the race before Kocinski overtook me. There was nothing I could do about it. And, as I tried to stay with him, I lost the front end in a pathetic first gear crash at a slow corner that I was trying to take too quickly. In the second race I was knocked out into the gravel at the start but came back on in last place and had made it up to seventh when the same crash happened again. From being five points behind, I was now 55 points behind. The championship was over.

In my mind, there was no point even travelling to the two final rounds in Japan and Indonesia. I tried to make the most of my injuries from the second crash, hoping that my finger was broken so that I had a good excuse to pull out. I was pissed off, more with the team than myself. I've never been a good loser, especially when I didn't feel that it was my fault. If Davide Tardozzi had been my manager that year, he would have pushed harder to solve the problems with the bike – and I am sure that I would have won the championship.

Predictably Kocinski clinched the championship in the second race at Sugo, after I had finished 13th in the first race and crashed out again in the second, when the bike jumped out of gear. All of a sudden,

Aaron Slight had closed the gap to third place to seven points, so there was some incentive for Indonesia. Amazingly, considering the championship was already won, Kocinski prevented him from winning the first race and Slight refused to stand on the rostrum with his team-mate. I watched Kocinski walk into the café at lunchtime, where Slight was sat with a face like thunder. Neil Tuxworth had to calm the situation before Slight stormed off. It was hilarious to watch but, with one race of the season remaining, I was hanging onto second place by just three points. But all I had to do, if I could be bothered, was finish ahead of Slight.

He was never in the race. I had settled for third while Kocinski and Simon Crafar battled it out in front. Then, just as Crafar looked set for his first superbike win before joining GPs, Kocinski tried to pass him at a hideous angle and they both crashed out. I rode through to collect an easy win. It was typical that Kocinski's one bit of bad luck all year had happened in a race that didn't mean anything. Someone up there must have decided, 'You're not having this one as well, mate!' Crafar was slightly injured and, because I had done nothing to earn victory, I gave him the trophy. It wasn't that nice, anyway!

Predictably, I wasn't in the best of moods but we still went for a meal with Neil Hodgson, Jamie Whitham and Andrea. Following that, there was a big end-of-season party organised at the Hard Rock Cafe in Jakarta, which was about half an hour away in a minibus. Neil was testing the following morning and went back to the hotel after the meal. I also wanted to call it a night. Michaela persuaded me to go to the party, but I didn't even want a drink. Scott Russell was singing on stage and Jamie got up to play the drums. Andrea was on backing vocals, with Aaron Slight's wife, Megan, on the keyboard. They wanted us to join in, but I said, 'Just forget it!'

We left after around 10 minutes and Michaela was furious. So there was a blazing row at the hotel. Sometimes, especially after races, she still doesn't seem to understand that I'm not always in the mood for being around the same people that I've spent the last few days working with. She feels that I should make more of an effort, for her sake, after all the work that she has put in over a weekend.

The fact that I had heard some bad news while out in Indonesia hadn't helped my mood. Towards the end of the season, I had made up my mind that I wanted to stay with Ducati. But I didn't want to spend another season under Virginio. Francis and Patricia Batta, who ran the Alstare team for Fabrizio Pirovano in the 600cc Supersport championship, came up with what seemed like the perfect solution during the round at Assen. They approached me to ride a Ducati for them, as they wanted to get their Corona-sponsored team back into superbikes. It was one of the biggest outfits in the paddock and I had dealt with the Battas before, when they arranged my sponsorship from Diesel clothing. It was very tempting, as a lot of their mechanics had worked with me for Raymond Roche in 1993. What's more, Virginio knew about the approach and didn't seem too bothered. A deal was agreed at Assen, but not signed. It was just as well.

A respected journalist, Alan Cathcart, approached me at Sentul and said, 'Just a word in your ear, Carl. I don't think this Ducati thing with Alstare is going to come off.' The last thing I wanted was yet another long, drawn out wrangle. The Battas weren't in Indonesia so, when we got back to England, I made a few check calls and it was obvious that their plan wouldn't get off the ground. I think they had been unable to strike an agreement with Ducati, especially as Suzuki had come in with a better offer. Even though the Battas were trying to back-pedal out of the Ducati deal, they made one last attempt to try and tempt me to ride a Suzuki. But there was no point in taking that risk.

In any case, I had already signed a new deal with Ducati when it had looked like Corona would be making a substantial contribution. When the Alstare plan fell through, and with it the Corona sponsorship, Ducati were left with the problem of how they were going to afford my new salary of £700,000, which was higher than they were used to paying.

Hoss Elm, of Ducati importers, Moto Cinelli, came up with a plan. He was involved in producing a line of 200 Foggy replica bikes for sale at around £20,000 each to the general public. He suggested that the price should be increased by £1,000 so that the extra £200,000 generated could be used to make up the shortfall. His idea worked as the bikes were quickly sold to fans including Douglas Hall, the chairman of Newcastle United, former England striker Les Ferdinand and £11.5 million Lottery winner, Carl Crompton, who lives in Blackpool and has become a friend.

After all the official functions were out of the way, we went on holiday to Mauritius with Alan Pendry and his family. The island was beautiful but we had obviously picked the wrong hotel. It was supposed to be all-inclusive but, when we went to check out at the end of the stay, they wanted an extra £800. Apparently, only the local drinks had been free. I had a right go at the manager and threatened to go to the papers about some rats we had seen near the kitchen and a light that was hanging out of its socket in the swimming pool. He soon reduced our bill to £300.

It was also around this time that rumours started to fly around that I was considering a move into driving cars. Vauxhall had arranged a day's testing at Oulton for their Vauxhall Vectra and asked me to turn up as a publicity stunt, in return for a new car, which I still have. They allowed me out in a Vectra, the car used in their celebrity Vectra Challenge, and I span off about a hundred times.

Then I took John Cleland, the British Touring Car championship driver, out for a spin. He shit himself. After three laps he was shouting, 'Pull in, pull in – you're going too fast.' I hadn't even got warmed up!

There still seem to be a lot of people interested in offering me drives when I retire from bikes. Peugeot have contacted me but, again, they might just be interested in the publicity. I was also only recently offered a deal to drive touring cars in South Africa. It came out of the blue from David Wong, the Singapore businessman who I rode for in Malaysia. I told him that he couldn't afford me. 'We definitely can,' he said. 'We have a very big sponsor.' I have no big plans but, for sure, I would have a go – as long as it didn't cost any of my own money. But, as always, I would have to be in with a chance of winning. And you cannot learn to run before you can walk. However, if there is one sport that you can become good at fairly quickly, it must be car racing.

Back on two wheels, Virginio had already secured his two riders for 1998 in Troy Corser, back from a wasted year in GPs where Davide Tardozzi's Austrian-backed team had gone bust, and Pierfrancesco Chili. Tests were arranged for November, in Albacete and Jerez, to try and solve the year's problems. I had been calling for a return to the 1995 bike and my point was proved when the lap times on that bike were only marginally slower than the 1997 model. I was also the fastest of the three riders and still very much Ducati's number one.

So Ducati had four problems to solve: to stop me running wide at corners, to improve grip at the rear, to make the throttle less aggressive and, oh yes, to find me a team. In the meantime, I had a major problem of my own to solve – my knee was knackered . . .

CHAPTER FOURTEEN

In-fighting

The problems with my knee can probably be traced back to the Bologna Motor Show of 1996. This is a huge event and includes an annual Supermotard race. The bikes are like motocross with smaller wheels and races are run on dirt-covered roads. At this show the track is set up in the car park in front of a big grandstand, so that the fans can see their road racing heroes trying their hand at a different kind of racing.

It was my duty to show my face at Bologna and compete. At one corner, as I was losing control, I put my leg down to try and stay on the bike. But, as it came round on me, my knee twisted badly, swelled up and caused a lot of pain for a few days.

Nothing much was made of it at the time, because the season had just finished. But, when I tried to play squash or football during the winter, my knee kept collapsing. It was agony. In those days I was doing a lot of motocross riding at a place near Doncaster with Jamie Whitham, Neil Hodgson and Jamie Dobb, a British motocross champion. Whenever I put my foot down in the soft sand, the knee would pop out and twist back in again, making me feel sick.

During the 1997 season, I had a scan, which showed that the cruciate ligament – the ligament which holds the knee together at the back – had snapped in half and was hanging loosely down at the back of the knee socket. I had not realised that I had done so much damage because you don't actually need the cruciate to ride a motorbike. My knee was swelling up after races but not really affecting my performance, so any treatment was put on hold.

The operation, by a South African specialist called Peter Turner at the Droitwich Knee Clinic, had been arranged for after the tests in

Spain in early December. Using keyhole surgery, he took part of a hamstring to make a new ligament for my knee, so it's probably not surprising that I now have problems with my hamstrings whenever I sprint – which is not that often – without stretching properly! The whole thing was videoed – I still have a souvenir copy – and he found that the joint was a bit of a mess, especially after the breaks in that leg earlier in my career.

Within 12 hours of the operation they wanted me to put weight on the knee and to try and walk with the aid of crutches. I wasn't so sure this was a bright idea, but I was persuaded into giving it a go. Later on, I asked the surgeon, who had done a fantastic job, how long it would be before I could get back on a bike and he assured me it would only be a few weeks. He must have thought I was going to be riding a Harley-Davidson down the streets of Blackburn, not cramped up on a racing bike.

'Trust us Carl, it's already healing really well,' he said.

'I bloody well hope it is,' I replied anxiously. 'I have to go testing in February and be fit for the start of the season at the end of March.'

The recovery took much longer than I thought, despite receiving expert help from the former physio of Blackburn Rovers Football Club, Mike Pettigrew, who had nursed England football captain Alan Shearer back to fitness following a similar cruciate injury. He took me mountain biking to try and build up the knee and gave me a series of exercises to do when watching the telly, such as lifting up a book on my foot or crouching against the wall. I couldn't be bothered to be honest. I didn't mind the biking, and still enjoy it, but I just didn't have the willpower to do the other stuff without Mike there to push me. 'Have you been doing your exercises?' he would ask. I couldn't lie and his look made it clear that he knew he was wasting his time.

While I was worrying about whether I would be back in action in time for the new season, the press were in a flap over how Ducati would be able to accommodate three riders. It was no big deal to me, as the contract was signed and sealed. The answer came in a phone-call from Claudio Domenicali, who runs Ducati's racing operation. 'How would you feel if Davide Tardozzi came back to be your new boss?' he said. I had a big, beaming smile on my face when I replied, 'That's perfect.'

The team, which would be run just for me while Virginio managed Corser and Chili, was to be sponsored by Ducati Performance, which had just bought an after-sales parts company called Gia Co Moto. Ducati were a bit worried that I would feel isolated in my own team and went to great lengths to explain that all three riders would be treated equally. But this was ideal for me. After 1997, I wanted to be on my own. Working with Neil Hodgson had been a waste of time and it was no surprise when he was ditched. For much of the year, the very fact that I had a team-mate had been a distraction.

Typically for Ducati, there was a big last-minute rush to get everything in place for the big team launch in Italy and we had to cut short our holiday in Tenerife. And, even then, the signs weren't good that I was going to be fit as I could barely sit on the bike for the photos.

Before the tests I made the trip down to Buckingham Palace in February to collect my MBE. The honour was announced in the New Year's list, and although we had been informed in November, we were sworn to secrecy. It was very strict and we were made well aware that the award would not be granted if news leaked out. Only our parents knew anything about it and Michaela had a special MBE cake made for our New Year's Eve party.

I am obviously used to collecting awards, but this was totally different and I felt very honoured. So I even bought a new suit for the trip to London to meet the Queen! You're allowed three guests, so I chose Michaela, my dad and a very proud Danielle, as Claudia was a bit young. I was not nervous, but I was worried that I would cock the presentation up. While I was waiting in line, the guy told me what to do – walk up, stop, turn and bow. My memory is terrible for things like that and I was sure I would turn the wrong way, trip up, butt her and knock her flying! In the event I was dead cool and she asked me what kind of motorcycle racing I did.

'It's circuit racing at places like Donington and Brands Hatch,' I said.

'And do you enjoy it?' she asked.

'Only when I'm winning,' I whispered sheepishly.

She almost grinned – before pushing me away ready for the next one! Then you step back three paces, bow, turn and go.

As I walked back, the video caught me punching the air with relief at not having messed up. It was a great day, but it could be run a lot better. We had to wait in a room for hours without food or drink and then they had the nerve to charge us for the video and photographs!

Meanwhile, Mike had stepped up my exercise programme for the troublesome knee but, when I tried to climb on the bike in Malaysia, the leg still hurt like hell. It wasn't the knee itself, which was now really stable, but lower down in the leg. I was on a new bike, with a new team and a new team manager. That made me very conscious that I might be letting everybody down. But I had to get off the bike after 10 laps. 'I can't ride yet, my leg is just killing me,' I told them.

Davide took me to the *Clinica Mobile*, but they couldn't really help. By the time I got back to the hotel, I was starting to panic and wondering what on earth I was going to do, as we had another test in Australia straight afterwards and only a month or so before the start of the season.

A phone call to Mike eased my fears. 'That doesn't sound too bad,' he said. 'At least it's not your knee that's giving you grief. Try and go through the pain. It's probably because you've not been using your leg properly for such a long time.'

The next day it was still sore during the morning's tests but, after a brief rest and another session in the afternoon, it started to feel okay until the knee started to ache again. This turned out to be just natural tenderness and, after the three days in Australia, I was confident that I was ready to race.

But first I had to pass the medical. They used to be held every five years, which was a bit of a joke, but now the FIM are a bit stricter and have one every year. The World Superbike championship doctors and medical facilities are very good. But that hasn't stopped me cheating the system just about every year. The problem is that I've got a lazy left eye and can only see blurred images out of it. Opticians told me that to try and correct it might actually affect the way I ride a bike. Funnily enough, the brain might adjust differently to braking with two good eyes rather than one. The medical board used to ask you to look at something from six feet six inches with both eyes and I could pass that test easily. Now, when I come to do the new one, I read the letters with my good eye and try to get the doctor talking so that he doesn't see me slip the board down while I remember the next set. It's a lot easier than going through all the hassle of explaining the problem or having to wear contact lenses!

While I was confident in my knee, what didn't fill me with a lot of confidence was the performance of the bike in the final test at Misano. All the problems from the previous year appeared to be still there. This, coupled with the knee problems, meant that motivation was a big problem approaching the first race in Australia. Instead of wanting to prove everybody wrong after missing out on the championship in 1997, I was still feeling sorry for myself. I didn't feel ready for the long hard drag of another season and would have been happy with a top five finish in both races.

That's where Davide's management skills came in. Virginio would have left me alone and let me sort myself out. But Davide, who is a lot like me because he can't keep still for a minute, was forever on my case saying, 'We will win this championship, Carl. I only want one thing from you – the title!'

My initial reaction was, 'I really don't need this', before I realised how badly other people like Davide wanted me to win. It was obvious that his hands-on style was exactly what I needed, because I won the first race at Phillip Island.

The hardest part of the race was trying to keep the bike upright in horrendous gales and my face was bright red as the wind was very hot and dry. I would probably have won the second if I hadn't had to settle for third when my tyre blew. There was no one more shocked than I was to be leading the championship with Noriyuki Haga, a fast but unpredictable Japanese rider. The package was right for him early on, but he did not worry me. He was too erratic to be able to sustain that form.

From the heat of Australia, the next round, at Donington, was freezing, the coldest conditions in which I've ever raced. It meant a real stop-start qualifying and, before Superpole, I was only 14th fastest. This was the first year of Superpole, the controversial way of deciding the starting grid. Each rider has just one lap against the clock. The fastest lap secures pole position for the two races, and so on down the grid. Riders don't like it because, after two days of good qualifying times, anything can happen in that one-off lap which could leave you on the third or fourth row. But at Donington it should have been a godsend for me because it gave me the opportunity of improving on 14th. The top 16 riders set off in descending order of their final qualifying times, so I was third to go. It was a great lap, one that would have left me in the top six, until it started to snow and the whole Superpole was scrapped. That left me on the fourth row for the race and with a mountain to climb.

Although my set-up was poor for the first race, I came through the field to finish a disappointing seventh. After a couple of changes –

smaller brake discs and a different rear tyre – the bike felt a bit better in the second race and I had moved up into fourth place before the race was stopped after a couple of crashes. But this time I was on the front row for the restart and managed to cross the finishing line ahead of Corser and Haga.

I had salvaged something from a miserable weekend with an overall position of third for the second race, and 40,000 or so fans went barmy. I even captured the MCN headlines with something like 'Foggy's late, late show'. Even so, the inconsistency was starting to worry me. And it was to be the same for a lot of other riders all season. Edwards, Slight, Haga, and even Chili were all fast but inconsistent. Only Corser looked capable of stringing good results together, but he didn't win many races.

The track at Monza, our next port of call, is one of the fastest circuits and was sure to suit the Hondas. Realistically, the best I could hope for was two third-place finishes. Brake problems in the first race relegated me to sixth but, in the second, I managed to hold onto third going into the final lap when Slight's engine blew up, spewing oil everywhere. My visor was covered in the stuff but I managed to tear off a rip-off, the disposable plastic sheets that cover the visor. Corser was still hanging onto me, but I held the inside line entering the final corner. I braked as late as possible but he braked too late and ran off into the gravel. Second place was a real bonus.

Then, all thoughts of racing were put on hold for a week as we moved into our new house. It was upsetting leaving Chapel's Farm, which had been the first home that we had built together, almost from scratch. But we needed somewhere bigger and more secluded. So Chapel's Farm had been put up for sale in October the previous year and, while we had a few people looking round – including former Wimbledon striker, Dean Holdsworth, who had just been transferred to nearby Bolton Wanderers – there were no takers.

So, with the season approaching, we had decided to take it back off the market and got an architect to draw up plans to alter the back of the property. But, out of the blue, the estate agent rang to say that another couple was interested. They fell for the place, put in an offer and, as always, the estate agent had another property lined up for us. 'It's just what you are looking for – privacy, 10 acres of land and stunning views,' he said.

A viewing was booked straight away, but I had already arranged a

I'm ahead of team-mates Neil Hodgson and Pierfrancesco Chili during my 40th WSB win at Donington in 1997, my first race back on a Ducati after my year with Honda.

Aaron Slight, who has been one of my biggest rivals down the years, on and off the track.

Troy Corser and Akira Yanagawa show their dejection in the press conference after I easily won the second race at Misano in 1999.

Scott Russell was at his best during 1993 and 1994 but changed as a rider when I beat him to the world championship in 1994.

A difficult day at a difficult track, Laguna Seca, during a difficult season with Honda in 1996.

This picture sums up my season with Honda in 1996. You can see the bike yet again losing rear traction mid-corner and the rubber left on the track from the skid at Brands Hatch.

Neil Tuxworth is no doubt pestering me yet again, this time at Laguna Seca in 1995, to ride for Honda the following year.

lick helps me make some
st minute adjustments at
ssen in 1995, on the day I
inched my second World
uperbike title.

Deep in discussions with
Virginio Ferrari during testing
of the new Ducati 916 at Jerez in
1994. Giancarlo Falappa is
listening in the background.

Davide Tardozzi joins in the
celebrations for my fourth world
title at Hockenheim in 1999.

This picture appeared on the back page of *The Sun* as I correctly predicted the 2-0 score of the first qualifying game between England and Scotland for Euro 2000.

A fan from Burnley shows his loyalty with a tattoo of me in action across the whole of his back. The picture was taken at an event to celebrate my third world title in Blackburn.

I was persuaded to wear this dress on the catwalk of a charity auction in 1998, but it's not really my style!

Above: I try to feed Aaronetta, the Vietnamese pot-bellied pig outside our home in Tockholes.

Below: Before moving to Tockholes we stayed at my dad's house for four months. This was one of the rare moments when the Great Dane, Bridget, and the Chihuahua, Arai, were not causing trouble.

Above: Michaela joins me and Ducati boss Frederico Minoli on the podium at Hockenheim in 1999 to celebrate my fourth world title. Aaron Slight refused to take his position because he thought he had won the race.

Below: In action at Kyalami in 2000 before crashing out of the second race.

Concentrating on treating my injured shoulder, hurt during a fall in testing at Valencia, in a break during qualifying at Kyalami in the 2000 season.

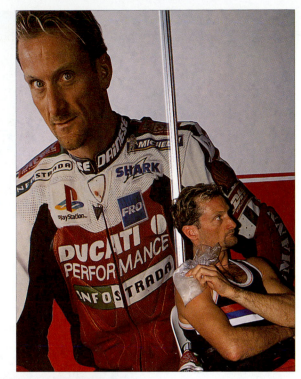

I enjoy a glass of champagne with Mick Doohan at the FIM prize giving in Rome after we won our respective world titles in 1994.

I take the mike at the surprise party Michaela organised for me after winning the world championship in 1998.

Those famous Foggy eyes.

Riding an enduro bike in the desert of Bahrain after being invited there by the country's crown prince. I'm not exactly setting a good example, without a helmet or any protective clothing, but I'm having a good time all the same.

cycle ride with Mike and was covered in mud when I met Michaela at the house just outside Mellor, a village on the other side of Blackburn. It didn't make much of a first impression. It was a bit old-fashioned inside because the house had become too big for the owners, a retired couple who only used one part of it. But Michaela loved it. When I visited for a second time, I realised there was scope to make a few alterations. Our offer of £350,000 was accepted before the first round in Australia and we moved in after Monza, the hottest week of the whole summer.

Michaela tried to insist that we should hire professional people for the move. 'There'll be things broken and smashed glass everywhere,' she nagged. But I stood firm because I love jobs like that. We hired a seven-and-a-half-ton truck and, with a trailer on the back of the jeep, moved everything from Tockholes to Mellor ourselves. On the way back to Chapel's Farm for the last load, I was explaining to my mate Howard that the speed cameras on the dual carriageway were never switched on when . . . 'Flash', the bastards got me. I was fined and docked three points for driving a truck at 65mph.

Apart from when I was caught in Scotland, the only other time I have been banned was for two weeks when I was doing 70mph in a 30mph zone in Bolton, a few years earlier. It was the best thing that could have happened to me because it meant I had a clean licence again. But the police were pathetic, hiding behind a bus shelter with a speed gun on a nice wide road with fields on one side and big detached houses on the other. Everyone gets caught there.

The traffic problems didn't end there. Having picked up the final truckload from Tockholes, I headed back to Mellor feeling a little nostalgic. Halfway down the road, our progress was blocked by a car that had rolled onto its roof on a sharp bend. A young girl was trapped but not badly injured. Four fire engines and four police cars turned up mob-handed and the road was blocked for more than an hour, with me impatiently wanting to get into my new home. It only needed a few blokes to roll it back onto its wheels.

When the emergency services turned up, including my cousin Chris who is a fireman, everyone was looking at me as if to say, 'What chaos have you caused here? You must have run her off the road!' 'It was nothing to do with me,' I laughed.

The girl was a fan, apparently, and was pretty chuffed when she found out that she had held up my house move. Michaela wasn't quite so chuffed when I finally turned up at our new home. 'Where the bloody hell have you been?' she snapped. What a welcome!

After a few hot days chopping down trees, starting work on the swimming pool and two extensions, not to mention lighting barbecues, it was back to the small matter of racing superbikes at Albacete. Corser was leading the championship but, already, there wasn't much information being swapped between the two Ducati teams. I had raced against Troy for a few years, but always found him a bit too cool and big-headed. He was the type to brag, 'I've been with this girl and that girl.' That didn't impress me, I just wasn't interested.

I was quicker than both Corser and Chili in practice but, halfway through Superpole, it started to rain. Stupidly, the last eight riders were forced to ride in the wet. Colin Edwards put his finger up to the organisers after his lap, to show his disgust. The whole thing should have been scrapped and the grid sorted out on qualifying times. I didn't know how hard to push and crashed out halfway round the warm-up lap, shaving a load of skin of my toes, almost down to the bone. There was even a small stone lodged in the skin, which had to be dug out and I still have the scars from that. It is one of the most niggling injuries you can have, as the foot never has a chance to heal properly when it's inside a shoe and sock. The first race was also rain-affected and, even for me in the wet, ninth was a bad result. I was pissed off and Davide was even less impressed. Things brightened up when the sun shone for the second race, and I won to pull the gap on Corser back to seven points.

The relief was short-lived. Germany's Nurburgring was the scene of my worst pair of single-day World Superbike results. I was 13th in both races – and it was partly down to bad luck. There was an unofficial practice day on the Wednesday before the races because this was a circuit new to the championship. I had a big crash and landed on my back and backside, when the back end of the bike let go and fired me over on an uphill curving section. At first, there didn't appear to be a problem and I walked away. But, while I was throwing the bike from side to side during qualifying on Saturday, my back just went.

I've always suffered slight problems with my back, but this time I was in absolute agony. And I've always had my doubts whether our race doctors were very good with back injuries. They tried to pull me round and twist the spine, when a couple of hours lying on a hard surface might have been better for it. Injections didn't make it much less painful and, come the rainy race day, when I also had to wear an uncomfortable bigger boot because of my toe injury, I really wanted to be back home in front of the fire.

And the reaction to my results was horrendous. When the crowd invaded the track one guy, who I assumed was English, gave me the wanker sign and another shrugged his shoulders as if to say, 'What's up with you?' Nobody had any idea the pain I was in. Everyone was quick to jump down my throat and the other riders loved it, especially when the press back home had their little digs. Apparently, it was disgraceful for a factory rider to finish so low down. If it had been any other rider, there wouldn't have been a mention. But with me, the expectations are higher.

My back was still hurting for the next round in Italy, so Davide tried to re-build my battered confidence. 'We just need some consistency. You might be sixth in the championship, but you are not many points behind,' he pointed out. Luckily, the other riders were also still struggling for form and the leader, Corser, hadn't even won a race. A third and fourth place in Misano was not spectacular, but did help to bring back a bit more of that much needed consistency.

Davide clearly still had faith in me because, during the Misano round, he approached me about an early deal for the following year.

'Look Davide. I think I'm going to quit,' I confessed. 'Unless I start feeling better and start winning regularly again, I'm going to stop at the end of this year.'

'Ok. We'll talk again after Laguna,' he replied.

The next round at Kyalami, in South Africa, another new venue, did little to improve my mood. The results were good, a couple of second places behind Chili. But it was now clear that the two Ducati teams weren't going to be able to work together. The first day of practice was riddled with problems. We expected to go slower in the altitude – but not ninth fastest. I was assured that there had been an oversight with the engine and that everything would be okay on the Saturday. But when I sent Slick round to find out what tyres Corser and Chili had been using, he reported back that they wouldn't give us any information.

There's always been some friction between Virginio and Davide. Virginio has always seen him as a rival to be Ducati's main man. But this was taking it too far. I was blazing mad and spat my dummy out of the pram. 'Right, we're not telling them a fucking thing from now on,' I fumed. Ironically, Chili saved his tyres better in the first race, although I was right up there with him. It was a similar story in the second. But, on the last lap, at the one point of the circuit where I knew I could take him, the low sun made a pass too risky because I couldn't see where I was going properly.

After racing most of the riders ended up in a restaurant called Montego Bay, where a 10-course meal cost around a fiver, due to the weakness of the South African currency. Jamie was back on the scene, riding a Suzuki, which meant that the night was always likely to be lively. Then Corser bought everyone a round of shots, and I don't normally drink shorts. That became the theme for the night and just about everyone was sick. Michaela spewed in our room and Jamie and Andrea were up all night honking their guts up. I didn't sleep well and, the following morning, all I wanted to do was sit round the pool before our evening flight.

Everyone else must have still been pissed because they decided to go on a tour of the area, organised by the Ducati importers based in Johannesburg. The roads to the local lion park were the most hideously bumpy I've ever been on. So, by the time we arrived there, I was desperate to be sick.

The security – or lack of it – at this place was unbelievable. In England, we would have electric fences and automatic gates for the cars. In South Africa, there was a guy with a stick, ready to shoo the lions back into the park! I could hardly stop the car and get out so I ended up sticking my head out of the window and spewing for England. Inside the car there were hysterics, outside the lions looked at me as if to say, 'What's this idiot doing here?'

We moved on from there to a rhino park, where I was sick again. In fact, it wasn't until I woke up in London after the flight home that I could keep any food down.

There was no time to return to Blackburn as the next round in California was the following week. We decided to spend a night in San Francisco and visited Alcatraz, where me and Jamie had our pictures taken behind bars. Michaela and Andrea thought it would have been a good idea to leave us there. They might as well have done for all the success I had at Laguna. I had a nightmare in qualifying and thought to myself, 'What the hell am I doing here? I can't even be bothered winning.' I had no motivation at all and, although I wasn't even interested about getting the best out of the bike, complained to

Davide. But he knew I was behaving like a spoilt child and told me so.

'You are wasting my time and the mechanics time,' he shouted. 'It's not the fucking bike, it's you. If you want to win, you will win. You know that you can win, but only you can sort yourself out.'

It was the first time anyone had spoken to me like that in racing. My dad might have said the odd thing in the past, but he was entitled to because he was my dad. It did the trick and pumped me up. From that moment on, we were far more consistent for the rest of the year.

I had come second in both races at Laguna in 1997 so I told the mechanics to set up the bike exactly as it had been the previous year. In the Sunday morning warm-up, I was a gnat's cock off the fastest time. The only problem now was to move up from the third row of the grid on one of the tightest tracks in the world, where it was notoriously difficult to pass. I managed to work my way up to fourth place, behind Corser and two Kawasakis ridden by Akira Yanagawa and Doug Chandler. There would have been no problem passing those two, until Chandler's bar snapped and he ran into Yanagawa at The Corkscrew, a twisty section with a steep downhill slope.

When I arrived it was like a scene from the Tom Cruise film, *Days of Thunder*, set at Daytona, where he drives into some fog. I couldn't see a thing for the dust and the debris, and just missed someone's wheel on the inside. Another rider crashed behind me but, suddenly, there was daylight again and I was in second place. But by the start of the next lap the red flags were out and the race was stopped.

For the restart I was on the second row of the grid, having been in fifth at the start of the lap before the crash. But it was obviously going to be one of those days for crashes. When it eventually got underway, a rider from the third row came through and clipped Aaron Slight, causing another big pile-up. Slight's ankle was badly injured and Piergiorgio Bontempi broke his arm. The organisers decided to scrap the first race and award half points. There was more bad luck in the second race. Having again reached third behind Corser and Haga from a third row start, my bike cut out and I was hit by Jamie Whitham. He stayed on his bike while I wobbled back to the pits and retired.

But the weekend had taught me a lot for the rest of the year. I left America 33 points behind Corser, with four rounds remaining. I would have to pull my finger out at Brands, Austria and Assen if I was to have a chance of the title. Davide's words were still ringing in my ears and I was determined not to make any more mistakes with the set-up. The only problem was that because the championship was so open, four or five other riders were thinking exactly the same thing.

To some extent, I was robbed of the chance to set the bike up perfectly at Brands through the heaviest rain I've ever seen in Britain, from Saturday night until the early hours of race day. The garages were flooded and the rain left a covering of sandy dirt on the track. It meant that all the hard work we had put into tyre choice during practice went out the window. I rode well to finish fourth but there was no way I could challenge the first three, the two Hondas and Scott Russell, who had all chosen the same tyre – a different one to the Ducatis. We obviously followed their example for the second race and it made a big difference. But, by the time I made it into second place, Corser had a three second lead. My attempt to pull that back was probably my best piece of riding of the whole year.

The problem that had caused me to lose points at Donington, Monza and Kyalami had returned. The rear wheel was chattering and coming round on me, but only at certain corners. It was horrendous at Brands and I had to ride round the problem to stand any chance of catching Corser. So, just as I tipped the bike into the corners, I opened the gas in an attempt to keep the back wheel down on the Tarmac and limit the chattering.

Jamie was behind me in third and could see exactly what I was doing for the best part of 22 laps out of the 25. It was not enough to win, but the massive 82,000 crowd really appreciated the effort. They loved it even more when I promised to be back the following year because it was the first time, in a trackside interview over the public address, that I had publicly stated that I wouldn't be retiring. I had never said that I wouldn't be racing. But I hadn't said that I would be and the press built up that uncertainty and speculated that it would be my last race there.

My adrenaline was flowing and I celebrated like I had won. First my helmet came off, hurled into row Z of the grandstand. Then I threw my gloves and boots into the stands and was left wandering around in my white socks, which stood out a mile.

Later that evening I was wearing even less. Every year the track's Thistle Hotel stages a charity bash which most of the riders attend. I wasn't really up for it and was having a few quiet drinks at the bar when the announcer shouted, 'Come on, Foggy, come and join us.'

Jamie Whitham, Scott Russell, Aaron Slight, Colin Edwards and Troy Corser had already been dragged up onto the stage. None of us knew what was happening, until one of the organisers threw us some hats and the *Full Monty* music started. The others were happy to strip down to their strides and flash their backsides. But me and Jamie went the whole hog and threw the hats away as well in full view of the audience, before turning round quickly and putting our underpants back on. We weren't the only ones flashing as cameras had started clicking all round the room. I thought, 'Oh no! Where are these photos going to appear tomorrow?'

It wasn't until everything had died down the next day that I started to feel a bit angry about the races. I had done enough to win them both, only to be let down by inconsistency with the bike or tyres yet again. It sounds like more excuses but, up to this point, there had only been two races where the bike had been spot on and when I didn't have other problems like injuries. Those were my two wins in Australia and Albacete. But Davide said, 'You can still win this thing, you know. Corser might have some bad luck and there are a lot of guys around who are capable of beating him.'

Not everyone shared Davide's confidence that I could pull back the 30 points on Corser over three rounds. But I had kept my self-belief and the next two rounds were the key. I needed to beat Corser in both Austrian races, as well as the two at Assen.

To add to the tension within the Ducati camp, there were no clear signals about what was going to happen for the following year. Davide thought he would be running the team and wanted me and Corser as his riders. But even he wasn't sure what was going on. All three riders were in the dark and Virginio also wanted to know where he stood. Ducati were trying to delay the decision until after the Assen round. I couldn't wait that long so I spoke to Claudio Domenicali at the A1 Ring. He was hardly reassuring. 'If you have another offer from another team, all I can say is take it,' he began. 'We are not sure what will happen next year. You have not had a brilliant year, Corser has not been fast and Chili has been inconsistent.'

Bloody hell, talk about telling you straight.

For the first time I realised that there was no loyalty in racing. The Battas had approached me again to join the Alstare Suzuki team and, although I didn't want to leave Ducati, it was tempting to play them off against each other. There have been times when I have planted stories in the motorcycle press, probably more than other riders. I don't know whether it worked, but it couldn't have done me a lot of harm to have Ducati wondering if Suzuki had made me a bigger offer! I've never been dishonest, but answering press questions with a cryptic smile can be just as effective.

Corser was also claiming that the whole situation was distracting him, although Chili didn't seem too bothered. Maybe, being Italian, he knew that he would be looked after. And the Austrian races gave us even more reason to believe that he was getting preferential treatment. Chili's bike was miles quicker than our bikes and, in the first race, he passed me at the second last corner to claim second place behind Slight. But, while my tyres were destroyed, his were like new.

In the second race, after I had altered the suspension, Slight got by on the last lap to leave me in second. I had closed the gap from 34 points to 19, but the other two contenders, Slight and Chili, had also made ground on Corser, who was blazing mad that his bike was also so much slower than Chili's. I sympathised with him. I didn't trust Virginio and I didn't trust Franco Farne, Chili's engine guy – who also worked in the factory. My suspicion was that he always provided Chili with the best engine.

The in-fighting at Ducati seemed heaven sent for Slight, who could keep chipping away while we took points off each other. And I knew that, if I didn't win at Assen, I wouldn't win the title. Sure enough I led the first race but couldn't shake Chili off my back. On the last lap he pulled out of my slipstream, almost before we got onto the straight. It was all too easy for him. But I felt as though I could get him back until I made a mistake at The Kinks, before the final chicane, and lost the tow. Again my tyre was destroyed and Chili's was like new. I was furious. On the podium Chili was trying to say, 'Don't be like that, someone has got to win.' I felt like telling him to 'Fuck off'.

At the press conference I said, 'I have to go out in front because no one else knows how to lead a race around this track, so everyone follows me.' I was annoyed that I had done all the hard work only for Chili to breeze past.

By the time the second race started, I was still burning mad under my helmet. The red mist was down again. 'There is no way that I am going to lose this race,' I said to myself. 'And I have to get someone between me and Corser.' It was the same story in the second race when me and Chili cleared off in front. I had to stop a repeat performance of the first race because his bike was definitely quicker. So this time, as soon as we came out of The Kinks on the final lap, I shot over to the left-hand side to stop him getting anywhere near my slipstream. At the next left corner he was coming up on the outside but I just let my bike run wide, pushing him right out, and we almost collided. He had no choice but to back off. I had to brake hard to make the next tight right-hander but, because he had eased off, he was not there on the inside, as expected. I was into the straight first.

'Yes, this is mine,' I thought, as I glanced back to check where he was. In fact, I was so concerned about where Chili was that I lost it in the final two corners. At one point I was in second gear, instead of my usual third, and riding erratically in a desperate bid to keep him behind. Chili seized his chance, came past me again but I was confident I could beat him on the brakes when we entered the final chicane. In fact, I was so late on the brakes that my back end was squirming round. And I even banged it into first to slow the bike right up so that I could get into the chicane first. Chili tried to come back on the outside but, having let go of the brakes, he put them on again and lost the front end. I had no idea that he had crashed, flicked my bike to the left, banged it into second gear and the race was mine.

When I looked back, punching and kicking the air, I couldn't see him. He must have been so pissed off at coming second that he shut off his engine immediately, I thought. The 20,000 Brits that had come across on the ferry went mental and invaded the track. I grabbed an English flag to carry round.

It has to be English because I'm not riding for Scotland, Wales or Northern Ireland. I have nothing against those countries but I'm an Englishman and it annoys me that more English sportsmen don't insist on carrying the Cross of St George instead of the Union Jack. Okay, Michaela wore a Union Jack dress at Brands Hatch the previous year, but that was only because we couldn't find one with the English flag design. We even thought about having one made specially. But, because Geri Halliwell had made them popular, it was easier to get your hands on the one she wore. It really caught on and even the blokes were wearing them at Assen!

As I entered the pit lane, I could see Chili marching towards me, pointing angrily. It was only then that I realised he must have crashed. I had barely come to a stop when he threw a punch at me, which glanced off my visor. 'What the fuck are you doing? I just passed you on the inside,' I yelled at him as everyone rushed over to pull him away. He was pointing in the direction of the corner at which I forced him to run wide.

As far as I'm concerned, it was nothing to do with that incident. The stupid idiot fell off at the last corner and blew his world championship hopes. He needed to blame somebody else. What did he expect, anyway? On the last lap of any race, you always weave about to stop someone coming past. But he wouldn't leave it alone and all hell was breaking loose, so I decided to wind him up even more by filling the pit lane with smoke from a burn-out and giving him the finger. Davide grabbed me before I lost control and told me to walk away. 'This is what we want to happen,' he said. 'It is looking bad on him and good on us if we ignore him.' When someone told me that I was now only six points behind Corser and five and a half behind Slight, I was even more pumped up.

Things had only just started to calm down by the time of the press conference. Slight had already come up to me and asked, 'What's Chili's problem? It was a clean move.' But Virginio had encouraged Chili to stir it all up again.

Chili turned up, halfway through the conference, wearing a tatty blue dressing gown and looking like he had just been dragged through a hedge backwards. It was a long way from the classic stylish Italian look. He sat on the front row and was staring daggers while I told everyone, 'Yes, I just passed him on the inside – a nice clean move to win the race.'

The interviewer then asked, 'Any more questions, ladies and gentlemen?' at which point Chili stood up and said, 'Yes, I have something to say. I would just like to say that what this man, Carl Fogarty, has done here today was a disgrace.' I had heard enough. I stood up and started to walk out, saying, 'Sorry, guys. I'm not staying to listen to this shit.' I had to walk past him to leave the tent and it all kicked off again with people piling in from all angles to separate us. It was all handbags at 30 paces but I was still blazing mad.

So I tried to forget it all by getting pissed out of my head while Jamie's band, The Po Boys, played in the tent at Assen. I managed to block it out, but there was no way this was just going to be forgotten by Ducati.

Their top brass were soon involved and heard Virginio's side of the story, as well as our version. I felt a bit left out of it all back in Blackburn, because Chili was in the factory every day, crying his eyes out. 'I didn't do anything. It was all Carl, he's so dangerous,' he whined. He was also quoted as saying that he would try to knock me off in Japan. Fortunately, Ducati saw sense and it all backfired on the other team. Chili lost his job and Virginio lost control of the team. That might have happened in any case, but they didn't do themselves any favours.

I think Ducati had always felt that they were banging their heads against a brick wall when they tried to get information from Virginio. He was a nice enough guy, but always disorganised. We would often nearly miss flights because he had left things until the last minute. Instead of looking after the important things, he would spend hours making sure that the stickers were in line on the bike. He was weird like that and it was interesting to see how he handled Anthony Gobert in the Bimota team in the 2000 season.

I also had a really good relationship with Chili, up until that season anyway. He has since ridden for the Corona Suzuki team and tries to be a kind of father figure to the riders, speaking up on their behalf on safety matters, money and things like that. In short, he's a typically temperamental and fiery Italian who has fallen out with a lot of sponsors and teams. Even at the start of 1998 we got on well, probably until he became a title rival at Austria – and on a quicker bike. We have buried the hatchet since then but I now keep him at arm's length. It's never a good thing to get too close to another rider, as you need to keep that competitive edge.

And I needed that edge more than ever at Sugo. The trouble was, I also needed to rest and the tension leading up to the final round was affecting my sleep. I had been seeing an osteopath in Blackburn called David Gutteridge because the crash at the Nurburgring had aggravated problems that I had been having with my back. He had already helped me to sleep in the past by telling me there was no point in lying on a hard mattress. This time he suggested I try acupuncture, so I gave it a go although I told him, 'This ain't going to work' after he stuck a load of needles in me. 'Just have a rest on there,' he told me as he left the room. When he came back in, I was still wide awake!

The tension was not being caused by contracts because, by the time we got to Japan, I had been told by Ducati that I would be riding for them the following season, with Corser as my team-mate and Davide as team boss. Although Troy was leading the championship, I didn't see him as the main threat. He had been unconvincing all year and I had beaten him in the previous four races. A lot of people were tipping Slight, mainly because the Honda was on home ground. I knew that all I had to do was concentrate and work hard on the set-up because I was in the best form.

But, after the first half-hour, the three fastest riders were Corser, Slight, Fogarty – in that order. It didn't bother me, though, because Corser always went well in practice but couldn't race. Slight was the one to keep an eye on. The rest of my practice went smoothly and I was confident with the bike and tyre choice. I qualified from Superpole in fifth, which wasn't bad considering there were a few quick local riders. Slight was left with a mountain to climb after only making the third row because starting had always been a problem for him.

After a good night's sleep I was quietly confident but keeping myself to myself. I posted a good time on old tyres in warm-up and then heard, just a few minutes later, that Corser had crashed out. I thought he might have winded himself, at worst. It soon became clear that it was much worse than that. The news from the hospital was that he had damaged his spleen and, luckily, the nearest hospital had the specialist equipment required for the surgery.

Suddenly, with Slight on the third row, the pressure was back on me and I lost all my earlier control and started to fall apart. In the same warm-up session a slow Japanese rider crashed in front of me and I literally ran over his head. Luckily he was okay but it really freaked me out. I became very emotional and, when I heard the 'It's Coming Home' song by the Lightning Seeds, which was playing on the CD in the garage, I started to lose it.

Michaela noticed straight away and went to fetch Jamie, who probably understood me as well as anybody.

'What's up with you?' he asked. 'All you've got to do is keep it together and you've won this.'

'I've run over a guy's head in warm-up,' I blubbered.

'Come on! This isn't like you. You're tougher than this. The only reason you are in this situation is because you are so tough,' he urged.

His words seemed to settle me down but I was still pumped up. As soon as the lights went to green, the tyre gripped hard and I was off to a good start, trailing Haga who was pulling away on his home track. When he crashed out, I was leading and my board told me that Slight was back in fifth. I knew that I needed to break the back of the points difference in this race.

A couple of Japs on Suzukis, Keiichi Kitagawa and Akira Ryo, came past me as my back tyre started to lose grip. 'I can't keep letting these guys come past or the points difference is going to be nothing,' I thought. I dug in deep and managed to hold off Yanagawa to clinch third place.

Slight finished in seventh behind Neil Hodgson and squared up to him on the cooling down lap. He accused Neil of brown-nosing and deliberately trying to help me, forgetting that Neil was still riding for a contract for the following year. Slight had also wound up Neil by confronting him on the second row of the grid before the race and saying, 'If you see my wheel, mate, give me a bit of room.' Neil was really pissed off that somebody he didn't particularly like had asked him to help stop another Englishman winning.

Even if Jamie Whitham was in front of me, I would never dream of asking another rider to do something like that. It probably made Neil doubly determined not to let him pass. And, suddenly, I was leading the championship by two points. All I had to do was finish in front of Slight in the final race of the year.

The wait before the next race was unbearable and I started to lose the plot again. After such an up and down year through injuries, lack of motivation, breakdowns, team fighting and what have you, it was just the same as in 1994. It was all down to the last race. Haga nearly knocked me off at the first corner, which wound me up, and I was pushing hard in second place. The signals told me 'Slight: p4, +1'. He was two places back but only a second behind. Soon those signals turned to 'P5, +2', then 'P5, +3'. I felt comfortable in second place and was closing in on Haga. My tyres were going off, but I felt strong enough to ride round any problem.

But with 10 laps to go the bike started vibrating and juddering like never before. It felt like a chunk had come out of the tyre. 'Please don't do this to me. Not now,' I pleaded. But, still, all I had to do was keep an eye on Slight. And he had lost the plot and was quite a way back. I have never seen the pressure get to anyone like it got to him. So I could afford to slow down and dropped back to fourth. And all the time I was shitting myself – praying that the tyre would not blow at any second.

I accelerated out of the last chicane, changed up to third and thought 'Yes!' Even if the tyre blew, I could have pulled the clutch in and freewheeled over the line. The title was mine.

It felt even more emotional than in 1994. All I could do was come to a stop and slump over the bike and cry my eyes out. I just wanted to be on my own. A couple of British fans came up, including a lad called Josh from British Airways who sometimes gets me an upgrade from business class to first class. They draped a flag over me and started to pat me but I was hardly aware that they were there. I just rode off and left the flag there. Back at pit-lane the priority was to find Michaela again.

The tears hadn't stopped from the moment I passed that chequered flag. To win this championship, after so many problems throughout the season, felt 10 times better than in 1995. People had said I would never be world champion again after 1997. How wrong they were.

CHAPTER FIFTEEN

Recognition

That third world title sparked my popularity explosion. There were about a hundred fans waiting for us back at Manchester Airport, plus a pack of journalists. It was all very flattering but we had been up until 5am the previous morning in a karaoke bar in Sendai and didn't have any chance to sleep before the coach picked us up to take us to the airport 45 minutes later. I was knackered but that was just the start of a hectic few days of interviews and celebrations.

I was invited to Old Trafford to watch Manchester United a few times, as a guest of the chairman Martin Edwards, who is a nice guy. But that didn't go down well with one person in particular. Before one game, David Beckham's wife, Victoria, or Posh Spice as she is better known, was giving Michaela the evil eye throughout the pre-match meal and during the interval. Even I noticed it, before Michaela said anything, and I don't usually pick up on these things. 'Look, she's staring at you again,' I kept telling her.

I can only think that Posh Spice, who was pregnant, was jealous because Michaela is better looking. Or maybe she didn't like us taking her place at the chairman's table. It made Michaela feel really uncomfortable. Posh Spice still kept up the staring match when Michaela was in the toilets, with all her mates to back her up. Michaela almost turned on her and asked, 'What the hell are you looking at?' But, because we were guests and because Beckham is such a big name at Old Trafford, she didn't make a fuss. Most of the guests there are very friendly. Michaela met Ulrika Jonssen at one game and they got on like a house on fire.

It was only just beginning to dawn on me that all the other sporting stars knew who I was. If I walked past Roy Keane or Ryan Giggs in

229

the corridor they would say, 'All right, Foggy!' Michael Owen is a big fan and nominated me as his most successful sportsman of the 1990s in the magazine *Total Sport*. I was actually chosen as their Sportsman of the Year in the last ever issue of the magazine at the end of 1999.

The likes of Ian Wright, Jamie Redknapp and Les Ferdinand are all really friendly. But it's funny that, living in Blackburn, I didn't bump into Blackburn Rovers players that often. I know and like Kevin Gallacher, who moved to Newcastle, as his kids go to the same school as mine. But I found Chris Sutton a bit rude. He would actually go out of his way to look the other way if he saw me at places like Blackburn's main nightclub, Utopia. It didn't bother me because I don't rate him as a footballer, certainly not worth £10 million anyway.

At another star-studded event, a charity fashion show staged by a designer clothes shop, Sunday Best, I stole the show. We were sat on the same table as Manchester United football player Phil Neville, the actor who played Billy Corkhill in *Brookside*, John McArdle, and the actress Jane Horrocks. On another table there was a hairdresser from Rawtenstall, called Freddie Cunliffe, who used to cut Michaela's hair. I was auctioning off some clothes with Steve Berry from *Top Gear* and Penny Smith from *GMTV*.

One of the main items of the night was a long dress, but there were no takers. Freddie said he would buy it for £200, as long as I modelled it. I told him there was no deal unless he coughed up £500. I knew I would get the price. Sure enough, Freddie stumped up and I had to go backstage to change. The place erupted when I appeared from behind the curtain. The next morning, pictures of me on the catwalk appeared in the *Daily Star*, and I never lived it down.

Sadly, I would be lying if I said that was my only time in women's clothing. I'm no David Beckham – I don't go around wearing Michaela's knickers, or anything like that. But there was one time when I got caught out. Michaela had ordered a designer bikini and left it lying in the bedroom. I stumbled across it and knew she was alone downstairs. For a laugh, I tried it on and wandered into the kitchen to surprise Michaela. But, by then, one of her friends had popped round for a chat. I'm not sure who was more embarrassed, me or Michaela!

The publicity surrounding that third world title meant that it was increasingly difficult to go out and relax in public. Utopia wasn't too bad because there is a VIP room, where you're not bothered too much.

But that isn't really my scene. Now I'm a lot happier having a few friends round to our house. At least, I can be guaranteed a bit of peace and quiet there.

In pubs it's virtually impossible to escape some kind of hassle. During one evening in Preston, when I was out with a few mates, including Howard Rigby, one idiot came up and slurred, 'Come over and meet my wife.'

'I'm okay here, thanks. I'm talking to my friends, but if you want to bring her over to say hello, then that's fine,' I replied.

'No, no,' he insisted, 'Come over to our table and I'll buy you a drink.'

'No, honestly, I'm fine here.'

Ten minutes later his wife turned up and growled, 'You are a fucking ignorant bastard. I'm going to tell my son to take his photographs of you in his bedroom down when I get home. And you,' she said, turning to Howard, who hadn't said a word, 'you're a right dickhead, 'n all.' I really don't need that.

It has now got to the stage where I feel like I've got something sticking out of my head whenever I leave the house. We took the kids and some of their friends, plus Slick, for a day out in Blackpool recently but I couldn't walk 10 yards without someone wanting an autograph. One of the Golden Mile stalls was selling big fuzzy wigs so I bought a blue one as a disguise. Surely, with my Oakley shades as well, nobody would be able to recognise me. I was kidding myself . . . The first person to walk past stared straight at me. I thought it was because I looked like an idiot until he shouted, 'Oi! That's Carl Fogarty!' I grabbed my wig, threw it on the floor and carried on walking while everyone else was in hysterics. You just can't win. It's great to have the size of following that I have attracted, but there are down sides.

I've been lucky enough to keep a close set of friends over the years and Michaela rounded most of them up for a surprise party just before Christmas in 1998. I knew that something had been organised, but I had no idea how much effort she had put into arranging the night at a hotel down the road called Mytton Fold.

The first clue as to the scale of it all was when a limousine parked up at the bottom of our drive. It was so long that it could hardly get round some of the bends near our house. I was met by a sea of faces that I hadn't seen for ages and everyone clapped me into the room. She had tracked down people like Taste, who I used to work with at

Holden's, and John Gibbons, my former mechanic. There were also a lot of television screens and a cameraman from Sky Sports. At first I thought it was being televised live, but it was only being transmitted throughout the hotel.

I was led into the hall, where a stage had been set up and Sky commentator Keith Huewen introduced a spoof *This Is Your Life*. Michaela, and my mum and dad were called up, followed by Jamie Whitham, then Neil Tuxworth. Then they started talking about Davide. 'No, he can't be here,' I thought as, sure enough, he walked in. Michaela had flown him over from Italy and he had just that second arrived.

At the end Keith presented me with the big red book, which contained a few cuttings that my mum had got together, plus a porno mag which said 'This Is Your Wife'. Jamie's band provided the music and Michaela sang a version of Blondie's *Sunday Girl*. She repeated it at the end of the evening, with me on backing vocals. It was a great night.

After Christmas we went on holiday to Disneyland, Florida as a break before the start of the 1999 season. It was a nightmare – and cold. After two days I wanted to come home. All we seemed to do was walk around, queue up for a ride, then walk to another and queue up again. Even the kids were a bit fed up. I would rather have been on a beach somewhere nice and hot.

Then it was time to start focusing on racing again. My contract had been sorted out within a matter of days of arriving home from Japan. The title win certainly helped, but without the fallback of their income from the replica bikes, I didn't want to make ridiculous demands of Ducati. In fact, I agreed to take a pay cut but with a very good bonus package built in depending on race wins. And my incentive to win another world title was very good. I might well have been able to earn more money elsewhere. But that was never a consideration. At that stage of my career there was no point undoing all the work I had put in with Ducati over the previous couple of years.

If I was in racing just for the money then it might have been an option, although it probably would have taken double Ducati's offer to tempt me away. But all I've ever been bothered about was winning and I didn't want to break up a winning team. If I improved, Davide improved and the rest of the team improved, then the bike would surely be that little bit better and we would walk 1999. When I signed,

232

Ducati were still considering Luca Cadalora as their second rider. Within a month, though, it was announced that Corser would stay. I was glad to have a team-mate again and realised that it had been a mistake to go it alone the previous year. It would have been better to have other people to share information with, especially on the new circuits. And when we hit tyre problems it would have been better to have another person testing different tyres.

All in all, my batteries had been recharged. Motivation was not a problem. In fact, it felt like the start of 1995 all over again. There were still doubters who thought I had been lucky the previous year, but that didn't alter the fact that I had the number one plate back. And I was ready to ram it down their throats that I was the best. The early signs were good. At the first test, in Kyalami, I was fastest on all three days and I broke the lap record. It was such a contrast to the testing and qualifying problems that had plagued us the previous year. And the confidence that I built up made me concentrate even harder. We were quickest again in the Phillip Island test and continued to work well together in the final test of that year's new 996 bike at Misano.

Throughout testing, I had been concentrating on the Superpole format of one fast lap, because the highest I had qualified all year in 1998 was fourth. At the first round, back in Kyalami, I was just pipped by Troy into second place. But the races were the easiest two wins I have ever collected. I controlled both from start to finish and was even pulling away when I was slowing down. The second race was my 50th career win while the first provided a good omen. In my previous three championship-winning years, I had won the first race of each season. I left South Africa thinking, 'Bloody hell. That was easy. This is like 1995 all over again.'

It was also like 1998 all over again that evening, as 10 of us crammed into one car trying to find a South African nightclub. Slick and Nori-yuki Haga were crammed into the boot, Haga jabbering away in Japanese and Slick drowning him out in pretend Japanese. It was one of the funniest things I have ever heard.

We never found the club and ended up back at the hotel pool where Michaela was messing around with Neil Tuxworth, nibbling his nipples as he loves that kind of thing. But he didn't enjoy it when Michaela and Troy's girlfriend Sam bit too hard and he had some explaining to do when he got back home to his girlfriend with a sore nipple. We sneaked off to bed after throwing him in the pool and missed all the commotion when Slick was accused of setting off all the fire extinguishers in and around his room. He got bollocked as usual but it turned out to be some of the Honda mechanics.

After a perfect start to the championship the season became a lot harder from those races onwards. The altitude near Johannesburg makes the bikes slower by around 15 per cent because the lack of oxygen starves the engine. It was the same in Mexico City in 1993 when it seemed like I was riding a moped down the straight. So, maybe, when the machines were back at sea level, mine became harder to control than the others.

But that didn't stop us from dominating the next round at Phillip Island. We were out of sight early on, which had the other teams moaning. It was the usual stuff. The Honda riders, Colin Edwards, but mainly Aaron Slight, spat their dummies and complained that the Ducatis had an advantage. The only thing different from the previous year was that the suspension had been changed a little bit. Even we couldn't understand why we were as much as 18 seconds better than the others. Troy made no mistakes in the first race, on his home track, and beat me. In the second race, I actually crossed the start line in front of him but he had better drive out of the last corner and, in the space of the few yards to the finish line, he won by five thousandths of a second. I've seen the video a few times and I'm still convinced I won!

It was a similar story at Donington. I won the first and was second in the second race. The Honda riders turned up at the pre-race press conference with faces like slapped arses. Perhaps they should have been doing as much work as we were in qualifying. I had blown two tyres in Australia, trying to find the right one. The other riders hadn't put in anywhere near as many laps as we did that weekend. They were in and out all the time and not doing race distances. I said at the time, 'I'm riding better than last year and we are working harder as a team. It's no surprise to me.'

As it turned out, I won the first race at Donington quite comfortably – but it was probably one of the hardest all year. Everyone thought I was cruising, because I kept a three second lead on Aaron Slight. They didn't realise that it was like riding on marbles as my tyre was completely destroyed and I pushed as hard as I've ever done in the final 10 laps because I wanted to win so badly in England. Slight said afterwards that there was nothing he could do to catch me. 'God man, if only you knew how hard it was to keep you at that distance,' I thought.

That effort took it out of me for the second race. Although we stiffened the suspension, I was always going to be hard pushed to repeat the win. I knew I had the beating of Troy when our tyres lost grip because I was always able to dig down deeper and find the necessary aggression. But there was no way I could compete with Edwards. If he had not had problems in the first race, he would probably have won that.

And, in some ways, I was glad he won the second. At least it would stop their moaning for a couple of weeks. Someone actually had the nerve to come up to me and ask me if I had let Edwards win that race because everyone was whinging about Ducati! I couldn't believe it. 'What do you fucking well think?' I snapped. 'Have I ever let anyone win a race? You're talking to *me* now. If someone offered me a million pounds to forfeit a race, I wouldn't do it.'

The performance of the Honda worried me a bit but I expected to win in Albacete, which has always been one of my stronger tracks. Sure enough, despite more problems with grip coming out of first gear corners, I achieved my first pole position since 1995 in Japan. It had been a standing joke around the paddock. 'He can't go fast in practice, but just wins races and world titles,' they said. As long as I've been on the front row, it hasn't really bothered me. One fast lap doesn't win a race or a world title. Very often I can do 25 fast laps better than just one.

On race day all the Japanese bikes were faster than our machines. In fact, Akira Yanagawa should have won both races on his Kawasaki, but couldn't pass anyone. Considering the problems, a pair of third places in races won by Haga, on a Yamaha, and Edwards, was not too bad for me and my championship lead was extended. Even so, I was disgusted and I had a face like stone on the rostrum. Davide recognised this immediately. 'That's the best I've seen you ride,' he said. 'We just didn't have the package for you to win the race.' Yet commentators and journalists continued to say that the Ducati had good drive coming out of slow corners. It just goes to show that they haven't got a clue what they are talking about. Ducatis are good coming out of third gear corners, but not first. That's where the Japanese bikes are so much better.

While I had been optimistic for Albacete, I didn't have good vibes about Monza. For the previous two years the Hondas had been miles quicker, on a track with long straights. In the past it had been important to be in the right position for a passing manoeuvre on the final lap. But this year our bikes were only a couple of kmph slower than the Hondas, so I wasn't too worried about qualifying on the second row. And, crucially, the start-finish line had been moved from the end of the straight to the exit of the last corner. It was perfect for me. Now the best rider would win and not the rider on the fastest bike, as happened in 1997 when I led out of the corner and was passed by both the Hondas down the straight.

The first race of the 1999 round with Colin Edwards was the highlight of the whole year. He had a slight speed advantage but I was all over him in the chicanes to win. Second time out I was behind Edwards going into the long final corner but gaining all the time. Just as we were exiting the corner, and lifting the bikes up, I timed the move perfectly and caught his slipstream the instant before we hit full power. I pulled wide and he dived inside to open the line up perfectly for me, and I nosed in front by half a wheel to win the race. If the finish line had been in its old position he would have won. It was so close. But I wasn't sure that I had nicked it. The first marshal that I saw put two fingers up to indicate second. 'No! I can't believe it,' I said to myself as I rode gloomily back to the pits. By the time I got round, the Ducati team were yelling,

'You're first!'

'What! I've won the race?' I replied.

'The times showed that you were first,' they insisted.

I started jumping up and down on the bike, as I knew how much it meant to Ducati to win at such an historic circuit in front of a passionate Italian crowd of more than 70,000. We drank until the early hours around the motorhomes, which is what usually happens at Monza. Stephane Chambon, who became the Supersport world champion that year, usually gets on a bike and starts doing one-legged and one-armed wheelie tricks, while other riders do burn-outs. And then I drove back to the hotel pissed out of my head, as nobody seems to bother about drinking and driving out there. It's easy to celebrate after a double win.

But, by the end of that week, racing no longer seemed to hold any importance . . .

CHAPTER SIXTEEN

Hannah

Nothing that I had seen in all my time in racing could have prepared me for the awful events at my home on the afternoon of Friday, 4 June, 1999. As I've explained, a racer becomes conditioned to deal with death and horrific injury on the track. But when the accident victim is a two-year-old girl, a friend of the family, and the tragedy takes place at your own home, it's impossible to cope in the same way. Hannah Walsh, the daughter of Michaela's dentist friend, Louise and her husband Graham, drowned in our swimming pool. It devastated us all.

I was up in the Lake District with a few friends, who had hired a log cabin near Windermere, when it happened. They were all staying for three or four days but I had travelled up that morning to spend a day trail riding with them. We had just got back after an exhausting ride and, while everyone was showering and winding down, I was getting ready to head off home when my mobile went at around 5.30pm. Michaela had been trying to contact me for the best part of an hour. She was desperate. 'Carl, come home as quick as you can. There's been an accident. It's Hannah. She's fallen in the pool and we don't know what's going to happen.'

The phone went dead before I had a chance to respond. But Michaela's words had knocked me sideways. It was serious – there was no mistaking the urgency and panic in her voice.

Having told the others what had happened as best I could, I chucked my bags in the back of the van that I had travelled up in with a mate, Austin Clewes, one of the managing directors of a motorbike business called CCM in Blackburn. I had parked my car at a hotel just next to the M6 near Preston but couldn't get a decent reception on my mobile phone until we got off the motorway.

'What's going on? What's happened?' I asked.

'We don't know anything yet,' she said. 'We're waiting to hear from the hospital. Please get home as quick as you can.'

'Is she all right?'

'No. She wasn't breathing when she left here. Louise tried the kiss of life and went to hospital in the ambulance with her,' she replied.

I told Austin what had happened and it was clear that we were both thinking the worst.

When I turned into the drive two police cars were parked at the end nearest the house. I stopped at the other end and ran inside, asking one of the policemen if there had been any news as I sprinted past. Michaela's dad, Alan, had taken the kids to the other side of the house and shut the door. Alan's wife, Pat, and Michaela were in the kitchen and both of them were totally distraught. Danielle, who was seven at the time, was a little bit more aware than the other two – Hannah's brother Matt, who was five, and four-year-old Claudia. They were too young to properly understand what had happened and just wanted to tell me what had gone on.

It appeared that all the kids had been playing inside and outside the house, watching videos in the playroom as well as running in and out of the garden. Michaela and Louise were making tea in the kitchen, which directly overlooks the garden and swimming pool. It was a horrible, rainy day but the doors were open and Hannah must have wandered off on her own. There was a full cover on the pool and, I suppose, one of three things could have happened. Either Hannah perhaps thought she could walk across, or she had lifted up the cover to have a nosey and fell in, or she tripped up on the ledge at the side of the pool and fell straight in. Nobody will ever know exactly what happened.

But when Michaela and Louise realised she wasn't with the others, they frantically tried to find her. Michaela spotted the shape of her body underneath the covering sheet and Louise immediately jumped in, dragged her out and tried to perform the kiss of life while Michaela rang for an ambulance. The wait for news was agonising. After I turned up, everyone just stood around waiting for perhaps an hour, nobody knowing what to say. Then a policewoman received a message on her radio. She came into the room to tell us that Hannah had died.

Michaela almost collapsed and was immediately sick in the toilet. I was in total shock. It just would not sink in. Louise and Graham arrived back from the hospital a couple of hours later. They had both wanted to come back to the scene immediately. There were very few words because everyone was just hugging each other and it was all unbelievably upsetting, even though everyone was still stunned and it hadn't fully sunk in at that point. Michaela didn't sleep at all that night. I eventually drifted off but woke up very early. I didn't know what to do with myself. Michaela spent most of the next morning with Louise, comforting her but also helping with all the formalities and investigations.

I was just trying to occupy my mind and was having a cup of tea outside when a car pulled up the drive. Graham got out but I had no idea what to say to him. He just wanted to come and spend a few minutes where Hannah had spent her last few hours.

I had only just started getting to know Graham, who owns his own steel company, a few weeks before. We had been out for a couple of meals and then started playing a lot of squash and tennis and were getting quite close. This was the type of incident that could either tear a friendship apart, or bring everyone even closer together.

Later that afternoon, I picked Michaela up from Louise's. She was in a terrible state. At one point I asked my mum to come up, because I thought another woman would be able to help her through it better than I could. On the Sunday evening, Michaela and Tracey went to see Hannah at the Chapel of Rest. It was their attempt to be able to remember Hannah as a person, and take away all the images of trying to revive her.

The press were quick to latch on and wanted to make a big issue of it, simply because it happened at my house. If it had been anyone else's house, it would have made a small paragraph. It was an attempt to make it a circus around me. That annoyed me, and really angered Louise and Graham. The coverage seemed to miss the point that a little girl had died in a tragic accident.

One reporter from the local paper, the *Lancashire Evening Telegraph*, turned up at my house during Saturday afternoon, but I told her I didn't want to say anything. They had also started hounding Graham and Louise. It is one thing expecting quotes from me – I'm used to dealing with the press and can look after myself – but what exactly was to be gained by going to the house of parents who had lost their daughter just the day before?

In any case, the police had told us not to say anything and there seemed to be a lot of conflicting advice. Both the local coroner and police had said that it might be possible to keep our names out of the papers. But the press wouldn't let it drop and, after a couple of days, I thought that by continuing to tell them to go away sounded like we had something to hide. It would be better to make a brief statement on behalf of us all.

On Monday morning, I asked Neil Bramwell, the sports editor of the local paper, who I was used to dealing with, to come up to the house so I could explain simply what had happened. He arrived just as the inquest, which we weren't required to attend, had opened. The police liaison woman was still, even at that point, trying to prevent all the names being released, but realistically that was never going to happen.

A Home Office pathologist called Dr William Lawlor carried out a post-mortem examination on Monday. He said that Hannah would have died the instant she entered the pool. He said at the inquest, 'I think the death was due to immersion in water associated with a mechanism which forensic pathologists refer to as dry drowning. The effect is that when water enters the nose and mouth, it causes almost instant unconsciousness and cessation of the heart. Once the heart had stopped it would not have been possible to restart it.'

In other words, there was nothing anyone could have done to bring her round and the coroner recorded a verdict of accidental death.

So try and imagine the horror we all felt when we picked up *The Mirror* newspaper the next morning and discovered their opinion column, 'The Voice of the Mirror', lecturing us all on how to look after children. These were their exact words, under the headline 'Children In Need':

'A child is the most precious of gifts for any parent. A never-ending source of unconditional love and joy. But today every parent in the land should reflect on the fragile nature of that gift. The shocking finding that 90 per cent of kids killed in car smashes die because of ill-fitted safety seats should shake us out of complacency. And the tragic drowning of a tot in the swimming pool of superbike champion Carl Fogarty reinforces the need for vigilance known only too well to all mums and dads. A moment of carelessness or distraction can lead to a lifetime of grief.'

Hannah's death was not down to carelessness or a lack of vigilance. It was an accident. Kids of that age have accidents all the time. Most of the time it is a cut finger or a bump on the head. This time the result was tragedy. You cannot tie a ball and chain around children, and you cannot watch them 24 hours a day. It just doesn't happen. Maybe there are circumstances, perhaps if a young kid has fallen in a canal, when you think, 'What the hell is a young kid doing next to a canal at that age?' Maybe the parents could be blamed in that situation because nobody allows a six or seven-year-old to play next to a canal.

This was different. Michaela and Louise were 15 or 20 feet away from where she fell in. I wanted to kill the pompous dick-head, sat behind a desk in London, who had tried to link Hannah's death with parents not using seatbelts in cars. It really sickened me and just added to all the hurt and upset, at a time when we could have really done without it.

And if the paper had been *that* concerned about the welfare of children, they might have taken a bit more notice of the court order that was made banning the identification of the other children that were present. Not only that, they were the only paper to publish a picture of the pool itself. To have been in a position to take that picture, the photographer could only have stood in one spot – at the very end of our drive and leaning over the gate. That was an invasion of privacy. Graham and Michaela, in particular, were furious and took the matter up with our lawyers, who thought we had a case. But that would have meant a long and drawn-out legal battle, which would not have changed anything that had happened. It would only have dragged out all the hurting for even longer.

The rest of the coverage was reasonable and, of the tabloids, *The Sun* was probably the most responsible for a change. The local paper had used a picture of our house, taken from the road, which was a bit stupid because I didn't want the world and his father to know where we live for obvious reasons.

The first half of the following week was just a blur. It had hardly occurred to me that I was due to ride the following Sunday at the Nurburgring in Germany. And, by Thursday, I was on my way to the biggest race of my life. I have never felt under as much pressure to win one single race, even when a world title has been at stake. This was not about gaining championship points, it was all about honouring Hannah.

It was my way of showing Graham and Louise that I cared and that I was hurting, in my own way. Everyone else's emotions had been out on display for all to see. I'm not like that. I tend to bottle things up. I suppose it's a typical man thing – you cannot be seen to be weak in these circumstances.

So I arrived in Germany feeling like an emotional pressure cooker. The rest of the Ducati team had obviously heard what had happened and were very concerned. But that didn't alter the fact that I had left Michaela behind in Blackburn and she would be attending the funeral as I started the first practice session on the Friday. The weather was grey and miserable, which was exactly how I felt, but I just tried to stay focused. And I managed to stay with the pace of the first timed session and clocked the fourth fastest time as we experimented with different gearboxes.

Michaela flew out in time for Saturday's qualifying and it was a relief to be with someone who was going through the same emotional turmoil that I was. She knew, though, that she had to behave normally so that I could try and approach the race in the usual way. That helped her as well. There was little point telling me about the funeral because I knew how horrible it must have been. But she did repeat something that Graham had told me before I left for Germany. He said, quite simply, 'Go out and win it for Hannah.'

That was easier said than done. I had never won at the Nurburgring before and had a disaster the previous year when I was 13th in both races. The odds seemed to be totally stacked against me and, on top of that, the weather forecast was awful. But, after the final timed session on Saturday afternoon, I was confident with the bike set-up although I wasn't producing anything special in the way of times and was only sixth fastest.

There were five riders to go after me in Superpole but my lap was inspired and no one was ever going to come anywhere near it. I set a new Nurburgring lap record for World Superbikes with a time of 1 minute 38.843 seconds, almost a full half a second faster than Colin Edwards in second place. It was one of the most incredible laps I had ever ridden for Superpole. I was quoted in *The Sun* saying that I had felt Hannah looking down on me and pushing me to better things. I didn't say anything like that but, all the same, this didn't feel like just any other meeting.

Religion, and life after death, are difficult subjects for me. I've never really gone to church but I do say a small prayer out loud before races – to whoever might be listening up there. It will only be a quick, 'Please help me through this one' or, 'I think I might need your help today' or just, 'Take care of me'. It would be a bit cheeky to ask for help in winning the race, as I haven't really put enough into religion to ask for that much out of it. But I guess I must believe in something. And I don't want to sound like Glenn Hoddle but I think there must be some form of life after death. Maybe, as soon as you die, you might come out as a baby somewhere else. I hope that's the case because otherwise it will be a bloody long time doing nothing. Surely it can't just be, 'Full stop, that's it'. There must be more to it all than that.

Come race day at the Nurburgring, I was desperate to just get out there and win the race. I'm intense enough during preparation for races in normal circumstances but, on that Sunday morning, I was in a world of my own.

And this was definitely one of those times, as I waited for the green light to signal the start of race one, when I asked for a little bit of divine intervention. I didn't have the best of starts and slipped into third place and I began to think there was no way I would be able to pass Chili and Edwards in front of me. I was not losing any ground to them, but I wasn't gaining either. But an early crash in the race had deposited oil at the bottom of the track and they both ran off into the gravel at that corner, leaving me back in the lead.

Five riders in total slid off at the same spot and there were official complaints about the standard of marshalling because no flags were shown warning riders of the oil. Even Davide got involved, storming up to race control and demanding an early finish to the race. All he was bothered about was the safety of the riders – he didn't care whether a Kawasaki, Suzuki or a scooter won the race.

To a large extent, I blamed the riders themselves. I can't remember seeing any yellow flags but I was aware that riders were crashing at the same spot. So I was careful to take a tighter line, avoiding the spill. Other riders could and should have done the same. During all this commotion, I was way out in front with a five seconds lead. But, if the race had been stopped early, not enough laps had been completed for me to secure the points. Edwards slammed the marshalling as 'amateurish and stupid'. It was appalling in some ways because, as I approached back marker Lothar Kraus, the marshals didn't show any blue flags to warn him so that he could move out of the way and let me through. And there was no way I was going to let him hold me up, so I decided to try and dive straight past him. We touched and he crashed out, but that was to be the last scare. I coasted home to win by more than seven seconds, with Slight in second and Corser in third.

The chequered flag usually triggers a whole load of emotions – relief, elation and exhilaration. This time it meant none of those. I buried my head into my bike, skipped the lap of honour and made straight for the pit lane. The greeting there was subdued and, as usual, the first hug was saved for Michaela. She was already weeping and, at that moment, the whole range of that week's events and feelings just erupted in a flood of my own tears. I was overcome by the feeling of pride and relief that I had done something for Graham and Louise and, more importantly, had honoured Hannah's memory.

In some ways, it was like a winning a world championship. Because to win this one race was a goal that had been eating away at me for what seemed like ages. It was difficult to find the right words to try and explain to the world's press exactly what the race had meant to me, and my family.

'This was the most important race of my life,' It told them. 'I had to win that race, no matter what, for somebody who is not with us any more. I wanted to win for little Hannah, who lost her life in tragic circumstances. I wanted to win for her at all costs. Her dad asked me to win the race for her.'

I didn't really want to take my place on the podium. It somehow didn't feel right but, in a way, I had to try to get back to normality. This wasn't an easy thing to do, especially on such a weird day. It always used to be a tradition in motorsport that the race winner was handed a laurel wreath, but that hardly ever happens now. But, at this meeting, the organisers had decided to restore that custom and I was presented with a huge garland, sprayed in gold paint. God Save The Queen was played and the Italian national anthem for the winning manufacturer.

I didn't have to explain to Troy, who was stood next to me on the left of the rostrum after finishing third, not to spray the champagne as a mark of respect. And I didn't think that I needed to tell Slight, on the right. I thought wrong and the idiot started to douse the crowd below. It made me hate the man even more.

The break between races was strange. It had probably been the worst week of my life and I felt exhausted. My energy had all been channeled into the first race. It wouldn't have been okay to come second in the first race and win the second. I had to win that first race directly after her death. Even a double win wouldn't have meant double the tribute to her memory, as all that had been sorted in race one.

To be honest, I really didn't care whether I won race two or not. It seemed like the meeting was over and that I had done all that was required of me. Yet I found myself winning comfortably again, by more than three seconds.

Then, with just five laps remaining, I slid off into the dirt at a totally harmless corner. Maybe the choice of tyre for the second race had been too soft, but it still shouldn't have happened. I managed to keep the engine going and, with the help of a marshal, rejoined the race but the leading pack were long gone and I had to settle for 15th place and one point. Many other riders would have thrown in the towel and not bothered to get back into the race. So, in that respect, I suppose my competitive instincts were intact after the draining events of the morning. But it was a fall that bugged me for the rest of the season. It was impossible not to think that, had I lost the championship by anything less than 24 points, it would have been due to that one stupid error that was totally out of character.

Within 20 minutes of the second race finishing I was dashing to the airport to catch an 8.30pm flight home. It was a meeting I was glad to see the back of, a weird weekend in every respect – when something or someone seemed to be controlling what was happening. The poor weather had held off and any obstacle that seemed to be in my way during the first race just seemed to disappear. When Chili and Edwards rode into the gravel, it seemed as though someone was saying, 'There's your clear track, Carl, go and do what you have to do.' Then there was the crash in race two. That appeared to say, 'We let you win the first race for Hannah; this is pay back time.'

It was also odd that the Nurburgring officials had decided to give podium finishers a garland, instead of the usual flowers. This was something I could give to Louise and Graham as a lasting tribute to Hannah and it has now been mounted in a gold frame, with a picture of her in the middle.

Graham and Louise had already decided, before the accident, to come and watch me in the next round at Misano. I suppose this was a make or break time for our friendship and it must not have been easy for them to see it through. Everybody was coming to terms with it in their own way. I had my racing to keep me focused and the Nurburgring experience had brought a lot of my deeper feelings to the surface. The fact that I had seen tragedies throughout my racing career also helped me to cope better than the others. But I found this very hard to deal with because it wasn't an adult, who was totally aware of the dangers of his sport, who had died. It was a beautiful little girl. Graham also threw himself into his work. But Louise and Michaela had been present and had to live with the images. It will stay with them much more vividly, and it was good for them to spend time together after the tragedy and talk it through.

I had actually flown out to Italy the week before the meeting for an aborted testing session at Misano. In the event, the track was in no condition for proper testing, so I took advantage of some spare time to visit Davide's home and we had our first chat about a contract for the following year.

I had also spent a couple of days trail riding around the mountains of Bologna with Slick and a few of the other Ducati lads. Two mechanics ended up in hospital with a broken thumb and badly sprained wrist, after falling off their bikes. I was staying in Cattolica, a resort on the Adriatic coast about 10 minutes drive (Italian-style) from the track and was already pretty chilled out by the time Michaela, Louise and the kids, arrived on the Sunday before the San Marino round. Graham had work commitments and joined us on the Wednesday.

We were all able to spend a lot of time together, just messing around on the beach during the day and enjoying the best Italian food and wine at night. Louise and Graham were naturally still grieving – deeply – but there were signs as the week wore on that the break was doing them some good. Sure, there were difficult moments that anyone who has experienced this kind of thing has to work through. For instance, it was strange watching their son Matt and the other kids climb into the hotel pool for the first time. I'm sure that Graham and Louise didn't want to take their eyes off them for a second.

Nobody had really known what to do about the swimming pool at home after the accident. Michaela has not been back in to this day and I wanted Graham's advice before I used it. 'What do you want me to do with that thing?' I asked, pointing to the pool. 'Do you want me to fill it in?' He told me to leave it as it was and I think that was the right decision. If we had filled it in visitors would always have asked 'What used to be there?' And then we would have had to go through the painful story.

Misano is not one of my favourite tracks and, going into that meeting, I had never won there. But I was unusually relaxed and I tend to feel pretty much at home in Italy, anyway. Graham and Louise spent a lot of time around the Ducati hospitality compound, which becomes almost home for a few days. And it didn't harm everyone's mood when I won both races. Misano was probably Corser's best track and it niggled him when I won Superpole.

I wanted to try the hardest tyre that Michelin had available. Michelin warned that it was too hard and too cold and Luca Gasbarro, who is effectively my chief mechanic, said, 'No, Carl, you're not using it. It's too cold and dangerous.'

'Put it in,' I insisted. 'Don't say another word, just put the tyre in.'

When it came to warm-up I was a bit nervous because I was out on a limb. But I was the quickest out there without even trying and the tyre looked perfect. I was way out in front in the first race but ended up just managing to fend off Troy because I had a gear selector problem, which was costing me time. People said that he had conserved his tyres better. That was bullshit. Riders don't conserve tyres – they ride as hard as they can for 25 laps. There were no such worries in the second race, which I won by miles. My friend Geoff, who owns a helicopter business, and his girlfriend, Mandy, had also flown out for the races and, by Sunday night, everyone seemed pretty relaxed. It was clear that, if anything, our friendship with Louise and Graham was even stronger.

It seemed, at that stage, that the kids had been pretty unaffected. They are probably at the best age to deal with something like this, when they don't really understand what's happened. Graham has two children from a previous marriage and his 10-year-old took things really badly. Matt didn't seem to mention the accident much at first and his mum and dad made a deliberate attempt to keep him occupied by maybe being a bit more lenient than usual. But he went through a bit of a bad patch later on. We have explained to our two what happened and they don't seem to have been too upset, although Danielle was concerned at first and wrote notes to Graham and Louise saying how sorry she was.

The next difficult time was the day Hannah would have been three. I think everyone wanted some kind of lasting memorial, so we decided to club together and buy some play equipment for the nursery she had attended. It wasn't meant to be a morbid occasion, although there were obviously a few tears when the equipment was handed over. It was our way of helping to keep Hannah's memory alive. Everybody has their own way of doing that. For instance, there is a picture of her on our kitchen cabinet, which Michaela wanted. Louise also has photos of Hannah all over the house. While it's impossible to say how you would react unless the same thing happened to you, I would probably have been inclined to take all the pictures down. I would find it too upsetting.

Time is the only real healer, though. I guess the first 12 months are probably the worst and then it might start to become a bit easier to live with. It is not something that will ever be forgotten – and we all wish we could turn back the clock.

CHAPTER SEVENTEEN

King Carl

Michael Doohan was on the same flight from London to San Francisco for the next round at Laguna Seca. He was going to see a specialist about the injuries from that big crash in Spain, which ended his career. He ran wide coming out of a corner and was heading for another left-hander when he clipped a white line, which was wet following early morning rain, and crashed at about 120mph. He suffered bad muscle and nerve damage to a wrist, badly damaged his knee ligaments and broke a collarbone.

Doohan looked terrible. 'He's never going to race again,' I thought. But he was very interested to hear about what was happening in superbikes and my plans for the following year.

'I might be running a team in Grands Prix. Would you be interested?' he asked.

'I don't know, Mick, I think I'm too old for that.'

'Bollocks man, it's not like it used to be. You could make the switch without a problem. The bikes are so much easier to ride nowadays,' he said.

I think that pissed him off a bit. He had mastered the bikes when they were difficult and won five world titles. When the fuel was changed to unleaded, people like Max Biaggi had just jumped on a 500cc and won straight away. Loris Capirossi and Valentino Rossi made the move from 250ccs and were among the fastest in testing straight away. I'm sick of these old pro-GP journalists saying that the 500s are so hard to ride. They should listen to Doohan, the man himself.

We helped Doohan with his bags at San Francisco airport and made sure he was okay getting into his hire car. As we drove down to Laguna, I asked Michaela what she thought about what Doohan had been saying. She said, 'Let's not go through all that again. It's nice and simple now and you've not got many years left.'

I had given Doohan the impression that I wasn't too interested, and that was how it was left. If the same thing had happened five years before then I would have pushed it all the way. But I can't help thinking that I would have been more motivated for the 2000 season if I was going into 500s.

I was glad to be taking a 55 point lead into the Laguna races as it's not a circuit where a rider like me can carry a lot of corner speed. If you tried to run fast through the first three corners, you would lose the front end. So I had to brake hard, then slide into bends like some of the other guys do, but that's not really my style. And I've always struggled in qualifying at that track. Putting a new rear tyre in didn't really make any difference, as it usually did, because I was always pushing the front tyre.

Where everyone else gains that extra half a second or more with a new tyre, I recorded the same times. That's why I was on the third row of the grid for the fifth year in succession. Still, by the end of the first lap, I was in front of Troy who had been on pole. He claimed that a few people had cheated at the start. Although I finished fifth it was a moral victory as my nearest rivals, Troy and Edwards, were sixth and fourth respectively. It was the only time all year when we all had tyre problems at the same time. Troy gambled on a different tyre for the second race, which worked because he was second while I swapped fourth and fifth with Edwards. But, overall, I had only lost a couple of points in the championship, which was as good as I could have hoped for.

Next stop, Brands! The build-up to the race was incredible. Almost every national newspaper did a full feature on me. I think it helped that Britain wasn't having any success in any other sport. Geoff flew me down to the Brands Hatch Thistle Hotel on the Wednesday before the race, and we flew into London on the Thursday for the big press conference and photoshoot in Trafalgar Square. I felt sorry for the other riders. It was as though they didn't exist in the eyes of the media. Not a single picture of them appeared anywhere.

While I was confident that we could win there, it was obvious during Friday's qualifying that we were struggling. Nothing that we tried seemed to be working. The pressure might have been starting to show because I was desperate to find the right set-up. When I tried to do a race distance on the Saturday, Davide pulled me in because my times were too slow. The tyre didn't seem to be the problem because I had noted that it looked good. I thought the slow times were being caused by the set-up. But I was told that they wanted to try a different tyre, which had helped Troy achieve better times.

By Superpole, I was still not confident that we knew what we wanted for the race. But a brief shower meant that Superpole was scrapped and riders were given 12 laps in which to set their fastest time. Davide had sensed we were struggling, and that the expectations were perhaps getting to me. So he grabbed me by the visor to shake me up. 'Just go out and ride,' he growled. My lap, in front of a massive 30,000 crowd who had turned up to watch qualifying, matched the one I had ridden at the Nurburgring – I was hanging off everywhere, on the limit at every corner. It was going to take something extra-special to wrestle pole position from me and no one came anywhere near it.

The hotel at the track had been too busy the previous couple of nights, so I decided to stay in the motorhome that we had rented. There were 100,000 people expected – although, come the day, it was more like 120,000 – and I didn't want to wrestle my way through the crowds first thing in the morning. But, because it wasn't my motor-home, I couldn't relax. There was no television to watch and nothing to make a brew with. It was all a bit of a cock-up and I had a rough night's sleep.

There was an important decision to make first thing the next morn-ing. The team wanted me to continue to use the harder 'P' tyre com-pound that Troy had chosen. I wasn't so sure and I should have stuck with my instincts, as I had at Misano, and opted for a softer 'M'. I had a great start but didn't really want to be in front early on. Edwards came past and I sat in behind him for three or four laps. 'There's not a problem here. This is very comfortable,' I thought. After 10 laps he was starting to pull away, because I was losing grip and running wide. Troy appeared to be having the same problems but, when I was back down in fourth place, my bike started to judder and bang. 'How the hell am I going to bring this thing home?' I asked myself, just as there was a loud bang at Dingle Dell. A huge chunk had flown out of the tyre and I went straight into the pits.

With a quick change I might have been able to salvage a few points in the lower positions. But the pit stop was a joke. It was like Laurel and Hardy. First the stand snapped on the welding. Then they couldn't get the wheel nut off, then the spanner. All I could do was stand by in embarrassment. When I rejoined the race I was a lap behind and out of the points. I have never been so gutted and livid. Why did this have to happen in front of an incredible crowd of 120,000 of my fans?

When I discovered that Honda had used the same tyre to come first and second, I was really stumped. But we opted to use a 16.5in, instead of the 17in, as that would run cooler. We also tried a new compound, which Michelin promised would not fall apart, although they weren't sure what the grip would be like. We changed our minds so many times between races but decided on the safe option. John Reynolds had used the same tyre in the first race to finish fourth, so I didn't think we could go too far wrong.

It was the worst tyre I have ever put on in my career. I was even sliding around on the warm-up lap. It just about got me through to the end of the race before it also blew on the last lap. I had to ride around the problem from the word go and I manhandled the bike into fourth place, which was a great result considering Troy was back in 13th on the same tyre. It didn't stop me feeling that I had let everyone down. This was the biggest single day attendance for any sporting event in Britain that year. Every time I moved a muscle, the crowds in the grandstand facing the garage were on their feet. I needed to tell them how much I appreciated their support, and why I hadn't been able to bring them the win that they craved. So I went out onto the track to say how much I loved them all and still got the biggest cheer of the day.

Then I needed some space. I hadn't been able to move all weekend and the last thing I wanted to do was sign a load of autographs. I went back to the motorhome and my room in hospitality and waited for the crowds to clear, which felt like ages. I had been expected at the hotel's annual charity night, but I was in no mood for a fancy dress party. I wasn't to know, but a surprise presentation had been arranged. The organisers had presumed I would be there and, if I had won both races, I probably would have been. In the event my mum had to go up and collect it – something which annoyed a few people – as I just wanted to be a million miles away from Brands Hatch.

I was snapping at everyone and felt very claustrophobic. The heat and humidity made things even worse. I couldn't stand having to talk to people when I was in such a bad mood. All I wanted was to shut my eyes, open them again and find myself on a deserted beach. The next best thing would be for Geoff to fly me to his hotel half a mile away, where I could dive into the pool. Eventually, when my dad took the kids, we decided to go for a Chinese with Graham and Louise, and Geoff and Mandy. We piled into a car and I crouched down in the front seat, so that nobody would spot me as we fought our way through the traffic. After the meal I sneaked back into the Thistle Hotel through a back door and went straight to my room.

Geoff flew us back home the following morning and, while we sunbathed around the pool in the afternoon, we decided to join both couples for a week in Ibiza – the first summer holiday that me and Michaela had ever had.

As it was a late booking, we were on a chartered flight but the airline looked after us and made sure that we weren't bothered because I tend to have a lot of hassle in those situations. We had found an apartment on the nice side of the island, not where all the idiots stay.

In a way, it didn't help having a four-week break before the next round because this was the only time in the year when doubts started to creep into my mind. Brands was still gnawing away at me, even though I still led the championship by around 50 points. But the break did help take my mind off things. One afternoon we were at a harbour filled with fantastic £2 million yachts. I said to Graham, 'I'm going to wander around to see if anyone recognises me.' The biggest and best boat had a Union Jack on the back and, sure enough, the owner came up and said, 'It's Carl Fogarty, isn't it? Do you want to come aboard?' I was on the deck waving at everyone before he finished the word 'aboard'.

It belonged to a really nice bloke called Klaas Zwart, a multi-millionaire who owns Ascari Cars in Scotland. He also produced components for oil rigs and raced ex-Formula One cars in the Boss series. He was also a big fan and invited the rest of us aboard, after we had taken our shoes off, and allowed us to use his jet-ski and his smaller boat. In the end, I felt like we had out-stayed our welcome a bit but we arranged to go for a drink with his family that night.

The holiday was supposed to be a break to recharge my batteries, but we ended up being up until 4am every morning. And it didn't get me away from bike problems.

We went to hire some bikes on the first day and, on the way to the rental shop, walked past a bar. The owner came running out.

'I can't believe it's you. We have about 100 people in here every

Sunday watching you race. Don't bother hiring a bike, you can have mine for the week,' he insisted.

'Fine,' I thought, 'that saves me paying.'

Throughout 1999 I seemed to get away without paying for anything!

He leant me his Yamaha V-Max, their version of a Harley-Davidson, which I thought I could potter around on without a problem. Geoff and Mandy hired a 600cc Yamaha Enduro bike and we set off around the island, finding nice beaches. I didn't like my bike one bit, as I'm not used to riding road bikes, whereas Geoff owns a Ducati. I could see he was itching for a go on the V-Max and I was more than happy to oblige. And he looked confident on it – for a few days.

On one of the last days, on our way back to hand in the bikes, we were on some winding roads about 8km away from the resort. Coming into one corner at only about 20–30mph, Geoff realised that he was running too wide because the bike was very difficult to lean over. As the bend tightened, he tried to lean further over but fell off right in front of me and I just missed Mandy's head (she was on the back) by anchoring the front and back brakes on. They both slid along the road. 'Oooooooh! Bare legs and arms on Tarmac. That is really going to hurt,' I cringed.

Luckily nothing was coming in the opposite direction and they stopped sliding just before the barrier, which separated the road from a sheer drop down to the sea. I parked up and ran back. Geoff had only scraped his elbow but Mandy's leg was like a slice of bacon, a big disc of raw steak. Her elbow was also a mess. She was jumping up and down shouting, 'You bloody pillock, you bloody pillock!' I thought he got off lightly. If it had been Michaela, I would have been over the cliffs.

The bike was an even bigger mess. Because it was so heavy, the bars were bent, the front brake lever had snapped off, the indicator and mirror were knackered and the exhaust was bent. Geoff and Mandy didn't want to get on it again, so it was down to me to ride it back with a very worried Michaela on the back. She nipped me every time I locked the back brake, while I struggled to steer the bent bars. To add insult to injury, we had to ride past a café packed with bikers who were at a Harley convention! They all started cheering, thinking I had been invited. As we limped back into the street the guy was stood outside his bar. At first he was smiling but, as we got nearer, his face started to drop as he noticed the damage. All I could do was state the obvious: 'There's been an accident.' He took it very well, as Geoff was not far behind and offered to pay for all the repairs.

The next job was to try and clean Mandy's wound, to prevent infection. She was climbing the walls as Michaela tried to scrub the dirt out. I knew that she wouldn't scream if I had a go. So I grabbed the brush and rubbed hard as she writhed in agony. A piece of Tarmac had even become lodged in her ankle, so we had to dig that out as well. The doctor gave her an injection to be on the safe side. It was only to be a matter of weeks before Mandy needed much more than an injection to repair the injuries from another bike accident.

All things considered, I was ready to race again by the time of the Austrian round. Edwards had tried to wind me up by saying, 'Carl always cracks under this kind of pressure.' I couldn't remember the last time I had cracked under pressure. He seemed to be forgetting that I had won three world titles in the previous five years. But what did stop me from sleeping was the rain on Saturday night. The heavens opened and it continued to rain on race day. Maybe things were starting to turn against me.

Parts of the track had started to dry by the start of the race, so we decided on cut slicks in the front and back. Edwards gambled on a cut slick in the front and a slick in the back. That would obviously suit him if the track continued to dry, which it did. Late on in the race my tyres were like destroyed slicks, but Edwards hadn't pulled away. Then it started to rain again, catching a lot of riders out, including Slight and Corser. All I had to do was keep the bike upright to clinch second, as Edwards slid all over the track in front of me to win a good race. It rained throughout the second race and we both started cautiously. But, after a few laps down in 11th, I thought, 'Bugger this! Even if I finish, I'm only going to collect four or five points.' So I started to lap about three seconds quicker and moved up past Edwards to sixth before two more riders fell off and I ended up in fourth. I had kept my cool and come through a big test.

Assen, the very next week, was my territory. If it stayed dry in Holland no one would come anywhere near me. And it was boiling hot – in front of an army of around 60,000 British fans. I was determined to concentrate on my own thing and even opted to use a tyre that nobody ever used, a different shaped 16.5inch. That also threw Troy's preparation because he had tried it but didn't like it. I was first away and led from start to finish.

Obviously, Troy switched tyre for the second race and pulled a 1.5 second lead until I was able to find a clear track in second place. The gap stayed the same for two laps until I reined in half a second per lap. He must have been thinking, 'What the hell can I do about this?' There was nothing he could do. I breezed past him and he was demoralised. It was just about the first time that I had heard another rider admit that he'd been totally helpless. 'On this circuit, there is nothing anyone can do to beat this guy,' Corser said. The crowd went bananas as I had one hand on the world championship trophy.

The sensible thing to do would have been to wrap myself in cotton wool before the following weekend's race at Hockenheim. Instead I went motocrossing on the Wednesday with a couple of mates called Garth Woods, who owns an engineering company in Blackburn, and Austin Clewes. Needless to say I had a horrendous crash. The bike landed sideways after a jump, threw me off and my wrist twisted under the bike. At first I thought it was broken, then I realised that I was dazed and my neck was stiff. I was sat in the sand at Preston Docks, four days before I could clinch the world title and suddenly thought, 'What on earth are you doing? Just put the bike back in the van, go home while you are in one piece and don't tell anyone.'

My wrist was still sore when I arrived at Hockenheim, with a lead of 71 points and needing just one more win to secure the title. I was starting to feel the pressure a bit. It seemed that everyone except me had it down as a foregone conclusion. I hadn't slept well for a few weeks, I was off my food and I didn't have a lot of time for people. That's part and parcel of my dedication. When you have such a big lead, there is always a nagging doubt that you could throw it all away. I just wanted to get down to business and, if things went well, start enjoying it all on Sunday night. But things never seemed to be that simple.

I was in the paddock on Thursday afternoon with Geoff, sorting out a few last minute details before practice started the following day. Michaela and Mandy had taken a couple of scooters around the track. Mandy looked nervous, because she hadn't had much experience of riding a scooter. The next thing I knew, Michaela was running towards me screaming. 'Mandy is really hurt. There's been a terrible accident,' she shouted. 'Mandy's had a crash, I thought she was dead,' she kept repeating, almost hysterically.

Me and Geoff jumped on scooters and set off to where Michaela was pointing. One of the doctors happened to be walking across the paddock at the same time, so he jumped on the back of my bike. By the time we reached the scene there was an ambulance already there, as it had been parked opposite the spot where the accident had happened. As Michaela and Mandy were riding down the straight, the driver of one of the machines that paints the markings on the track must have just turned towards them.

Michaela, who is used to riding a scooter, managed to swerve out of the way. But Mandy panicked. The truck had a bar, to attach a lamp to, sticking out of the side and it smashed into her leg, practically slicing it off just above the ankle. Both bones had been sheered through and her foot was hanging on by a bit of muscle. She had also been thrown down the track and had landed on her head. There was blood everywhere and her teeth were smashed. She was just conscious, although Michaela said she had been knocked out at first.

I thought the worst when I saw the blood around her head. But then she groaned, 'Oh Carl, I'm never riding a bike again.' I realised then that she would be okay. I knew that the leg would heal. It's when you bang your head that you can have real problems. Within an hour everything had settled down and I had almost forgotten about the whole incident. It was the start of a big weekend for me and, to be perfectly honest, it didn't affect me in the slightest.

Mandy was taken to the nearest hospital, had a long operation to pin her leg back together and stayed in Germany for the next week. Obviously we checked on her condition every day but it wasn't something that preyed on my mind in the build-up to the races. By the time we were back in England, it was something I could even joke about.

I told everyone that Michaela had tried to kill Mandy, although I'm not sure that Michaela appreciated the joke. Mandy is on the mend now, but needed a bone graft from her hip to help the fracture heal properly. The gap between the two ends of bone had been too wide for it to knit together and calcify properly. In many ways she was lucky, although she probably wished she had never met us after this and the fall in Ibiza.

Qualifying was none too smooth, either. A clutch problem during Superpole meant that I was seventh on the grid, at a track where I wouldn't be able to go easy on the bike and just pick up the points. The long straights at Hockenheim mean that there is maximum strain on the engine for long periods, and that's just to stay in the draught of other bikes. During the Sunday morning warm-up I was obviously a bit tense.

One particular fat little German marshal had annoyed me the previous day by not letting me out of pit-lane, which meant I had to stop the bike and get the mechanics to run down and start me up again. On the Sunday, I had been out on one bike and was about to go out on the number two bike. Just as I was approaching the end of pit-lane, the red light, which signals the end of the session, came on. All I wanted to do was go out, do one lap, and come back in. But the steward leapt out with his red flag and he was determined not to let me out at any cost. I almost ran into him. I was swearing like a madman although he couldn't understand a word I was saying. I backed the bike up a few yards and pretended to run straight at him, stopping just short, of course! By this stage he was crapping himself because I was still furious and giving him the finger. A woman was stood close by and she was indicating that she had seen everything that had happened. She was obviously going to love grassing me up.

When the first race eventually arrived I was confident with our choice of tyre. Again I went for the hardest that Michelin had, similar to the tyre we used throughout 1995. From what I had seen, the others were struggling and I thought I was the only one who had done a race distance in practice – and I had done it twice. Davide, watching from pit-lane, didn't think that I got off to a good start. In fact I had charged through from the second row and was leading going into the first chicane. That made me uneasy. All the time I was wondering where Troy was, because I only needed to beat him to win the title. Yet again I had to talk to myself to keep focused. 'Look, just do what you do. Keep your head down and keep putting in fast consistent laps,' I told myself.

At the start of the last lap I thought my board was telling me that Troy was in ninth. That was perfect, there was no point getting into a dice with Slight in second place. He came past and was weaving all over expecting me to come back at him. I wasn't interested in him in the slightest and was looking behind just to make sure Troy wasn't there – but knowing that the world title was mine. For once in my life I wasn't bothered about winning the race and crossed the line in second with a big wheelie. I stopped the bike in front of the grandstand, where there were around 30,000 Brits who had made the journey. I punched the air and then dropped to my knees in the sand saying little prayers of thanks.

The T-shirts were out in pit-lane saying, 'Carl Fogarty: Four times world champion' and I noticed, behind the podium, that Aaron Slight was furious. Someone came up to me and said, 'You've won the race!'

'No, Aaron won the race,' I said, confused.

It turned out that the red flags had been out on the final lap after an accident, which meant that the result stood from the start of the last lap when I was leading. It was a bit embarrassing but I didn't care because I had won the title.

Slight didn't appear on the podium and I probably would have done the same because he won the race fair and square. He made a protest but it was rejected. And, as far as I was concerned, the trouble with the marshal from the morning had also been forgotten. But team manager Davide Tardozzi had been ordered up to race control. The organisers originally wanted to fine me 3,000 Swiss Francs, until I was talked into going up there to apologise to everyone and they settled for 1,000 Swiss Francs, about £400. It was no skin off my nose.

The relief during the break between races was amazing. Davide had to remind me that there was another race because I turned up at the garage with a big grin.

But, as soon as my helmet was on, there was no smiling. It was back to business as usual, although Chili just edged me into second in a good race. The Alstare Suzuki team threw a big party in the paddock, with some strippers, but I had an early flight in the morning and there would be plenty more celebrations back home. So we didn't have a really late night in Germany. A few press were waiting at the airport again, including a right nugget from the *Manchester Evening News*. He knew that I had won a world title, but did not know whether I rode a bike or a snail. I could have won the tiddlywinks world title for all he cared.

I had been in a mischievous mood after the Hockenheim races and told the press that I wouldn't be travelling to Japan for the final race a month later. There was never any doubt that I would be going, but Ducati took me seriously and had a quiet word. As it turned out, there was some doubt the week before the final race because a nuclear leak threatened the event in Sugo. We were due to travel on the bullet train from Tokyo through the affected area, but Ducati made a lot of checks and we were promised that everything would be okay. It was a pity, as I really could have done without that extra round.

Michaela felt exactly the same . . .

CHAPTER EIGHTEEN

Teamwork

Michaela picked her moment to suggest that there was no point in her travelling to Japan, but I was busy with something else, so I ignored her. She tried again,

'Carl, you don't really need me in Japan, do you?'

Again I didn't respond.

'I guess I'm coming to Japan, then!'

'Yep, you're coming to Japan,' I grinned.

She was right, there was no real need for her to travel halfway across the world for a meaningless race. But I've come to rely on her company at races and she has been at every round for the last couple of years. That's a measure of the strength of our relationship. Unlike many couples, who go off to work at the start of each day and maybe spend a couple of hours together in the evening and at weekends, Michaela and I are in each other's pockets for the most part of most days. It's got to the stage that I don't feel right at a meeting if she is not there.

It can be a very lonely time in a foreign country, and especially somewhere like Japan, during a race meeting. The mechanics stay behind at the track working on the bike, so the rider has to go back to a hotel room or go out and eat alone. It's so important to have somebody there to share a joke with or provide a shoulder to cry on. Michaela and I know each other inside out and the relationship has matured over the years. Anyone who knows us will say that we are two very strong characters. We both let people know exactly what we think about them. That can be a potentially explosive combination and obviously there are flash points. It has occasionally come to blows but I always warn her that I'll never let the fight end until I've won!

There was a period when a big row meant we could go for days without speaking. But, the more Michaela has become involved with the business side of things, the harder it is to ignore each other and now we don't argue as much as we used to. Nowadays I can recognise when I've been unreasonable. Perhaps I might have snapped at her if she was in my chair in the garage after I had been out during qualifying when things hadn't gone to plan. But her mood will soon tell me when I've overstepped the mark and I usually end up eating humble pie.

It might be a sign that I am mellowing because, more often than not, I'm now the first to apologise – in my own way. I might mutter, 'Dickhead!' as we pass in the corridor, to try and break the ice. I actually try to avoid arguments at all costs but she sometimes pushes me to the brink and forces me to say something nasty. Days later, when it's all forgotten as far as I'm concerned, she will throw it back in my face and force an apology out of me.

Michaela loves to be involved with the team. Ever since around 1993 she has been a regular on the pit wall, noting down my lap times for the records. A lot of the wives and girlfriends take a back seat, but Michaela is always in and around the garage and therefore on television. So she has a high profile of her own now and is often recognised in England when I'm not there. The Italians love our public shows of emotion after races and that's perhaps one of the reasons I'm so popular in that country.

Her presence also serves another purpose. Biking has always attracted a glamorous female following. Around the time I first started seeing Michaela, I found it quite hard to pull girls even though I was racing all over the world. I'm no model – I suppose I'm just an average looking guy with distinctive features. It's a similar thing with Mick Jagger – people either think that you're good looking or that you're an ugly git. Either way, it doesn't bother me. I've always had good-looking girlfriends and I've got a beautiful wife, so there must be something there that women like. Now it would be relatively easy to pull birds because I'm well known and have a bit of cash. But, because Michaela and the kids are always around, everyone sees that I'm a big family man. So perhaps girls don't want to get involved and leave me well alone. Sure, they occasionally give me the eye, but there have certainly never been crowds of them rushing into the garage trying to rip my pants off.

That's not to say that Michaela doesn't get a bit insecure. Perhaps

I do sometimes have wandering eyes. Show me a man who hasn't. So Michaela will ask, 'What's she got that I haven't?' I'll say 'Nothing. I'm married to you, though.'

It's just not in my nature to tell her she looks beautiful all the time, so she hates it when I say that some stranger looks sexy. When a girl once asked me in the Isle of Man to sign her boob right across the nipple, she went apeshit. And she hates it whenever I'm asked to do something like squirt water on the contestants in a Miss Wet T-shirt contest (although it's okay if she's allowed to judge the Mr Willy competition). But that's about the only temptation that is put in my way, which is fine by me. There is just too much to throw away, even if I was tempted. Many sportsmen can't resist affairs and you read about it in the papers every Sunday morning. It's not as bad in motor-cycle racing as many people think, and nowhere near as bad as it is in football.

A lot of the other superbike riders are in the same boat, as most have wives or steady girlfriends. The younger riders, who haven't got someone in tow, are generally not famous enough to attract the interest in the first place. One or two who do have partners still play the field and get away with it, but that's their business. Sometimes I wish it had been laid on a plate when I was younger and still in the market. But if that had been the case I would probably be washed up and living in some flat in Monaco with a drug problem – with a different woman every night. You can't have your cake and eat it and I think I'll settle for what I've got, thanks very much.

Michaela's involvement with the team is a way of controlling her nerves, more than anything. It's always worse for people who are watching because they can't do anything about what's happening on the track. At least I'm in a position to influence things. It's not that she's scared, just anxious that I don't injure myself and, at the same time, keen for me to do well. She knows only too well that I'm not a nice person for a couple of days after a bad result. But, while I know she's a nervous wreck, it's calming for me to have her around and especially when things get tense.

I realise that I'm not always the easiest bloke to be around, as I want everything done to perfection. And if I were to ask for a cup of tea at home I would probably be told to go and get it myself. At first she was like that at races, and a proper pain in the arse. Now she appreciates the pressures that I am under, with everyone wanting a slice of my time, and knows that it's not worth arguing. So she now does more and more stuff, such as mixing up drinks or fetching tablets from the doctors – the type of things that I always used to do for myself. But there are certain things, like seeing to my helmet visor, which I still prefer to do on my own so that nobody else can be blamed if it's not done properly.

Michaela has also got a lot better at the business side of things, which she hated at first but is now very comfortable with. She can be a very tough negotiator and runs my diary. I've never seen the sense in employing an agent and having to give him a 10 per cent cut of every deal, although I do have a publicity agent called Jane Rose, who handles the media commitments and tries to bring in sponsorship. That was becoming too big a job for us to handle, so it's nice for someone to take that pressure off us. Michaela is also my first line of defence from the telephone. So she was heavily involved when all the shit kicked off with my uncle Brian, my dad's brother.

The problem dated back to around 1994 when Brian asked me if he could try and make a bit of cash selling pieces of pottery, plates and mugs with my name and pictures on. I was only too pleased to help out because he seemed to have struggled for most of his life. Even when he did enjoy a rare bit of luck, Brian always seemed to do something stupid and blow it. For four or five years, he would set up a stall at race meetings and sell a few items – so everyone went away happy. I never asked for a cut and didn't want a share of the proceeds. He then fell in with some people who set themselves up as Foggy Promotions, an offshoot of Motorsport Enterprises, claiming to be the official suppliers of Carl Fogarty merchandise.

A professional outfit called Clinton Enterprises, run by Tim Clinton, who also represented Castrol Honda, had handled all my official merchandising for a number of years. But suddenly they were being told that Foggy Promotions had the sole rights to my merchandise. That was bullshit but Brian and these guys were by then driving round in a car with all kinds of slogans painted on the side, not to mention producing caps and T-shirts which they had no right to do. They even used the logo of my eyes, which Alan Pendry has exclusive rights to use after copyrighting the logo, which was based on the design owned by No Fear and looks like a Polo mint broken in half and pulled apart. They also spent thousands of pounds trying to register my name.

Then they set up a new Web site on the Internet with the message, supposedly from me, saying, 'This is my official range of products that I endorse. Welcome to my Web site. I would also like to thank my Uncle Brian for supporting me throughout my career.' This was totally untrue.

This had all blown up in the middle of the 1999 championship and I didn't want it to distract me from my racing. So I told Brian, 'You can't do this. I'll have a meeting with you and your people once the season is over.' In all honesty though, I had no intention of getting involved. I just wanted to shut them up for the time being. So, during the week after my victory at Hockenheim, it all kicked off when I was out in Italy helping to promote the Milan Show. I had enough mayhem to deal with out there, without all this. Shark had asked me to sign some helmets on a specially constructed stage but had advertised the time that I would be there. It was a big mistake because Italians never form an orderly queue. I had only signed one before the crowd burst through the security and the stage collapsed. I was practically picked up by my bodyguards and carried to safety!

That night, Michaela rang me to say that Brian had warned Clinton that he wouldn't be able to sell merchandise at an event that was being organised by Blackburn Council to commemorate my fourth world title. A similar tribute night had been held every championship year, but the previous year's had turned into a big autograph session. I was uncomfortable with this because people had paid for tickets and thought I was profiting, which was not the case. But this year the night had become the focus of this running battle for my merchandising rights.

I went ballistic, so Michaela rang Brian to tell him exactly how I felt. He flew off the handle with Michaela. 'I can do whatever I want,' he said. 'I have a contract with Carl that gives me his worldwide rights. Anyway, it's got nothing to do with you. I have got permission off the Fogarty family.' Again it was all bullshit.

The day after I returned home I received a recorded delivery letter from Motorsport Enterpises, which was also sent to Ducati, Action Performance and Clinton. It claimed they held all my worldwide rights because I had signed a piece of paper in 1995 allowing Brian to sell 'pottery'. Apparently, I had signed it because Brian was getting hassle from some of the circuits who were asking for official documents before allowing him to sell his stuff. But Motorsport Enterprises went on to claim that 'pottery' was just a trading name, which included all forms of merchandise. And *they* threatened to take *me* to court if I didn't co-operate.

265

I flipped. Just at that moment, dad rang. The timing was all wrong.

'What are you doing about this celebration evening at Blackburn? Alf Wright from the council is trying to get it all sorted,' he asked in all innocence.

'I am not going to that fucking thing because of your bastard brother. I'm going to kill him,' I shouted. 'And if you've got anything to do with it, you can fuck off as well.'

Dad was obviously upset with the way I had spoken to him. But I thought that he'd taken Brian's side. I didn't speak to dad again until Christmas Day, when he turned up with presents for the kids. You could have cut the atmosphere with a knife. 'There's a present for you. That should cheer you up,' he said and off he went. The Blackburn event was eventually cancelled using the legitimate excuse that the council hadn't even checked whether I was available for that particular night.

Actually, I had already decided to switch to Action Performance for the year 2000 before all this blew up, as they handled a lot of World Superbike and Ducati merchandise. There is the potential to make a lot of money on the back of my name but, in the wrong hands, there is also potential for a lot of people, including the public, to be ripped off. So my lawyers, and those of Action Performance and Ducati, were on the case in an increasingly complicated battle. 'Brian said you would let us do this and Brian said we could do that,' a guy called Warren Cox, from Motorsport Enterprises, moaned before backing off and offering to try and come to an amicable arrangement, claiming that no one would benefit in the long run. 'I don't give a fuck what Brian said, you're getting nothing out of me,' I said. I couldn't understand how anyone, least of all my own uncle, would have the nerve to sell my stuff without my consent.

Out of the blue, towards the end of January, dad phoned up and asked if he could come round so that I could sign some posters. He turned up, I signed the posters and, again, he left with hardly a word said between us. I couldn't believe that this was happening. Dad rang again a couple of weeks later but this time to say that he had been in contact with Barry Marsden, a Blackburn businessman who had a history of being involved with failed companies. Marsden said he was something to do with a company called Harvest.

This company had offered to buy the agreement off Motorsport Enterprises. Harvest claimed to have offices in Blackburn, Texas and

Singapore and dad told me they had great ideas to make all sorts of products like a Foggy Plug, Foggy Flex and a Foggy Watch.

'I want nothing to do with them,' I said. 'You haven't been around for the last four months, so how would you know how far this has gone and how much trouble Brian has caused.'

'Well you said all those bad things to me,' he replied.

At last we had started a conversation and it was clear that dad had no idea of the scale of the problem. He went mad and went straight round to Brian's and told him to stop it all. Brian refused and whined that he hadn't been able to sleep for four months. It was obvious that Brian had misled everyone and dug himself into a big hole. I'll never speak to him again and he has also pissed off the people he got involved with, as they had spent money on the back of his promises.

Meanwhile, some of my people had been doing some digging on Harvest. Apparently, it wasn't until they had read a story in the *Lancashire Evening Telegraph* that they realised my uncle was acting without my consent. So I spoke to their main man, a Cheshire-based businessman called John H Gee, to try and make some progress. He seemed nice enough but, by then, I didn't know who to trust. I told him that, if he had commercial ideas, I was prepared to listen to them as long as they had nothing to do with Motorsport Enterprises or Brian Fogarty. But, after another story in the *Telegraph*, Harvest quickly disappeared out of the equation.

By then I didn't care if I never sold another piece of merchandising. I was determined not to let these people make any money from my name. At one stage, just a month before the season, I was considering not racing in the year 2000. The previous four months had been a living nightmare. It had caused tension between me and Michaela because, as is often the case, you take things like this out on those closest to you. And that wasn't fair on her. I told Ducati, 'I really don't want to race this year. What's the point in me racing when all this is going on. I'm not riding round a track and risking my life when these bastards could make money out of me.' That pricked up Ducati's ears and they sprang into action. A crisis meeting was called between their lawyers, those of Action Performance and my own legal team, when it was agreed to take Motorsport Enterprises to court.

At least everything was cleared up with dad. He had played a big part in my career and was always there to support me in the early years. Before all this blew up, he'd always been easy-going, laid back and, apart from the odd row at race meetings in the heat of the moment, we had never really fallen out for any length of time before. He has obviously been very proud of me from the day I was born – you can tell that by my middle name, George. Personally, I think middle names are snobby and cannot see the point of them because you're never going to lose your first name so our two do not have them.

Generally, he doesn't have a bad word for anyone and nobody seems to have a bad word for him. That wasn't always the case. While he was building up his business, dad and Philip had a reputation as being pretty ruthless. Dad is certainly not the type to let anyone stand in his way if he wants something badly enough. Throughout their early life, all four brothers were in trouble for one thing or another like fighting.

That business developed into a very successful haulage and storage business with huge clients like Star Paper Mill, the Thwaites brewery, and Walkersteel, run by Jack Walker, who is now the owner of Blackburn Rovers and worth £600 million. It became a bit of a goldmine, especially when they moved to a site nearer to the town centre and right next to a rail link.

Phillip gradually lost interest and, in 1989, they decided to sell out to a company called Gilbraith's. Dad stayed on as a consultant for another five years before packing up altogether. But he isn't the type to sit around kicking his heels and helped a lot with work on our last two houses. Even now he helps a couple of people with their gardens, always wearing his Carl Fogarty T-shirt!

In fact, everything he walks round in is the old stuff that I've thrown out. He begrudges buying anything for himself, and thinks it's disgusting if I buy a pair of pants for £60 or £70. Dad is much happier going to some cheap shop and picking up a pair for £10.99. He's not tight, because he loves to buy the kids stuff. It's back to the work ethic thing. He hates thinking he is making someone else well off, without them doing anything for it. So he will always try and repair something rather than call in an expert, which usually results in it costing him more money in the long run when it breaks down again. If, for instance, he wanted a new tennis racket, he'd pay £14.99 thinking he has got value for money even if it only lasted a few games. So I've tended to buy him things like that for Christmas.

I was also sick of seeing him driving around in a heap of a car, a

Land Rover, that he had bought from the auctions. It was always breaking down and, whenever dad went into a garage, he tried to flog it in part exchange for another 'bargain'. So, one Christmas, I bought him a Land Cruiser Colorado jeep from a dealer in Northampton (because I wanted one as well!)

It was a £30,000 turbodiesel automatic and a gorgeous deep blue colour – and I threw in an 8 FOG number plate. On Christmas Eve I made an excuse that I wanted to borrow his heap to pick up some presents for the kids, but took it away and flogged it for around £7,000. That evening I told him that it was too late to return his car and that he could pick it up when they came for Christmas dinner. When they arrived on Christmas Day I said, 'Can you go and get your bloody car out of my garage. I can't get that pile of shit to start.'

'Why? There's nothing wrong with it. You've just got to turn the key the right way,' he muttered as he trudged off to the garage.

When he opened the door he saw this brand new jeep, all carefully wrapped up with ribbons and a big message 'Merry Xmas Dad'. He thought I had bought it for myself, and couldn't figure it out that it was for him. 'It's yours, you daft git,' I told him. It is the only time I have seen tears in his eyes. And I've got the moment on video to prove it. It made me so happy because he had done so much for us down the years. My relationship with mum has never really been that close.

Mum and dad split up around July 1998. It was not a bitter divorce and didn't affect me at all. They were just two people who had grown apart and out of love. The only thing they really had in common as a couple was his racing and that had obviously finished. When their kids left home they realised there was no real reason to stay together any longer. But they are still on friendly terms and, at Brands last year, dad turned up with his new younger girlfriend, Bev, and mum didn't bat an eyelid.

Mum has actually just moved into my sister Georgina's old house but I'm not sure how she will cope. She might not even know how to pay a gas bill because dad seemed to do everything like that. It's strange because, as an orphan whose two brothers live in South Africa and the States, you would expect her to be able to stand on her own two feet. But it hasn't worked out that way.

The same goes for Georgina. We were always fighting as kids and nothing much seems to have changed. She was an annoying little sister and I probably picked on her a bit. I'm not sure that many boys get on well with their younger sisters as a general rule. But it was probably quite cool for her to have an older brother, although she would probably not admit that. There were the obvious benefits for me in meeting her friends but that worked both ways because she went out with a couple of racers, Nigel Bosworth and Darren Dixon, while I was riding 250ccs. Now she seems to copy everything we do. She married Simon Bradshaw, who runs a car valeting and dry cleaning business in Blackburn, seven months after we were married. She had children soon after we had children. Like my mum, Georgina seems incapable of doing anything on her own.

Mum and my sister can both be a bit childish and have caused a few problems down the years. Perhaps they have always been a bit spoilt because dad did too much for them. They are constantly falling out with each other, their own friends, and Michaela. That's because they don't seem to realise that Michaela leads a busy life and likes to see her own friends. But, out of the blue, they will ring up and say, 'You haven't rung for ages. I find that really annoying.'

This has gone on for about 10 years and there's no need for it. Maybe they, and my sister in particular, are jealous of our lifestyle. I've tried to help financially where I could, lending Georgina and her husband some money to set up their business and helping mum to buy that house. If I thought they appreciated that help as much as dad appreciated his jeep, I would probably help more often. Again, it's sad to say, but they seem to put their hand out and expect. I would now rather help my mate Howard, who works his balls off day-in, day-out, to buy a tractor for his farm rather than help some members of my own family.

It has reached the point when something will happen one day, as we are sick of it all. We are considering moving down to the South Coast, when we can find a suitable time in the girls' education, to escape all the hassle. If it hadn't been for the kids we would probably have done it before now. There are more important things in life than tittle-tattle gossip, or moaning about your hair, weight or clothes, not to mention other people's hair, weight and clothes. I'm sure that they don't realise that their comments upset people a lot of the time.

But I am sorry to say that it has reached the stage where we have got very little in common and I don't have much to say to them. Mum might come round and say, 'Well done at the weekend.' But, before you know it, she is straight into, 'My back is hurting from all the tennis I've been playing' or, 'What do you think of my new haircut?' I'm glad I haven't turned out that way, although it could well have happened if I hadn't gone out and achieved all that I have done.

My dad and Michaela's dad, Alan, are two very different people. But we would be knackered without Alan and Pat. Whenever we're away they move into the house and keep the ship afloat. We don't even have to ask them to help out, fixing and organising things and even cleaning up. Without their help and support Michaela wouldn't be able to travel to the races because we would have to pay someone to look after the kids. They are also always babysitting and the girls love it when they stay. So that's another reason why it has made sense to stay in Blackburn, as the girls mean everything to us.

Danielle and Claudia are like chalk and cheese. Danielle is the prim and proper lady and has to win at everything she does. She was competing in a running race at a village fete a few years ago and was winning until another girl passed her shortly before the finishing line. Danielle stopped dead in her tracks and started crying. I asked her, 'What did you do that for?'

'I wasn't going to win. That other girl was,' she said.

'You can't just do that, you have to take part,' I lectured.

Michaela sniggered in the background, 'I wonder who she takes after?' She was right. I would never take part in individual school sports that I didn't think I was any good at. And, like Danielle, I used to be quite shy and guarded with strangers.

She also seems to have been born with my inability to concentrate for long periods of time at school. She is not bad at any subject, although they are both having private maths lessons during the week, but tends to be middle of the class rather than excelling. The other kids at her school, a private school for girls in Blackburn, are at the age when they see me on telly and realise that their friend's daddy is famous. That tends to make our two both pretty popular in the playground. Neither of them would bat an eyelid if I appeared on the screen out of the blue. In fact they would probably look the other way!

My fame has helped bring Danielle out of her shell to a certain extent. She can see that being in front of the cameras is not unusual and she is now happier joining me on the rostrum, whereas a couple of years ago she wouldn't have dreamed of it. When I did the double in Misano, the two of them became separated after the first race and Claudia was plonked in front of the cameras wearing a silly red crown while Danielle was trapped behind the barrier. It would have taken an army of stewards to prevent her from squirming between the legs, under the cordon and into the limelight.

In contrast to Danielle, Claudia is a bit of a tomboy and they react so differently, even to very ordinary situations. For instance, one day Geoff flew us all up to Lockerbie for Sunday lunch and the waitress asked the kids what they wanted to drink. Because it was a nice place, Danielle ordered a cup of tea while Claudia went straight for the Coke. She tends to be much more open and comfortable with other people, especially strangers.

There is a portrait photograph of the four of us hanging over the mantelpiece in the living room, taken by a photographer from the Lake District called Annabel Williams. It captures the difference between them perfectly. Claudia has her arms draped around Michaela's neck, while Danielle sits like a grown up next to me. Claudia is much more loving, like her mum, and will always remind you of how much she loves you. But she is also very clumsy (like her mum). If there is anything to break or knock over, Claudia will find it and there are very few days that go by without something coming to grief. But she will have a go at anything because she has no fear of losing. The worrying thing is that she already drinks like a fish (again like her mum). Even at four years of age, she can down a glass of wine or beer in the blink of an eye and not show any effects (unlike her mum). Danielle would never go near the stuff.

A lot people have the impression that, because I am away racing all the time, I might not be able to spend enough time with the girls. In fact, the opposite is true. During the season I'm often abroad from Thursday to Monday. But, for the rest of the time, I'm at home a lot and can take them to school and pick them up. Many dads leave for work before their kids are out of bed and get home after they are in bed.

I actually spend more time with them when they come to watch me race, because they realise I am the centre of attention and they want a piece of the action. They want to ride on my scooter and help out in the garage. They love to hand out posters in front of the hospitality area and serve people with drinks. When we're back home, their attitude is, 'Dad's here again. I'd rather play with my toys.' I suppose I can be quite strict with them, perhaps more so than Michaela, and it drives me daft when they fight. More often than not it's because Danielle is bossing Claudia, trying to stop her being a pest. If sending them to their rooms doesn't work, then they know that a slap is on the way. But the result is that we can take them anywhere in public and they will be as good as gold. There are perhaps not that many parents who could say that with confidence.

CHAPTER NINETEEN

Race Weekend

Winter used to be a time when I could wind down and recharge my batteries for the season ahead. Away from the day-to-day pressures of racing, I could try and be a nice person again. Not any more. Even without all the upset caused by the battle with my uncle, it felt like I didn't get a minute's peace after the 1999 season. If anything, I was even more in demand than I am during the racing season.

Luckily, my contract for the 2000 campaign had been sorted out long before the end of the previous season. The figures were agreed at Brands and it was a lot easier getting the right money out of Ducati than usual. It was basically agreed in a 10-minute phone call to Domenicali, but the deal was kept quiet until Hockenheim because Corser's future was not as clear. All the way through the season there had been press reports suggesting I would move away, including one that Suzuki had offered me £3 million. I might have made it sound as though they were interested, but there was no approach.

It was no great shock when the news was announced that I would be returning to Ducati. But there was one surprise still in store. Following the final races in Sugo, Ducati announced that Corser would not be re-signed for the following year. Instead they went for a talented young American rider called Ben Bostrom, who had looked fast at the Laguna Seca round.

There were suggestions that the American owners of Ducati wanted to expand the profile of their company in the States. But Troy had also asked for stupid money, and you can only do that if you are the world champion. On top of all that, Ducati were not impressed by his performance in Japan. While I battled away, with nothing at stake, to finish second and fifth, Troy was way down the field in eighth and

14th. He had still been in with a chance of making it a Ducati one-two at the top of the championship, but allowed Edwards to draw level on points and become runner-up because he had more race wins.

I also realised that Ducati were about to make another change to the team. Every year I'd had a battle to keep Slick on and there had been more problems again during 1999. Some of the other mechanics had complained about his work and Davide was not happy with some of his behaviour at hotels and his appearance on race day. I could have dug my heels in and insisted that he stayed but I had already sensed that Slick was no longer happy. His heart wasn't in being somewhere that he wasn't wanted. His role had changed so much that he was almost just in the background. And I felt sorry for him. 'I don't want you just to be there for me. I want you to do something for yourself. You know that Ducati don't really want you, so I don't think you really want to be there either,' I told him. He came to stay in Blackburn for a few days and was pretty upset. But racing has changed and maybe Slick hasn't changed with it.

He has made it hard for himself at times, although he was always dedicated to Carl Fogarty more than any other person in racing. That might not have gone down well with people at Honda or Ducati because he always wanted to do what was right for me and not necessarily the team. And he didn't care who he upset along the way. But it was sad and strange to start the 2000 season without him. Ducati offered him a job in the factory, but that wasn't Slick. He also had a few other options and I would like to have seen him set up his own business on the back of my success. Instead, I think he has taken the easy option by going to work for another team, Level 3, run by Ray Stringer, with Michael Rutter and Paul Young riding Yamahas.

Almost straight after the Sugo round there was a test in Croatia. It rained for the whole two days and was a waste of time. Then it was Foggy Day at the NEC Bike Show, organised by MCN, where a lot of people were disappointed because I couldn't cope with the demands on my time. I had a 20-minute slot racing someone on a video game, then a 15-minute auction, and then autograph sessions when I knew I wouldn't get through half the queue. It became one mad rush with four big bodyguards keeping people away. And that doesn't go down well with the fans. I tried my best in an exhausting and hectic schedule but there is only so much you can do in a day.

Some of the money raised from the auction went towards Princess Anne's Riders For Health appeal, which I presented to her in London at a later date. She tried to tell me that the Badminton Horse Trials are the biggest single day attended sporting event in Britain. I put her right! Auctions are the best way for me to help charities because I am just too busy to do personal appearances and visits to injured riders in hospital. I get letters every day, addressed to 'Carl Fogarty, Blackburn', asking for signed photos but I have to admit that most don't get a reply. There are just too many to go through.

But I did manage to start a leg of Ian Botham's walk from John O'Groats to Land's End in Bristol. When I was chatting to Botham, and picking up a few blisters, it was clear we had a lot in common. When he was at his peak, he didn't train anywhere near as hard as the others. He was able to beat them because he was the best. The same went for me for a long time, although I do a bit more preparation these days.

For instance, this year I did a week's motocross riding during a break in Tenerife between the Misano and Valencia tests, which set me up nicely. It's the only thing, along with trail riding, which I can motivate myself to do, as I don't like mountain biking and, while I've built a gymnasium at home, it bores the shit out of me. I'm trying to do more enduro riding and now have even more incentive after Michelin bought me a brand new KTM bike for winning the world championship and a Blackburn company, CCM, gave me a trail bike. And Michaela's latest idea is to get a road licence for riding bikes, so that she can come with me. I can't ever see her riding a bike on the road – she's not even safe driving a car! And we would only fall out because we're very competitive at sport. We play a lot of tennis and I always win, despite the fact that she has had lessons for two years. She reckons she's a better swimmer and sprinter – but it's not true!

The highlights of my TV dates were my second *A Question of Sport* appearance and *Through the Keyhole*, which must have been a nightmare for Lloyd Grossman to film as he wandered round our house.

The first thing you see as you walk through the door is my 1998 championship-winning bike in the hallway. And the rest of the house is packed with biking stuff like my leathers, trophies, a wicker bike and a lethal little two-stroke mini moto, which Danielle rides up and down the drive. Sure enough, the panel didn't take long to say, 'There has only been one racer who has done anything since Barry Sheene and that's . . .' I was sure they were going to say something like Ron Haslam!

Before a week's testing in Australia we managed to squeeze in a few breaks for ourselves. In January I went skiing for the first time in Italy. I absolutely loved it, despite a big fall on the first day in which I damaged my left shoulder ligaments because I was trying to keep up with Davide. If the scheduled first round in Valencia had not been cancelled because of the Spanish elections, I might not have been ready for the season.

But the highlight of the winter was a visit to Bahrain, as guest of their Crown Prince, to help promote the launch of a new powerboat by watching an attempt to go round the island in a record time. There was no existing record to beat, so it seemed a bit pointless. I was quite nervous when we arrived at the palace but the Prince broke the ice straight away when he said, 'Hi Carl. I've been following your career since 1992.' Somehow, I couldn't see Prince Charles knowing so much about his sporting guests. Formula One driver Mika Salo and his Japanese wife Noriko were also there and we were treated like royalty the whole week. They took us riding bikes in the desert, and provided a horse for Michaela.

One morning we went diving for pearls. We just snorkelled on the surface but Salo and Noriko had scuba licences. When they toppled backwards over the side of the boat, she went down headfirst with her feet stuck out of the water, flapping around. Everyone else was really concerned but I had to run to the other side of the boat, crying with laughter. Then they couldn't get her weights right and she kept bobbing back up to the surface.

All this made her seasick and, when she clambered back on board, she looked like a drowned rat. 'Ooooh, seeeek, seeeek,' she groaned, as she puked everywhere. She curled up in a corner, as sick as a dog and shivering. The devils in my head were telling me to go ahead and laugh aloud, but I managed to cover my head in my hands and run to the other end of the boat again.

There's no doubt that I've got an evil streak because I always tend to laugh at other people's misfortunes. If someone had broken a leg, it wouldn't be funny, but anything like that, which is not too serious, I always find amusing. Salo was a decent bloke, but a bit of a dominant character with his wife. And, if we ever said something was nice like a jet-ski, he was quick to say, 'Yes, I've got one at home – well, two actually.' I don't tend to bump into the Formula One guys too often but, when I do, I always get on well with Eddie Irvine. He is also a friend of Alan Pendry.

When it came to the end of March, I had almost forgotten that I had to go out and race. The test at Phillip Island was also pretty much a waste of time because I caught some kind of virus out there. At first I thought it was the food on the plane but I realised it wasn't food poisoning when I was constipated for three days. It wasn't until the final day that I began to feel better and I nearly killed Colin Edwards in the end of testing press conference when I let off three days' worth of farts.

At the next test in Misano things started to click for us. I was joint fastest with Edwards after the three days and continued that form in Valencia when I was fastest until I had a big crash on the afternoon of the second day. When I realised that I wouldn't be able to take one corner I ran off into the gravel, expecting it to slow me down. It didn't and I ditched the bike with the barrier fast approaching. I must have fallen awkwardly because I damaged ligaments in my right shoulder and knocked myself out for a few moments – for only the second time in my career. It meant that I missed the final day of the Valencia test, when Edwards on the new twin cylinder VTR1000 set a faster time. He was obviously going to be the one to look out for. And, for the first time, the Honda riders would not be able to moan that the two cylinder Ducatis were better than their two cylinder bikes.

Honda had to change Edwards' team-mate at the last minute after Aaron Slight was taken ill following the tests at Phillip Island. It was discovered that he had a small brain haemorrhage and he needed brain surgery in Sydney. At the time, I couldn't really see Aaron racing again, which was sad, even though I didn't get on with him. No one would have liked to see a good rider finish his career like that. Simon Crafar was hired by Honda to take Slight's place for the first few races. My shoulder injury meant that I had to cancel another brief skiing trip, to Bormio in Italy, to present the trophy on behalf of our sponsor Infostrada to the winner of the World Cup downhill. That trip was planned for just two weeks before the opening round in Kyalami, so it was perhaps for the best. Even so, when it came to leaving for Kyalami, the shoulder was still very sore and worrying me.

I don't think many people realise the drag that these long journeys can be. Bike racing is certainly not always the glamorous lifestyle that it's cracked up to be. For instance, this trip started on the Tuesday afternoon before the race and it upset Michaela when Danielle burst into tears when she dropped her off at school in the morning. We took a connecting flight from Manchester to Heathrow, where British Airways at least try to make life a bit easier. They had spotted that I was on the flight and a guy met us at the other end to bypass the transfer between terminals by driving us there directly. Then we were upgraded from Business Class to First Class, which often happens, so at least we had a bed and some free pyjamas! But I didn't sleep too well on the 11-hour flight to Johannesburg because I couldn't get comfortable with my shoulder. To add insult to injury the captain wished the Honda team, who were on the same flight, the best of luck for Sunday's race!

We were met at the airport and, in pouring rain, driven to our hotel in a Bentley by a guy who owns a Ferrari dealership near Johannesburg. Then I went straight up to the track in the afternoon to see the doctors about my shoulder. The injury had meant that I hadn't been able to do any motocross riding in the build-up to the first race so I made a token effort and went for a run around the track with a friend.

Davide was also worried about the shoulder and arranged a scan in Pretoria. After hanging round at the hospital for hours, the machine broke while I was inside! So all the next day was spent back at the track with the doctors and physios, trying to find out exactly what was wrong. The initial diagnosis was that I had torn some cartilage in the rotator cuff of the joint and I had a painkilling injection in my backside – which I hate –but it seemed to help.

South Africa, and Johannesburg in particular, is not a place where you can wander round and experiment with where to eat and drink. All the hotels and houses are protected by barbed wire and the crime is so high that you stick with what you know. So we went back to Montego Bay in the main square of the huge Sandton City shopping centre, where you feel safe enough – apart from one waitress who was after tickets for Sunday. When we went back on the Thursday, the owner gave us the meal on the house. My new team-mate, Ben and his girlfriend, Leeann Tweeden, a model and TV presenter from Los Angeles, also ate there on the first night. We had all been winding Michaela up that she now had some competition on the pit wall. I was told later that Leeann thought I was sweet, which is the first time I've ever been called that!

Ben seems a typical Californian, very laid back although he takes his preparation seriously. He is always mixing high-energy drinks and eats a high protein diet right up until race day. I tend to eat what I want – although I won't touch alcohol for about a week before a race – and I discovered oysters for the first time at Montego Bay. The next day, Ben had an upset stomach and I felt fine. He's a talented rider who was bound to go fast at some tracks, but I also felt that he would struggle on others.

Thursday was also the day of the pre-meeting press conference. The FIM told us about some new fines and Chili stood up as usual to do his grandfather bit. He has a point, though. These things are always imposed on the riders without any discussions. We should have a representative on the governing bodies. But the most bizarre question came from one journalist who asked, 'Why do all the riders wear their sunglasses on their heads?' The answer is obvious, because most of us are sponsored to wear them.

My shades are provided by Oakley, and I had already done them one favour that year. For Christmas, Michaela bought me a solid gold Oakley watch that weighed a ton. The strap was too big for my wrist at first and I had to have a couple of links removed. This proved handy for Oakley as Mike Tyson bought the same watch when he was in Manchester to fight Julius Francis. But his strap was not big enough to fit round his wrist so we gave them back the links to add to his watch.

I bought Michaela some diamond earrings. Her presents get more and more expensive every year, but what do you buy someone who has everything? One year I bought her a solid gold Rolex and put it in a massive box filled with rags and her knickers. I videoed her searching for the small box, which was wrapped in wallpaper and stuck together with duct tape. Her face was a picture.

It was actually getting quite difficult fitting all the sponsors' badges on my leathers. But I had just done a deal with Motorbikes4U, a company that I had invested some money in along with a few other riders like Barry Sheene, to wear their new caps that advertised my new Web site. I also stuck a small strip across the top of my visor because, due to the problems I'd had with Brian, it was important to get the message across that I now had an authentic official site.

In the first free practice session on Friday morning I had a few suspension problems and Edwards was quickest, with Haga also going well. He always seems to be good early in the season when his Dunlop tyres suit the first few circuits. I did 18 laps and the shoulder was still troubling me at three points on the circuit – two chicanes where I had to flip the bike over quickly and at one hard-braking corner. In the first qualifying session that afternoon, we tried some new forks because the track seemed bumpier than the previous year and they seemed a lot better. I also used a 16.5 tyre, which I had never raced on before. I haven't liked it in the past but it felt good and I reduced the difference between Edwards' fastest lap from 1.5 to just 0.3 seconds. I would probably have gone quicker than him if a slow rider hadn't got in my way on my last lap.

It was another long day at the track, with a lot more physiotherapy on the shoulder plus more injections. After each session there is also a technical meeting with the engineers to discuss plans for the next day. And the BBC also wanted to do a piece with their presenter Suzi Perry, out on the track before the light faded. The very fact that it was their first race added to the pressure on me because I was aware that a lot more people would be watching back home. By the time we left the track in our hire car it was dark. You are always fairly nervous driving around over there, as the latest crime wave is car-jacking. So, when we drove past some flashing police lights at the side of the road, with what looked like a dead body sprawled out in the middle of the road, we didn't stop to see if it had been a shooting or a car accident!

In Saturday morning's final qualifying session I tried the tyre again and finished third fastest behind Edwards and Chili's Suzuki. But I was beginning to feel like I was going round in circles with all the different things we were trying and it might have been better to put the bike back to how it had been set up the previous year. My shoulder was not much better but I needed full movement in it during the final free practice of Saturday afternoon to give the finger to a slow guy called Massimo De Silvestro, who could have killed me when he turned straight into my path while pulling into the pit lane. I had to swerve just to miss running in the back of him. It was no surprise to me when Corser clinched Superpole. He's probably the best rider at doing one fast lap and Dunlop also produce a special tyre for it. I was third, just under a tenth of a second slower than Edwards, so at least I was on the front row of the grid at a track which is difficult to pass on.

It had already been a trying week. For these long-haul meetings, there's no point in Ducati bringing over the full hospitality set-up so we are all forced to share a room at the back of the garage. There's not much privacy and I even had to change into my leathers in front of everyone. After the press conference following Superpole, I just wanted to go through everything again with the mechanics to make sure we had covered all the bases before Sunday.

My mind was now totally on the racing. So it wasn't the best time for Ducati to have arranged a profile piece with *Sports Illustrated* at 6pm, just when I was ready to get back to the hotel room and shut myself away. Then there was a queue of autograph hunters waiting at the back of the garage with a pile of calendars to sign. Still, Michaela cheered me up when she rang her dad, then told me that Blackburn Rovers had won 5–0 and Manchester United beat West Ham 7–1. Michaela has a lot of time to kill at the track and she does her best to try and keep me as relaxed as possible in the build-up to a race. So she stayed in the room with me that night, instead of going out for a meal.

A crowd of nearly 60,000 turned up at the track for race day which, thankfully, turned out fine. That was twice the size of the previous year and four times that of the South African Grand Prix race the previous week at Welkom. A few Brits made the trip and had been shouting themselves hoarse, across the track from our garage on the finishing straight behind their English flags, for the previous two days. After morning warm-up I made my final visit to the *Clinica Mobile* to have about seven more injections in the shoulder area and a few pills. But they could not prevent some pain during the race, which soon boiled down to a three-way fight with Haga, Edwards and me.

For the first time ever I used a 16.5in front tyre and the grip was not the best. Also, I was struggling to change gear and eventually had to do it manually, which used even more energy. And, while my top speed was good, I was losing some acceleration coming out of a few corners. So, on the last lap, I just wasn't able to make in-roads as Edwards won the race. I donated my trophy to the doctors at the track for putting up with me for the last few days, as I had not been the easiest person to deal with. It also saved me carrying the thing back on the plane!

In some ways, the result relaxed me for the second race because I probably couldn't have asked for much more, all things considered. But I got a terrible start and, after touching the back wheel of a

Japanese rider called Haruchika Aoki, dropped down to eighth. I had swapped the front tyre back to a 17in and the grip was better, even though I lost the front end two or three times. Still, I managed to fight it and worked my way back up to the leading three pretty easily and was confident of getting past them with plenty of laps available.

Then, on the 11th lap, I lost the front end and slid into the gravel. The bike was still running and I tried to get back on but the gear lever was snapped and the brake line severed. So that was that. I had a mountain to climb so early in the season as Haga went on to win and join Edwards on 45 points, while I had just 16. Maybe I should have just ridden round the problem with the front end and settled for fourth. But that's just not me.

Luckily, we had brought our flights back to England a day forward, keen to get back home and surprise the girls. There wasn't a lot of time to spare so I was able to get away from all the stupid questions and just hibernate with Michaela, who knows exactly how to handle me after a bad result. Danielle burst into tears again when her mum picked her up from school on Monday afternoon. But there was only a gap of less than two weeks before we were off to Australia and Japan for back-to-back rounds.

I have always had problems sleeping in the build-up to races, and especially in Australia because of the jetlag. So this year we decided to go out a couple of days early and visit Sydney. What a shithole! Everyone goes on about how fantastic a place it is but it pissed down most of the time we were there and, if you're like me and not into sightseeing, there's not much to do. It's not as though I'm going to queue up for tickets to see something at the Sydney Opera House. We had a look round the aquarium and took a couple of ferries around the harbour but I was glad to get away, especially when, for the first time in Australia, people started coming up and asking for autographs in the street. To make up for the disappointment, we decided to book a couple of days up on the Great Barrier Reef near Cairns on the way up to Japan, to try and see a bit of real Australia, as there was a chance we might never get back there.

The frustrating thing, though, was that the plan to get me into an Australian sleep pattern hadn't worked. I'd had about one decent night's sleep and was knackered by the time we made it down to Phillip Island, a couple of hours' drive from Melbourne. South Africa had been difficult for Michaela because there had not been many of the girls around. But Troy's girlfriend Sam and Aaron Slight's wife, Megan, were there, Ben's girlfriend had flown over to see him and Michaela's best mate on the circuit, Andrea Cooke, was back on the scene as Jamie was racing in the Supersport series. But, even with all the gossip that lot produces, I still wasn't sleeping well.

So, the evening after qualifying, Barry Sheene had a quiet word with me and suggested I tried taking a Valium tranquiliser. I wasn't so sure. People think you're a looney when you say you're on sleeping pills. But he swore by them and said that the Formula One driver Gerhard Berger always used to take them before races. I asked the doctors and they told me not to go near them. But it had been a difficult first day. A wet morning had prevented me doing more than five laps but I still managed to set the fastest lap. The wind was so strong in the afternoon that I was continually fighting it just to pull the bike in, which aggravated my shoulder, and I finished that qualifying session third fastest. As usual, I was totally wrapped up in the racing and finding it really difficult to relax. So I decided to give one of the pills a go that night and slept like a log.

I felt great the next morning and was fastest by a long way in the final morning qualifying session. That meant I was last out for Superpole. Just as I started the lap, I saw a few spots of rain on my visor and completely lost the plot. I panicked and rode round like there was a wasp in my helmet, trying to get the lap out the way before the rain set in. I was still quick in a couple of sections but was only sixth fastest, which meant a second row start for race day when more rain was predicted. For good measure, I took another Valium that night and slept better than I usually do.

As feared, the Sunday was wet and windy. If it had been a dry race I would have won without a problem because I was riding so well. We initially decided to use full wet weather tyres but changed them at the last minute to intermediates. As it turned out, it would have been better to stick with them because local rider, Anthony Gobert, used his local knowledge of the weather and won by a mile on wets. He was a bit lucky, though, because at one point it looked as though I might be able to claw back his 33 second lead.

The track had started to dry, which was destroying his wet weather tyres and I was gaining a couple of seconds a lap with enough of the race left to catch him. Just then it started to rain again and I had to concentrate on staying upright to collect a comfortable second place.

The showers hold off towards the start of the second race at 3.30pm and it's declared 'dry'. That means that, once the race is started, the result will stand if more than two-thirds of the laps are completed should it start raining again. So this time we nearly all go with the same tyre combination, a cut intermediate on the front and a slick on the rear. With that decision made, I can concentrate on the job in hand, knowing that my British fans are crawling out of their beds early on Easter Sunday morning to watch the live coverage. Some stupid cow tries to get my autograph while the bike is started and revved up by the mechanics, as I sit next to a fan at the back of the garage to keep cool. But she is stopped by some of the team. I would have just ignored her anyway because, by now, I'm in my own bubble. I've been in this position hundreds of times, but it's always tense.

After taking our positions on the grid, Luca and the other mechanics spend the final 10 minutes checking that everything is okay and putting the warmers on the tyres to make sure they stay heated. Michaela stands alongside me holding the umbrella to keep the sun, which keeps bursting through the clouds, off my head. The photographers and television crews buzz around, getting their final close-up pictures of my piercing blue eyes. Some riders allow interviews – but the reporters know better than to even ask me.

That famous Foggy stare is fixed on the track ahead as the hooter sounds and the grid is cleared of everyone but the riders. Michaela is last to leave me. She hugs me and tells me that she loves me. And her last words are always the same . . . 'Come back!'

Career Record

1983

Venue/Race	Class	Place
Aintree	Formula 500	2nd, disqualified
Ouston	Formula 500	2nd, 1st
Mallory	Formula 500	1st, 2nd, 1st
Cadwell	Formula 500	crashed
Mallory	Formula 500	1st
Oulton	1000cc	4th
Aintree	Formula 500	1st
Cadwell	Formula 500	1st

1984

Venue/Race	Class	Place
Snetterton	250cc	retired
Thruxton (ACU)	250cc	10th
Cadwell	250cc	2nd, 3rd
	trophy	6th
Donington (ACU)	250cc	crashed
Oulton	250cc	5th
	350cc	5th
Oulton (ACU)	250cc	12th (heat)
Cadwell (ACU)	250cc	1st, retired
	1000cc	3rd
Aintree	250cc	2nd
Mallory	250cc	1st, 1st
	trophy	1st
Cadwell	250cc	8th

Venue/Race	Class	Place
Aintree	250cc	1st
	350cc	9th
Carnaby (ACU)	250cc	5th
Oulton	250cc	1st
	champs	3rd
Mallory	250cc	5th
Silverstone (ACU)	250cc	4th
Aintree	250cc	1st
	350cc	1st (heat)
Oulton	250cc	12th (heat)
Cadwell	250cc	1st
	350cc	2nd

1985

Venue/Race	Class	Place
Oulton	250cc	1st
	350cc	2nd
	500cc heat	1st
Cadwell	250cc	crashed
Snetterton: Sat	250cc	1st, 1st
	350cc	4th, 4th
Snetterton: Sun	250cc	retired
(ACU)	350cc	retired
Darley	250cc	1st
	350cc	3rd (ACU Star)
Donington	250cc	crashed
Oulton	250cc	6th
Aintree	250cc	1st
	350cc	1st (heat)
Thruxton (ACU)	250cc	1st
Brands (ACU)	250cc	7th
	350cc	8th
Mallory	350cc	crashed
Cadwell (ACU)	250cc	6th
Aintree	250cc	1st (heat)
	350cc	1st
Lydden: Sat	250cc	1st
	1000cc	4th

Venue/Race	Class	Place
Lydden: Sun (ACU)	250cc	1st
Donington: Sat	250cc	3rd
Donington: Sun (ACU)	250cc	9th
Aintree	250cc	1st
	350cc	1st
Mallory	250cc	retired
Aintree	250cc	1st
	350cc	1st
Carnaby (ACU)	250cc	4th
Mallory (ACU)	250cc	11th
Manx GP	250cc newcomers	3rd and 1st
Aintree	250cc	1st
	350cc	2nd
Silverstone (ACU)	250cc	1st
Cadwell	250cc	9th
Darley	250cc	1st

1986

Venue/Race	Class	Place
Oulton	250cc	1st
	350cc	1st
Cadwell	250cc	7th, 8th
Brands	250cc	11th, 5th
Donington	250cc	3rd
	Formula 2	1st
Oulton	250cc	6th
	350cc	2nd
	champs	2nd
Cadwell	250cc	3rd
Thruxton	250cc	1st
	350cc	crashed
Mallory	250cc	retired
	Formula 2	2nd
Brands	250cc	2nd
Aintree	250cc	2nd
	350cc	1st
Isle of Man TT	250cc	retired

Venue/Race	Class	Place
	350cc	retired
	400cc	17th
	600cc	12th
Mallory	250cc	2nd
Donington	250cc	4th, 5th
	Formula 2	1st
Aberdare	250cc	1st
	1000cc	1st
Scarborough: Sat	350cc	2nd
Scarborough: Sun	250cc	1st
Snetterton	250cc	2nd, 2nd
Mallory	250cc	2nd
British GP	250cc	11th

1987

Venue/Race	Class	Place
Jerez	250cc	did not qualify
Donington	250cc	did not qualify
Scarborough	250cc	1st
	350cc	1st
North West 200	250cc	crashed
Isle of Man TT	350cc junior	4th
	750cc	9th
Donington	350cc Super 2	retired
	King of Donington	4th
Aberdare	250cc	1st
	1000cc	1st
Cadwell	350cc Super 2	4th
Scarborough: Sat	250cc	1st
	350cc Super 2	1st
Scarborough: Sun	250cc	1st
	1000cc	5th
Knockhill	350cc Super 2	2nd
	1000cc	9th (heat)
Snetterton	350cc Super 2	5th
Mallory	250cc	1st
	350cc Super 2	1st
British GP	250cc	did not qualify

Venue/Race	Class	Place
Thruxton	250cc	3rd, 4th
	350cc Super 2	1st
Mallory	250cc	1st
	1000cc	5th
Scarborough: Sat	350cc Super 2	1st
Scarborough: Sun	250cc	1st
Silverstone	250cc	crashed

1988

Venue/Race	Class	Place
Donington	250cc	did not finish
Thruxton	250cc	3rd
Scarborough	250cc	1st
	Superbikes	3rd
Snetterton	250cc	2nd
Brands	250cc	7th
Pembrey	250cc	1st, 1st
	Superbikes	3rd
North West 200	250cc	2nd
	Superbikes	5th
Carnaby	Formula One	9th
Isle of Man TT	600cc Super 2	12th
	Formula One	4th
	1000cc senior	7th
Donington	250cc	6th (heat)
	Superbikes	5th
Assen	Formula One	9th
Aberdare	250cc	1st
	1000cc	1st
Cadwell	Formula One	3rd
Vila Real	Formula One	retired
Knockhill	250cc	2nd
	Formula One	6th
Kouvola	Formula One	4th
Mallory	Formula One	5th
Ulster GP	Formula One	1st
Pergusa	Formula One	1st
Donington	Formula One	5th (world title)

Venue/Race	Class	Place
Cadwell: Sat	Superbikes	3rd
Cadwell: Sun	Formula One	4th
Kirkistown	1000cc	1st, 2nd

1989

Venue/Race	Class	Place
Brands	Eurochallenge	11th, 10th, 8th
Donington: Sun	Eurochallenge	3rd, 2nd
Donington: Mon	WSB	7th, 13th
	Eurochallenge	11th, 2nd, 4th
Mallory	1000cc	crashed
Castle Combe	1000cc	1st
Thruxton	1000cc	did not finish
Sugo	Formula One	13th
Mallory	Formula One	5th
Isle of Man TT	1000cc	4th
	125cc	3rd
	junior	4th
	750cc	1st
Cadwell	Formula One	1st
	Superbikes	1st
Donington	Formula One	2nd
	Other	1st
Assen	Formula One	1st
Vila Real	Formula One	2nd
Kouvola	Formula One	1st
Donington: Sun	Superbikes	2nd
Donington: Mon	Superbikes	2nd
Ulster GP	Formula One	2nd (world title)
	Other	1st
Thruxton	Formula One	4th
Suzuka 8 hours	Endurance	33rd
Mallory	Superbikes	3rd
	Other	4th
Scarborough: Sat	250cc	1st
	Other	1st, 1st
Scarborough: Sun	250cc	1st

Venue/Race	Class	Place
	Other	1st, 1st
Cadwell	Formula One	1st
	Other	2nd
Donington	Formula One	1st
	Superbikes	1st, 1st
Darley	Other	1st, 1st
Kirkistown	1000cc	2nd

....

1990

Venue/Race	Class	Place
Daytona 200	1000cc	crashed
Jerez	WSB	14th, retired
Donington	WSB	6th, 6th
Sugo	Formula One	5th
North West 200	Superbikes	2nd
Snetterton	Superbikes	did not finish
Isle of Man TT	Superbikes senior	1st
	Formula One	1st
	400cc	2nd
	junior	4th
Donington	Superbikes	3rd, 2nd
	Formula One	1st
Vila Real	Formula One	1st
Knockhill	Formula One	1st
Kouvola	Formula One	1st (world title)
Suzuka 8 hours	Endurance	crashed
British GP	500cc	crashed
Swedish GP	500cc	6th
Czech GP	500cc	10th
Hungarian GP	500cc	8th
Oulton	Superbikes	3rd, 1st
Cadwell	Superbikes	8th, 1st
Le Mans	WSB	retired, 8th
Donington	Formula One	2nd
Kirkistown	1000cc	1st, 2nd
	Other	2nd
Darley	Other	1st, 1st

Venue/Race	Class	Place
Brands	Superbikes	3rd, 4th
	Formula One	

1991

Venue/Race	Class	Place
Daytona 200		crashed
Donington: Sun	Formula One	retired
Donington: Mon	WSB	retired, 9th
Jarama	WSB	9th, 8th
Mallory	(UK v USA)	4th, 4th, 2nd
Brands	(UK v USA)	7th, 7th, 9th
Donington	Formula One	6th
	Supersport	7th
Isle of Man TT	Formula One	2nd
Brainerd	WSB	11th, 11th
Brands	1000cc	8th
	Supersport	6th
Cadwell	1000cc	2nd
	Supersport	1st
Suzuka 8 hours	Endurance	3rd
Misano	WSB	7th, 8th
Anderstorp	WSB	4th, 4th
Oulton	1000cc	3rd, 2nd
	Supersport 400	1st
Mallory	WSB	11th, 8th
Sugo	1000cc	10th, 5th
Shah Alam	WSB	8th, 7th
Hockenheim	WSB	9th, 10th
Magny-Cours	WSB	6th, 7th
Mugello	WSB	7th, retired
Kirkistown	1000cc	1st, 2nd

1992

Venue/Race	Class	Place
Albacete	WSB	12th, 10th
Oulton	Superbikes	2nd, 2nd
Donington	WSB	crashed, 1st
Le Mans	Endurance	1st

Venue/Race	Class	Place
Donington	1000cc	1st
Brands	1000cc	did not finish
North West 200	Superbikes	4th
Hockenheim	WSB	retired, 11th
Spa	WSB	retired, 8th
Isle of Man TT	senior	2nd
Jarama	WSB	5th, crashed
Spa	Endurance	1st
Zeltweg	WSB	6th, 7th
Snetterton	1000cc	6th
Mugello	WSB	7th, 4th
Suzuka 8 hours	Endurance	did not finish
British GP	500cc	crashed
Silverstone	Superbikes	6th, 6th
Assen	WSB	4th, 2nd
Bol d'Or	Endurance	1st
Monza	WSB	retired, retired
Philip Island	WSB	7th, retired
	Endurance	1st (world title)
Johor	Endurance	1st
Macau GP	1000cc	1st
Malaysia		1st, 1st, retired

1993

Venue/Race	Class	Place
Brands	WSB	crashed
Hockenheim	WSB	3rd, 7th
Oulton	Superbikes	retired, retired
North West 200	Superbikes	1st, 1st
Albacete	WSB	1st, 1st
Donington	1000cc	1st, 1st
Misano	WSB	5th, 3rd
Osterreichring	WSB	4th, 4th
Brno	WSB	1st, 2nd
British GP	500cc	4th
Anderstorp	WSB	1st, 1st
Shah Alam	WSB	1st, 1st
Sugo	WSB	1st, crashed

Venue/Race	Class	Place
Assen	WSB	1st, 1st
Monza	WSB	4th, 4th
Donington	WSB	2nd, crashed
Estoril	WSB	crashed, 1st
Mexico	WSB	did not race

1994

Venue/Race	Class	Place
Donington	Superbikes	1st, 1st
Donington	WSB	1st, 3rd
Hockenheim	WSB	did not start
Misano	WSB	retired, 5th
Albacete	WSB	1st, 1st
Zeltweg	WSB	1st, 1st
British GP	500cc	did not start
Sentul	WSB	retired, 1st
Sugo	WSB	4th, 2nd
Assen	WSB	1st, 1st
San Marino	WSB	2nd, 1st
Donington	WSB	14th, 5th
Phillip Island	WSB	1st, 2nd (world title)

1995

Venue/Race	Class	Place
Daytona		2nd
Hockenheim	WSB	1st, 1st
Misano	WSB	2nd, 2nd
Donington	WSB	1st, 1st
Monza	WSB	1st, 2nd
Albacete	WSB	2nd, 1st
Salzburgring	WSB	1st, 2nd
Laguna Seca	WSB	5th, 7th
Brands	WSB	1st, 1st
Sugo	WSB	crashed, 1st
Assen	WSB	1st, 1st (world title)
Sentul	WSB	1st, retired
Phillip Island	WSB	4th, 2nd

1996

Venue/Race	Class	Place
Misano	WSB	7th, 6th
Donington	WSB	9th, 7th
Hockenheim	WSB	5th, 1st
Monza	WSB	1st, 3rd
Brno	WSB	2nd, 3rd
Laguna Seca	WSB	8th, 4th
Suzuka 8 hours		3rd
Brands	WSB	5th, crashed
Sentul	WSB	2nd, 3rd
Sugo	WSB	8th, 4th
Assen	WSB	1st, 1st
Albacete	WSB	5th, 7th
Phillip Island	WSB	4th, 6th

1997

Venue/Race	Class	Place
Phillip Island	WSB	2nd, 4th
Misano	WSB	3rd, 3rd
Donington	WSB	2nd, 1st
Hockenheim	WSB	4th, 1st
Monza	WSB	3rd, 4th
Laguna Seca	WSB	2nd, 2nd
Brands	WSB	crashed, 1st
A1 Ring	WSB	1st, crashed
Assen	WSB	2nd, 1st
Albacete	WSB	crashed, crashed
Sugo	WSB	13th, crashed
Sentul	WSB	3rd, 1st

1998

Venue/Race	Class	Place
Phillip Island	WSB	1st, 3rd
Donington	WSB	7th, 3rd
Monza	WSB	6th, 2nd
Albacete	WSB	9th, 1st
Nurburgring	WSB	13th, 13th
Misano	WSB	4th, 3rd

Venue/Race	Class	Place
Kyalami	WSB	2nd, 2nd
Laguna Seca	WSB	5th, retired
Brands	WSB	4th, 2nd
A1 Ring	WSB	3rd, 2nd
Assen	WSB	2nd, 1st
Sugo	WSB	3rd, 4th (world title)

1999

Venue/Race	Class	Place
Kyalami	WSB	1st, 1st
Phillip Island	WSB	2nd, 2nd
Donington	WSB	1st, 2nd
Albacete	WSB	3rd, 3rd
Monza	WSB	1st, 1st
Nurburgring	WSB	1st, 15th
Misano	WSB	1st, 1st
Laguna Seca	WSB	5th, 4th
Brands	WSB	19th, 4th
A1 Ring	WSB	2nd, 4th
Assen	WSB	1st, 1st
Hockenheim	WSB	1st, 2nd (world title)
Sugo	WSB	2nd, 5th

2000

Venue/Race	Class	Place
Kyalami	WSB	3rd, crashed
Phillip Island	WSB	2nd, crashed

Index